The Holy Trinity

The Holy Trinity Revisited

Essays in Response to Stephen R. Holmes

Edited by T.A. Noble
and
Jason S. Sexton

Paternoster:
thinking faith

21 20 19 18 17 16 15   7 6 5 4 3 2 1

First published 2015 by Paternoster
Paternoster is an imprint of Authentic Media Limited
52 Presley Way, Crownhill, Milton Keynes, MK8 0ES.
authenticmedia.co.uk
Authentic Publishers, PO Box 185, West Ryde, Australia

The right of T.A. Noble and Jason S. Sexton to be identified as the Editors of
this Work has been asserted by them in accordance with the
Copyright, Designs and Patents Act 1988.

British Library Cataloguing in Publication Data

A catalogue record for this book is available from the British Library

ISBN 978-1-84227-900-7
978-1-84227-901-4 (e-book)

Cover Design by Paul Airy (www.designleft.co.uk)
Printed and bound by CPI Group (UK) Ltd., Croydon, CR0 4YY

CONTENTS

Abbreviations

AugStud	*Augustinian Studies*
CD	**Barth**, *Church Dogmatics*
CTQ	*Concordia Theological Quarterly*
EP	*Ekklesiastikos Pharos*
HTR	*Harvard Theological Review*
IJPR	*International Journal for Philosophy of Religion*
IJST	*International Journal of Systematic Theology*
JRT	*Journal of Reformed Theology*
LQ	*Lutheran Quarterly*
LXX	Septuagint
Mod Theol	*Modern Theology*
NCCS	New Covenant Commentary Series
NGC	*New German Critique*
NPNF	*Nicene and Post-Nicene Fathers*
OT	Old Testament
PG	*Patrologiae cursus completus: Series graeca (ed. J.P. Migne, et al.; Paris, 1857–86)*
PL	*Patrologiae cursus completus: Series latina (ed. J.P. Migne, et al.; Paris, 1844–64)*
ProEccl	*Pro ecclesia*
RelS	*Religious Studies*
SJT	*Scottish Journal of Theology*
ST	Aquinas, *Summa Theologiae*
StPatr	*Studia Patristica*
SVTQ	*St Vladimir's Theological Quarterly*
TJ	*Trinity Journal*
TS	*Theological Studies*
TynBul	*Tyndale Bulletin*

Contributors

Michael F. Bird is a biblical theologian and lecturer in theology at Ridley College, Melbourne, Australia. He holds a PhD from the University of Queensland and has authored *Evangelical Theology: A Biblical and Systematic Introduction*, and is a popular blogger at his Patheos-hosted blog, Euangelion (www.patheos.com/blogs/euangelion/).

John Colwell has recently served as pastor of Budleigh Salterton Baptist Church, and is tutor in doctrine and ethics at Spurgeon's College, London, where he is a senior research fellow. He holds a PhD from King's College, London, and is the author of *Promise and Presence: An Exploration of Sacramental Theology*.

Kevin Giles is an ordained Anglican minister who served in parish ministry for forty years. On the Trinity, he has published *The Eternal Generation of the Son: Maintaining Orthodoxy in Trinitarian Theology* as well as *Jesus and the Father: Modern Evangelicals Reinvent the Doctrine of the Trinity*. He has also served as a consulting theologian for World Vision Australia, and lives in Melbourne.

Stephen R. Holmes is senior lecturer in St Mary's College, University of St Andrews. He is an ordained Baptist minister and holds a BA degree from the University of Cambridge, an MTh from Spurgeon's College, London, and a PhD from King's College, London. He is editor of the *International Journal of Systematic Theology* and author of *Listening to the Past: The Place of Tradition in Theology*; and also *The Holy Trinity: Understanding God's Life* (US version: *The Quest for the Trinity: The Doctrine of God in Scripture, History and Modernity*).

Robert Letham is director of research and senior lecturer in systematic and historical theology at Wales Evangelical School of Theology. He holds a PhD from the University of Aberdeen and is a Presbyterian minister with twenty-five years' pastoral experience. Among a range of books, he has written *The Holy Trinity: In Scripture, History, Theology, and Worship*, winner of the Gold Medallion award of the Evangelical Christian Publishers Association.

Jon Mackenzie is a PhD candidate in Corpus Christi College at the University of Cambridge writing a thesis entitled, 'Phenomenology of the Word: The Place of the Subject in Protestant Theology'. He holds an MPhil from the University of Cambridge along with an MTheol from the University of St Andrews where he subsequently spent a year as an adjunct lecturer.

R.T. Mullins has completed a postdoctorate at the Center for the Philosophy of Religion at the University of Notre Dame and is research associate in philosophy of religion at the University of Cambridge. He holds a PhD from the University of St Andrews, and is the author of articles in the *Heythrop Journal, Journal of Analytic Theology, Journal of Reformed Theology, and Ars Disputandi*.

T.A. Noble is professor of theology, Nazarene Theological Seminary, Kansas City, and senior research fellow in theology, Nazarene Theological College, Manchester. He holds a PhD from the University of Edinburgh, was president of the Wesleyan Theological Society 2009–10, and is the author of *Holy Trinity: Holy People: The Theology of Christian Perfecting*, based on his 2012 Didsbury Lectures. He is a visiting lecturer at Nazarene Theological College (Brisbane), a co-editor of the revised edition of the *New Dictionary of Theology*, and chair of the Tyndale Fellowship Christian doctrine group.

Jason Radcliff is a teacher at the Stony Brook School, a college preparatory boarding and day school in New York. He also serves as Assistant Editor for *Participatio: The Journal of the Thomas F. Torrance Theological Fellowhip*. Jason holds a PhD from the University of Edinburgh and has authored the book *Thomas F Torrance and the Church Father..*

Fred Sanders is professor in the Torrey Honors Institute, Biola University. He earned a BA from Murray State University, an MDiv from Asbury Theological Seminary, and a PhD from Graduate Theological Union, Berkeley. He has authored *The Image of the Immanent Trinity* and *Embracing the Trinity: Life with God in the Gospel* (US version: *The Deep Things of God: How the Trinity Changes Everything*).

Jason S. Sexton is lecturer in the Honors Department at California State University, Fullerton, and adjunct professor at Fuller Seminary. He holds a PhD from the University of St Andrews and has taught at Cambridge as a visiting scholar at Ridley Hall. He is the author of *The Trinitarian Theology of Stanley J. Grenz*, general editor of *Two Views on the Doctrine of the Trinity*, secretary of the Tyndale Fellowship Christian Doctrine group, and a contributing editor to *Marginalia Review of Books* (http://marginalia.lareviewofbooks.org/).

Graham J. Watts is tutor in Christian doctrine and ethics at Spurgeon's College, London. Originally a teacher of science and music, he trained while a minister of two churches, in Sussex and Wales, before being appointed to his current position. While in local church ministry he gained a PhD from King's College, London, published in 2005 as *Revelation and the Spirit*.

Introduction

T.A. Noble and Jason S. Sexton

Stephen Holmes's book, *The Holy Trinity: Understanding God's Life*, has given focus to recent discussion on the doctrine of the Trinity. While it is a history of the development of the doctrine over the whole history of the church, it presents a succinct thesis. Holmes argues that the 'revival' of Trinitarian theology over the past six or seven decades is not a 'revival' at all, but a distortion of the doctrine articulated by the fathers of the church on the basis of Holy Scripture. He states his thesis at the outset:

> I see the twentieth-century renewal of Trinitarian theology as depending in large part on concepts and ideas that cannot be found in patristic, medieval, or Reformation accounts of the doctrine of the Trinity. In some cases, indeed, they are points explicitly and energetically repudiated as erroneous – even occasionally as formally heretical – by earlier tradition.[1]

This is not to deny that the doctrine of the Trinity was either rejected or perceived as 'useless orthodoxy' by the end of the nineteenth century. Nor is it to deny that Karl Barth and Karl Rahner turned the tide of modern opinion which had marginalized the doctrine along with other Christian distinctives in the interests of accentuating those features of 'religion' which were common to all humanity. But original features in the Trinitarian thought of both of these major theologians, the development of the so-called 'social analogy' by others, the way in which some have reconstructed the traditional accounts of the relationship of God with history, the way in which the doctrine of the Trinity has been connected with ecclesiology, and some developments in 'analytic' theology, have all recast Trinitarian theology in ways which depart to some extent from the classical theology of the church fathers.[2] Holmes sums up his charge in the final sentence of the book: 'We called what we were doing a "Trinitarian revival"; future historians might want to ask us why.'

Given the list of significant names associated with the 'revival', this is an audacious claim: Barth and Rahner, Moltmann and Pannenberg, Zizioulas and LaCugna, Gunton and Jenson. Of course Holmes is not rejecting everything written by these influential theologians. But he does criticize the tendency to overemphasize the differences between East and West, the development of the so-called 'social analogy' to such a degree that divine unity appears to be almost discarded by some, and the failure to ground these newer versions of the doctrine in Holy Scripture. Holmes draws on recent scholarship in his critique of these theologians, but he brings together so much recent scholarly research in a succinct way which enables us to engage theologically with the issues.

This book is a collection of papers engaging with Holmes sympathetically but critically so as to carry on the conversation. It originated in the Christian Doctrine study group of the Tyndale Fellowship for Biblical and Theological Research, meeting in Cambridge from 4 to 6 July 2013. Several of the papers published here were read at that conference and several of those have since been published in the *Evangelical Quarterly* 86/1 (January 2014). Others have been added to give a much more robust engagement with Holmes's work.

In the first chapter Fred Sanders identifies Holmes's central thesis as a historical one: that the Trinitarian thought of the past six or seven decades is fundamentally different from that of the fathers, and proceeds to examine the implications of that historical judgement for constructive theological work. The first major question he discusses is the scriptural basis for the doctrine. That has often been poorly done in the past by assembling proof texts, but scholarly exegetical work is necessary and the contribution which systematic theology can make to that task is to draw attention to two larger structures within which the skilled exegete can work – the relationship of the Old and New Testaments, and (an even more comprehensive structure) the nature of revelation as a union of historical event and inspired textual witness. The second major question is the question of what has been revealed: 'What does the sending of the Son and the Spirit reveal about the eternal life of God?'

Sanders also offers brief commentary on the need for greater reflection today on the unity of the three persons as well as on the unity of the economic Trinity with the immanent Trinity. He recommends greater engagement by theologians with analytical theology, reflects on the handling of the historical development of the doctrine (with particular reference to the so-called 'de Régnon thesis' about East and West), and on the authority which should be accorded to the ancient central tradition of the church.

Robert Letham expresses broad agreement with Holmes, but of course points of disagreement are always more enlightening and so he develops several of these. First, he contends that it is not wrong to speak of a Trinitarian 'revival'. He agrees with Holmes's criticism of major trends among the 'revival' theologians, but since the doctrine of the Trinity has in fact been largely ignored in the life of the church – especially among evangelicals – a revival of the doctrine, and indeed of Trinitarian worship, was and is needed. Second, he agrees with Holmes's embracing of the work of Lewis Ayres demonstrating that there is much in common between Eastern and Western Trinitarian theology, but he argues that this is overdone. The dispute about the *filioque* may be obscure, but it cannot be dismissed as insignificant. Third, he challenges Holmes on 'the case of the missing theologian', T.F. Torrance, whom he regards as 'pre-eminent in recent Trinitarian theology.' Finally, he expresses the concern that in reacting against the so-called 'social analogy', Holmes fails to give enough weight to the significance of the concept of the relational in the patristic theology he seeks to champion.

In the third chapter, Kevin Giles begins with his strong agreement with Holmes and his delight in his book. But there are some details he wishes to question before going on to more major matters. The first of these (as with Sanders) is the biblical basis of the doctrine. In reaction to Holmes's criticism that the church fathers are often obscure on this, he advocates strongly that contemporary theologians have a lot to learn from the hermeneutics of Athanasius. Second, he presents a more positive evaluation of some twentieth-century developments, particularly the thinking about the significance of the word 'person'. He would also like to have seen some trenchant criticism of what he does not hesitate to call the Trinitarian heresies of some contemporary evangelical theologians, notably Wayne Grudem.

Jon Mackenzie provides a Lutheran response to Holmes in the fourth chapter. He notes that there is only a very brief mention of Luther in the book and that he is included in the great consensus of everyone East and West from the fathers right up to the twentieth century who embrace the orthodox doctrine of the Trinity. But Mackenzie suggests that there is a far more fascinating Luther lurking beneath the surface of Holmes's account. This is the Luther whose *theologia crucis* had such an influence on Barth's doctrine of the Trinity in *Church Dogmatics* I/1. After Barth, it is the development of theologies entangling the triune God with history which Mackenzie identifies as showing the influence of Luther – the writings of Moltmann and Pannenberg, which both betray evidence of the influence of Hegel, and the theology of Robert Jenson. Holmes may avoid bringing simplistic charges of Hegelianism against them, but the influence of Luther lies deeper in this group of Lutheran theologians. Mackenzie introduces the work of the Luther scholar Christine Helmer, and develops the argument that Luther's innovative Christology, particularly his approach to the *communicatio idiomatum*, was the root of later questioning in the Lutheran tradition of the viability of the fourth-century Trinitarian settlement. This was not just an approach which appealed later in the nineteenth century to the neo-Kantian preference for an epistemology which began with the phenomenal (and thus with the incarnate Christ) and not with the noumenal (and so with the immanent Trinity), but may be seen in Luther's own concern, reflected in his eucharistic theology, to develop an ontological account of God's presence in the world. Mackenzie thus argues that there is a tension between Luther's orthodox doctrine of the Trinity and his radical christocentric approach – a 'double-headed Luther'.

Jason Radcliff devotes his chapter to developing more fully the comment made by Robert Letham (and also incidentally by Kevin Giles), that Holmes should not have omitted the significant Trinitarian theology of T.F. Torrance. Radcliff argues that Torrance is not a patrologist or simply a historian, but that he is a theologian who creates a Reformed and evangelical version of the patristic tradition on the doctrine of the Trinity. He examines differences between Torrance's approach and that of Holmes and argues 'that Torrance's reconstruction of the fathers on the doctrine of the Trinity offers a dogmatic-theological approach, complementing Holmes's book and his more historical-exegetical approach.' Torrance agrees with Holmes that 'the fathers are the answer, not the problem.' He sees an evangelical tradition or 'stream' through history from Athanasius and Cyril through the Reformers to Barth. He recommends Rahner's rule that the immanent Trinity is the economic Trinity and vice versa, but at the same time, like Holmes, he notes the ambiguity in it. If it is epistemological, it is helpful: we come to know that God is triune in himself through his revelation in the economy. But if it is understood ontologically, then problems arise. Certainly Torrance does not merely repeat the patristic doctrine, but is this all we are to do? He may be creative in his insight (as a theologian should be), but not in order to further some modern agenda. Radcliff argues that Holmes the historian and Torrance the theologian are thus complementary.

R.T. Mullins begins with thanks to Holmes for explaining lucidly the ways in which contemporary Trinitarian theology has misread the doctrine of the fathers, but he wishes to pursue the question whether the fathers rebutted the heretics sufficiently, and to examine specifically their arguments against the subordination of the Son to the Father. Writing as an analytic theologian, he presents evidence that, contra Holmes, analytic theologians do discuss religious language. Not all analytic theologians reject the doctrine of analogy, yet he himself wishes to defend univocity – that there is a univocal core to the meaning of words that apply to

God and creatures. He comes then to the main focus of his chapter on divine simplicity, pointing out first that while Holmes wishes to retain the doctrine (in opposition to many in the Trinitarian 'revival'), he does not offer a sufficient account of it, tending instead to speak of divine ineffability. Mullins offers a full account of the concept of divine simplicity while rigorously rejecting the doctrine of divine ineffability as untenable because it is logically incoherent. Our speech about God must conform to the same logic as our speech about anything else in 'the world'. (This means of course, although he does not say so, that he is rejecting the apophaticism which is an integral part of the patristic approach.) This being so, ineffability cannot be used to refute the heretic's argument for the subordination of the Son to the Father. Since the Father is the cause of the Son according to the doctrine of the eternal generation (Mullins is apparently following Cappadocian rather than Athanasian theology here), this implies subordinationism. It appears then that Eunomius won the argument, and Mullins ends with a plea to contemporary theologians to come with a better argument to defeat him.

By contrast, John Colwell takes his stance firmly on the apophaticism which is integral to the patristic doctrine of the Trinity. He begins from John 17 as the outstanding instance of a passage in which we overhear the conversation between the Father and the Son in a way which we must understand to be a true revelation of their eternal relationship. And yet we cannot fully understand what we hear, for the language is necessarily and inherently analogical. Colwell considers the different analogies now associated with the Cappadocians and with Augustine and agrees with Holmes that both had a doctrine of divine simplicity and unity that did not capitulate to the philosophical notions of their day. But along with Robert Jenson, Colwell departs from Holmes somewhat in wanting to respond to the 'bashers' of the 'Augustine bashers'. There are features of Augustine's doctrine which so stressed divine unity as to lead to an undermining of the distinctions among the persons of the Trinity, and Colwell entertains the possibility that in pursuing the so-called 'psychological analogy' in the later books of *De trinitate*, Augustine is actually 'more concerned with a doctrine of humanity in response to a doctrine of the Trinity than with the doctrine of the Trinity itself'. Colwell continues to agree with Colin Gunton that the legacy of this 'monadic' oneness includes the 'Western predisposition to individualism'.

Michael Bird provides in his chapter a professional biblical scholar's assessment of Holmes's chapter on the biblical basis for the doctrine of the Trinity. He endorses Holmes's approach and adds a synopsis of his own thinking on this. In dealing with the Old Testament we must remember that revelation is progressive and that doctrine emerges deductively from the scripture. The catalyst for the reinterpretation of the Hebrew scriptures by this Jewish sect was 'the event and experience of the gospel of Jesus Christ'. This supports Holmes's thesis that what makes Christian exegesis of the Old Testament plausible is 'that it was working with a different hermeneutic.' Bird agrees that the Old Testament does not have a developed metaphysical monotheism, and yet he does think that to say that God is One is a metaphysical claim. He endorses Holmes's four-fold taxonomy of arguments for the doctrine of the Trinity from the New Testament, but the treatment is brief and Bird would like to develop the taxonomy with more rigour and depth.

Finally, Graham Watts's chapter is the Tyndale Christian Doctrine Lecture for 2013 given at the meeting of the study group in Cambridge. Watts takes Holmes as his starting point, but rather than engaging in critique, he thinks constructively about the implications. Focusing on the relationship between God and creation, couched often in the modern era in terms of the relationship between God and history, Watts explores the ontological implications of the Nicene *homoousios*. Comparing and contrasting the thinking of Wolfhart Pannenberg and T.F. Torrance, he concludes that Pannenberg is vulnerable to Holmes's criticism of the Trinitarian 'revival' but that Torrance is not. The influence of Luther's Christology is examined once again, particularly with reference to Pannenberg, and it is argued that whereas Pannenberg works with meta-physical notions such as the concept of the infinite, Torrance tries to develop the implication of the incarnation for our concepts of time and space in the light of post-Einstein physics. With other contributors, Watts recommends a further examination of Torrance's Trinitarian thinking as pointing to a way forward which develops rather than contradicts the Trinitarian thinking of the fathers.

In response to these essays, Stephen Holmes gives a substantial rejoinder. It is to his credit that he has not only provided substantial crit-ical reaction to recent innovations in Trinitarian theology, but that he has stayed around for the necessary conversations on the major issues. He addresses concerns from senior scholars, including one of his former teachers, and from some of his former students. As such, this book provides a familial conversation.

This collection of nine responses to Holmes's book, then, along with his response in the final chapter, witnesses to a lively new debate among evangelical theologians. While critical of much of the development of the Trinitarian 'revival' of the last seventy years, the contributors are agreed in trying to think biblically and constructively about a doctrine which is not just one among many, but the comprehensive, overarching doctrine of the Christian faith. They demonstrate that complacent orthodoxy and creative heterodoxy are not the only options, but that lively debate and discussion can facilitate the further development of that central Christian tradition of Trinitarian thought whose trajectory can be plotted through the formative thinking of the fathers, the Reformers, and on into our present day.

T.A. Noble
Jason S. Sexton
Lent, 2014

Part I

Critical and Constructive Responses

1.

Redefining Progress in Trinitarian Theology: Stephen R. Holmes on the Trinity

Fred Sanders

In various ways, much of the best new work on the doctrine of the Trinity can be considered counter-revolutionary: Nicaea was more doctrinally holistic than merely a refutation of one heresy; Augustine was not nearly as bad as Colin Gunton alleged; Aquinas did not sever the treatise on the one God from the treatise on the Trinity; de Régnon was overly schematic with his East–West distinction, and so on. The new wave of counter-revolutionary Trinitarianism begs to differ, and is finding ways to leap over the orthodoxies of the recent past to get back in touch with a longer narrative that makes more sense. Steve Holmes's book is the feistiest of this new wave of counter-revolutionary Trinitarianism, and serves as a kind of clearing house for all the recent moves, stating them more succinctly, more coherently, and more explosively.

In particular, it is the historical claims and schematic generalizations about the past that are being called into question, and this is where Holmes begins his book: his opening pages take up the status of the Trinitarian revival of the twentieth century, and then he doubles back and covers biblical and patristic material in later chapters. Holmes has to start with recent discussions because his book is, I think, primarily an intervention in the current conversation. And I do mean intervention, as in the kind of uncomfortable meeting where somebody with a substance abuse problem finds themselves suddenly confronted by a group of friends who sit them down and say, 'You can't go on like this'. Modern Trinitarian theology, Holmes is insisting, cannot go on like this.

Modern Trinitarian theology has been all abuzz for decades about how everything is radically different now and we have revived and renewed and reimagined and reoriented the whole mass of Trinitarianism. There is a vast and self-congratulatory literature on the subject. A lot of that literature is in fact very exciting to read. I think of Moltmann's *Trinity and the Kingdom*,[1] the book that first lit a fire for me to start researching the doctrine of the Trinity, or LaCugna's *God For Us*,[2] which brought together so many different ways of arguing, or Robert Jenson's whole *Systematic Theology*,[3] which I would call drastically Trinitarian in its intentional revisionism. Colin Gunton in a number of publications was a major proponent of a renewed passion for Trinitarian theology that required significant revision of what had gone before.

Holmes admits to having been under the influence of that mighty movement of 'the new Trinitarianism' of the late twentieth century, but he has turned a corner and now claims that 'the explosion of theological work claiming to recapture the doctrine of the Trinity that we have witnessed in recent decades in fact misunderstands and distorts the traditional doctrine so badly that it is unrecognizable'.[4] He is sympathetic, fair, and even-handed in his criticisms of particular authors throughout this book. But he also ends up telling what he admits is 'a catastrophic story of loss',[5] which is the exact opposite of the conventional wisdom about this avalanche of Trinity books.

So Holmes leads with that claim, sketches three of the most significant themes within the revival (the historicizing of the Trinity, an extension of the life of the Trinity into the life of the church, and recent analytic theological proposals regarding the Trinity), and then turns back to examine the older tradition from which we have recently departed. He has to work this way because part of his thesis is a purely historical observation: that 'the twentieth-century renewal of Trinitarian theology' depends 'in large part on concepts and ideas that cannot be found in patristic, medieval, or Reformation accounts of the doctrine of the Trinity.'[6] In fact, some of the modern concepts were 'explicitly and energetically repudiated as erroneous' by the earlier consensus.[7] For all Holmes the historian knows, maybe the moderns are right and the ancients wrong. 'But if so,' he warns, 'we need to conclude that the majority of the Christian tradition has been wrong in what it has claimed about the eternal life of God.'[8]

In this book, though writing with an unsuppressed dogmatic clarity, Holmes carefully restricts himself to historical judgements about how modern Trinitarianism compares to classic Trinitarianism. In what follows, I would like to consider where we stand now theologically if Holmes is right in his main judgements, and what sort of shape the next wave of constructive Trinitarian theology ought to take. What follows are notes for the kind of constructive Trinitarian theology that is possible and necessary in the new situation brought about by the successful counter-revolution, that is, Trinitarian theology post-Holmes. I hope it is obvious that in taking Holmes as the dividing line between the two ages, in describing the course of modern Trinitarianism as the epochs pre-Holmes and post-Holmes, I do not mean to suggest that he has single-handedly changed the history of Trinitarianism, or even its historiography. *The Holy Trinity* is a remarkable book, but not that remarkable! What Holmes has accomplished in this eminently timely book is to focus and articulate a backlash against the recent orthodoxies of the Trinitarian revival, a backlash that has been developing in a more diffuse way for some time now. If one were to seek another symbolic culminating point for this backlash, it might be 2012's rather massive *Oxford Handbook on the Trinity*.[9] That volume, however, does a great deal of the actual historical work and as such is rather too compendious to serve as a symbolic rallying point. Holmes's work is remarkably concise, and presupposes or leverages a great deal of historical work more nimbly.

The Scriptural Basis of Trinitarianism

In his already-classic, already-widely-quoted final paragraphs, Holmes laments that in the modern revival, 'we returned to the Scriptures, but we chose (with Tertullian's *Praxeas*, Noetus of Smyrna, and Samuel Clarke) to focus exclusively on the New Testament texts, instead of listening to the whole of Scripture with Tertullian, Hippolytus, and Daniel Waterland.'[10] The scriptural foundation of Trinitarian thought is indeed a major sore spot for Trinitarian theology, and future systematic work on the doctrine of the Trinity will need to give more attention than usual to exegesis and hermeneutics. This is not something that can be outsourced to the biblical studies department any more; for theologians of the Trinity, the exegetical questions must now be handled as part of the systematic task.

One of the chief obligations laid upon Trinitarian theology in our time is that it render the doctrine of the Trinity with unprecedented clarity as a biblical doctrine, or, to speak more precisely, as a doctrine that is in the Bible. If there ever was a time when theology could afford to hurry past this task, with an impatient wave of the hand in the general direction of Scripture, that time is not now. It is not enough to show that the doctrine is capable of harmonizing with biblical themes, or to settle for the double-negative claim that it is at least not unbiblical. Nor can we any longer afford to displace the weight of this burden onto a temporary resting place like tradition or the consent of all the faithful, lest that prop suffer the strains of bearing what it was never intended to support. Nor, finally, can we encumber this doctrinal field with a jumble of unworthy and unserious arguments and illustrations. For we have come to a stage of crisis with regard to this doctrine. A prominent feature of the current era is the growing unpersuasiveness and untenability of the traditional proof texts that were used to establish and demonstrate the doctrine. In this context, it is imperative that whenever we handle the doctrine of the Trinity, we handle it as a doctrine that is both known to be, and shown to be, biblical.

In the Middle Ages, theologians like Thomas Aquinas warned against using weak arguments for sacred doctrines, lest the believer be exposed to the *irrisionem infidelium*, the mockery of unbelievers, when they see us believing Christian claims on risibly inadequate grounds. It is the task of this chapter to show that the doctrine of the Trinity is in fact well grounded in the gospel and well attested in the Scriptures, and furthermore that this doctrine was not waiting for any new arguments from the theological journals before it attained credibility. Considered in itself, the doctrine is already credible and biblical. Nevertheless, Trinitarianism as it exists in the minds of most believers, many biblical scholars, and some theologians in our time is a jumble of highly suspect proof texts, unarticulated assumptions, buried premises, loud non-sequiturs, and obtuse analogies. It is a congeries of Hebrew divine plurals, shamrocks, Melchizedeks, ice cubes, and random occurrences of the number three in Bible stories. In the field of biblical studies, the overall trend of sober historical-grammatical labours has been towards the gradual removal of the Trinitarian implications of passage after passage. Some of these passages were in fact never anything but Trinitarian mirages: 1 John 5's 'three that bear record in heaven',[11] for example, was rightly dismantled by the first generation of textual criticism. Other texts, like those where the word *monogenes* is used, are still matters of contention because of the disparity between the traditional and the modern translations. But all the proofs have descended into the valley of divided details, without clear connections that would bind them into a recognizable doctrine, much less warrant the average New Testament scholar, acting in his or her professional capacity, to believe that God is the Trinity.

The service that systematic theology can provide in the present state of disorder is not to do the exegesis itself, nor to dictate in advance what the exegetes are required to find. The lines of authority in the shared, interdisciplinary task of Christian theology do not run in that direction, nor with such directness. But the theologian can draw attention to the larger structures within which the exegetical labourers can do their skilled work. My hope is that a survey and description of the proper foundation of the doctrine of the Trinity can make it plain where meaningful work is to be done by qualified investigators. It is these larger structures that make sense of the individual bits of information that go into the doctrine of the Trinity. We will come at last to those bits of information, but there are two primary dogmatic structures we must first attend to. One is the

Trinitarian hinge between the Old and New Testaments, the canonical nexus which is the happy hunting ground for Trinitarian theology. But that hinge is situated within another, more comprehensive, structure, which is revelation. By 'revelation' I mean the character of biblical revelation itself as a manifold union of historical event and inspired textual witness.

In his classic essay on the doctrine of the Trinity,[12] Warfield rather oddly affirmed that the doctrine is biblical, but denied that it was revealed in either the Old Testament or the New Testament. 'We cannot speak of the doctrine of the Trinity', said Warfield,

> as revealed in the New Testament, any more than we can speak of it as revealed in the Old Testament. The Old Testament was written before its revelation; the New Testament after it. The revelation itself was made not in word but in deed. It was made in the incarnation of God the Son, and the outpouring of God the Holy Spirit. The relation of the two Testaments to this revelation is in the one case that of preparation for it, and in the other that of product of it. The revelation itself is embodied just in Christ and the Holy Spirit.

Historically speaking, this observation is trivial enough: first comes Jesus, then the gospels. But two significant corollaries follow from the sequence event-then-document. First, the sequence accounts for the oblique way in which the New Testament contains Trinitarian elements. The authors of the New Testament seem to be already in possession of a Trinitarian understanding of God, one that they serenely decline to bring to full articulation. The clearest Trinitarian statements in the New Testament do not occur in the context of teachings about God or Christ, but as almost casual allusions or brief digressions in the middle of discourse about other things.

The second corollary is that we should not seek to construct the doctrine of the Trinity from the words of the New Testament alone, where it is not properly revealed so much as presupposed. Instead, we must develop hermeneutical approaches and exegetical skills that let us read the New Testament in the spirit of its own composition: with constant reference back to the revelation in Christ and the Spirit. Our Trinitarian theology should be demonstrated from Scripture, but in a way that recognizes the priority of the actual revelation in events, and the dependent character of the inspired texts.

The third corollary is that we should expect the strongest arguments for the doctrine of the Trinity to be found along those seams where the Old Testament's prospective witness and the New Testament's retrospective witness are both present in overlap. That is, the doctrine of the Trinity is best established in an extended thematic study of the way the New Testament uses the Old Testament in its talk of God and salvation. This happy fact is a link between the state of scholarship in the twenty-first century and the second, as we are currently living in a kind of golden age of mature studies of the use of the Old Testament by the New Testament. And in the second century with the ancient Jewish canon and the recent documents of the New Testament before him, Irenaeus of Lyons wrote a short, classic theological work in which he argued two major points:[13] the Bible is one coherent book in two testaments, and God is triune. The prophetic and apostolic witnesses, together, determine the shape and certainty of the doctrine of the Trinity.

C. Kavin Rowe has argued that 'the two-testament canon read as one book presses its interpreters to make ontological judgments about the Trinitarian nature of the one God *ad intra* on the basis of its narration of the act and identity of the biblical God ad extra'. Indeed, he says that 'it is safe to say that the doctrine of the Trinity would never have arisen on the basis of the Old or New Testaments in isolation'.[14]

Systematic theologians working today with critical-historical-grammatical tools may not be able to endorse the details of patristic exegetical moves, but it seems to me we have got to get into a position to make the same overall move they made: to leverage New Testament revelation in our reading of the Old Testament. We must give a strategic priority to the New Testament (since that is where the lights come on with regard to the revelation of the Son and Spirit as distinct persons), but it will not do to set aside the Old Testament altogether. Or at least if we do so – Holmes's main point – we will be constructing a Trinitarian theology that is not the same as what the church believed before modernity.

This approach to the use of Scripture in Trinitarian theology suggests a few options for organizing the doctrinal material, options that will be evident even in the table of contents, or the ordering of chapters. There is an unhappy tradition in books on the Trinity of beginning with the Old Testament and then moving to the New Testament. This ordering places an intolerable burden on the exposition of the Old Testament texts, and causes many otherwise helpful arguments to appear in their weakest possible light. The shadows, premonitions, and adumbrations of triunity are brought forth as if they are proofs or demonstrations, but they make no sense until the definitive revelation of the Son and Spirit is discussed in a later chapter. Perhaps it would be better to treat the New Testament first, and then assess the Old Testament witness in light of it. Even better, following Warfield's lines, would be a theological account of the economic presence of Son and Spirit that remained at the dogmatically descriptive level, expounding the meaning of incarnation and Pentecost, before plunging into the New Testament's textual witness to them.

Starting a Trinitarian theology at some remove from the biblical material, precisely to guarantee the right angle of engagement with the biblical material, also suggests that an initial orientation should include an account of why Christian believers approach the Bible with the goal of discerning Trinitarianism in it to begin with. There is some drive or motivation at work before the detailed task of exegesis begins. T.F. Torrance described it as 'the Trinitarian mind' of the church in a Polanyian mode;[15] Bernard Lonergan had an even more abstract epistemological account of it;[16] while Lewis Ayres has explored the 'Trinitarian culture' or cultures that underwrite hermeneutical strategies and exegetical moves.[17] There is something substantive to the charge that not just any reader of the Bible would necessarily come up with Trinitarianism, and a good presentation of the doctrine would account for this in advance. I would prefer to do so by drawing attention to a certain implicit soteriological vision that drives and motivates the work of Trinitarian exegesis: Christians have a sense of what salvation is, and it is readers working from within this sense of the size, scope, nature, and shape of salvation who succeed in reading the texts rightly. There are great advantages to beginning the teaching of Trinitarian theology with this kind of attunement, before moving to the event of historical manifestation, before then moving to the New Testament and Old Testament in that order. Certain dangers will have to be avoided, of course: beginning either with a 'Trinitarian sense of the church' or with the Christian experience of salvation could easily be mistaken for grounding the doctrine on these beginning points. We have all been down those blind alleys in early modern Trinitarianism, and need not repeat the journey.

Other organizational schemes are possible, of course, that would equally recognize the priority of event over witness, and of revelation over adumbration. We will see shortly that there exists a compelling doctrinal reason to place the Old Testament exposition before the New Testament: because the total shape of the canonical narrative is the story of the one God who discloses, in the fullness of time, a constitutive threeness. The Bible is, narratively speaking, the story of One who is Three, not vice versa. In terms of order of exposition, trade-offs will have to be made. There has been a great deal of exegetical work done in recent decades on the use of the Old Testament by the New Testament, and a direct investigation of these numerous 'canonical hinge' texts could also be an instrument for establishing proper order in the appeal to the biblical witness. It would also enable modern expositors simultaneously to make use of contemporary biblical studies while hewing closer to certain venerable patristic tropes.

The Question of What Has Been Revealed

One reason this biblical task must be dealt with, insofar as possible, at the systematic level, is that it arises from the perception that what we have in Scripture is the record of an economy in which God has not only taken action but has taken revelatory, self-communicative action. The doctrine of the Trinity has always been an attempt at a comprehensive assemblage of biblical materials based on the conviction that it is possible to offer a single, comprehensive interpretation of the entire scope of biblical revelation, answering the question of what God has revealed about his eternal being by making himself known in the economy of salvation as Father, Son, and Holy Spirit. It was not a small-minded misreading of the etymology of *monogenes*, only-begotten, that led to the doctrine of the eternal begetting of the Son. It was an attempted answer to the very large question of how the economic Trinity is correlated with the eternal, immanent life of God, how the missions make known something about God that goes back further than the missions. The dynamics that gave rise to the doctrine of eternal processions arise from the larger question of how the economy of salvation is to be correlated with the eternal being of God, and that question is the central task of Trinitarian theology. The doctrine of the Trinity is a description of how the economy of salvation correlates with the eternal being of God.

A good way to see this is to pose the question openly – what does the sending of the Son and Spirit signify about the eternal life of God? – and to consider the range of possible inferences from the economy of salvation. As R.W. Dale said, the most important question in Trinitarian theology is, 'have we the right to assume that the historic manifestation of God to our race discloses anything of God's own eternal being?'[18] He answers yes – all Trinitarians do – but Trinitarians have developed different opinions about what precisely is revealed.

Consider the possible answers as ranged on a spectrum with the classic answer at the centre: the sending of the Son signifies the eternal relation of generation from the Father, and the sending of the Spirit signifies the eternal relation of the breathing of the Spirit from the Father. Ranging to the left are more minimal positions, and to the right are more maximal positions. What is revealed? Is it threeness? Thickly interpersonal ('social Trinity') threeness? Is it eternal generation, or eternal sonship without eternal generation, or is sonship a messianic and merely economic category? Is it hierarchy having a command-and-obey structure? Or does the cross reveal God's eternal and essential tragic suffering? Or does the Spirit's immanence reveal that the world is the history of God's self-realization? I would like to lay these options out along a spectrum from defect

(Unitarianism: the economy reveals nothing and God is unipersonal) to excess (Hegel or pantheism: the economy reveals that God is the unity of the course of events), with a range of plausibly orthodox positions clustered in the middle.

It seems to me that for a long time Trinitarian theology was able to take for granted a middle position on this question of revelation, but that the time has come for it to return to a place of greater prominence in Trinitarianism. It is the point of the doctrine of the Trinity: to correlate the economy of salvation with the being of God.

The Unity of the Trinity

Though Holmes does not deal with this topic at length, the treatment of divine unity is a major point of contrast between classical Trinitarianism and the recent revival. It is not the case that the classical tradition handled the divine unity one way and the recent revival handles it differently. It is more accurate to say that the recent revival has shown minimal interest in handling divine unity at all. The venerable topic, which certainly seems to be something that would be high on a list of issues to be dealt with by Trinitarian theologians, seems to be presupposed as already taken care of, or as not worth attending to. It is not considered a fruitful topic for elaboration, apparently. Bruce Marshall has pointed out this blind spot, especially among the Roman Catholic participants in the revival:

> Since ancient times, Trinitarian theology has thought it essential to dispel the specter of incoherence at this quite basic point, and offer a plausible explanation of the unity of the triune God. All the more remarkable, then, that Trinitarian theology for a half-century or more has paid so little attention to this question. At least two generations of Catholic and Protestant theologians alike have thought of their own time as one of great renewal and vitality in Trinitarian theology, after a greater or lesser period of inexcusable and destructive neglect. Yet a striking feature of this self-described renewal has been the neglect of a matter perennially considered indispensable to vital Trinitarian theology.[19]

Again, if we are thinking only at the superficial level of which chapters belong in a book about the Trinity, we would be hard pressed to find a chapter on divine unity in any of the recent treatises on the Trinity:

> This neglect goes beyond the evident demise of the treatise *de Deo uno* in Catholic theology, by whatever name it might be called, as well as of its

Protestant parallels. The admonition to 'start' with the Trinity has had the effect, it seems, not so much of relocating sustained reflection on the one God as of killing it off altogether, though we can hope the effect is temporary. The deeper problem lies within Trinitarian theology itself. Though a great deal is now written about the Trinity, surprisingly little of this writing pauses to consider in detail how it is that the three distinct persons are one God, let alone to regard it as a fundamental question of Trinitarian theology. For the most part, the unity of the triune God seems simply to be assumed, or insisted upon as a kind of afterthought.[20]

In place of this treatise on the one God, modern Trinitarianism has invested heavily in a covert treatise on the God–world relation, in the form of a consideration of how the three persons in the economy of salvation are identical with the three persons of the transcendent God. As Marshall puts it, 'Recent Trinitarian theology has, however, been greatly concerned about a different problem, a unity of a different sort. Most writing on the subject, especially among Catholic theologians, has regarded the unity of "the economic Trinity" and "the immanent Trinity" as the main problem facing Trinitarian theology.'[21]

In the most radical accounts of this unity between economic and immanent Trinity, it is easy to see how the latter unity eclipses the former. Consider Moltmann, whose treatise on *The Trinity and the Kingdom of God* is devoted precisely to starting with the three economic persons, and only working out their divine unity in an account of God's involvement in the consummation of world process: the kingdom. Moltmann is explicit and intentional about relocating the divine unity from the divine life in itself (whether as a single substance or single subject) to a perichoretic event of world-involvement. Moltmann also proved fully prepared to accept the consequences: divine passibility, panentheism, and if we take him at his word, the explicit denial of monotheism. Not many have followed him all the way in these decisions. But most in the revival have agreed to focus on the unity of economic and immanent Trinity, ignoring the venerable topic of divine unity. It is a striking lacuna, and I must confess that, having been theologically trained in the culture of the recent revival, I have written more about the economic–immanent relation than about divine unity. This means I have inadvertently run afoul of the very lines Holmes lays down, and have participated in constructing a doctrine of the Trinity that has a very different form from the classical doctrine. Marshall warns against this heavy investment in the language of immanent and economic Trinity: 'The language of "immanent" and "economic" has become so pervasive in Catholic Trinitarian theology that to question it might seem tantamount to questioning faith in the Trinity itself. But that cannot really be right, since Trinitarian doctrine and theology got along quite well for most of their history without thinking in these terms.'[22] Trinitarianism, after this salutary, Holmesian scolding, must re-engage the topic of divine unity. The task of relating divine unity to economic–immanent unity is a project still in need of elaboration, scarcely having been attempted by the revivalists.

Re-Centring on the Economy of Salvation

Having just confessed to having written too much on this topic, I will pass over it briefly. Careful specification of how the immanent Trinity is related to the economic Trinity is crucial for next-wave Trinitarianism. Instructive errors have been made on all sides, and simple answers will not suffice. If classic Trinitarianism occasionally lapsed into too much abstraction in its way of portraying the immanent Trinity, the revival of Trinitarianism reacted by paying nearly exclusive attention to the economy. Progress in this area will be a matter of balance: keeping the economic focus of the moderns without sacrificing the immanent Trinity. My own previous proposal has been that the economic Trinity is the exclusive image of the immanent Trinity, and that the key to interpreting them correctly is to recognize the special and hypostatically particular way the Son is present among us as himself (utilizing the categories of anhypostatic-enhypostatic Christology to emphasize that the subject operative in the incarnation is identical with the subject of the *Logos*), and the parallel way the Holy Spirit has a special and proper office in the economy of salvation. The way forward in the discussion of the economic and immanent Trinity is to show how it aligns with the more classical doctrine of the eternal Trinitarian processions and the two temporal missions which extend from them. Discussion of economic and immanent Trinity should be recognized as a valuable development of doctrine, an addition and enrichment of classical categories that enables us to speak more broadly of the total implications of the old procession–mission conceptuality. Materially, it is hard to improve on the work of Gilles Emery on this front, but what he has accomplished with heavy Thomistic equipment could perhaps be carried out in other terms that would translate more immediately for non-Thomist discourse.

Classical Theism and Analytic Theology

One sentence of Holmes's stinging conclusion runs, 'We addressed divine simplicity, and chose (with Socinus and John Biddle) to discard it,

rather than following Basil and the rest in affirming it as the heart of Trinitarian doctrine. We thought about Father, Son, and Holy Spirit, but chose
(with Sabellius, Arius, and Eunomius) to affirm true personality of each,
rather than following Augustine and John of Damascus in believing in
one divine personality.'[24] There is a great need for theologians to develop
their arguments in conversation with philosophy, especially with practi-
tioners of analytic theology. Theologians should frame their proposals in
ways that can be grasped by philosophers and translated into the terms
and conventions of that allied discipline. In particular we will increasingly need to take positions on a range of issues that seem less central to
the dogmatic task, but which loom quite large in analytic theology. We
need not declare ourselves on every contentious issue that flits through
the journal pages. But it is to our advantage to enlist philosophical help
selectively. For example, the Trinitarian revival was cultivated at some
remove from the regions of classical theism, and went its own way. In
departing from classical theism, the Trinitarian revival also departed
from the patristic, medieval, and Reformation consensus. Theologians
negotiating a retrieval of that consensus should avail themselves of the
latest movements in philosophical theology to this end. One reason this
will be helpful is that much of the abandonment of classical theism was
based on unsound or at least unexamined philosophical commitments.

The great case study would be divine unity, and especially its cutting
edge of divine simplicity. Classic Trinitarian theology developed as an
exposition of divine simplicity. Much modern theology has approached
Trinitarianism as if it were an alternative to divine simplicity, or the
massive counter-example that the church fathers must not have noticed:
if God exists as three persons, how could we ever have claimed that he
is one? But Holmes traces the Nicene logic in a way that makes it clear
that none of this Trinitarian stuff works at all unless 'the divine nature is
simple, incomposite, and ineffable', as well as 'unrepeatable, and so, in
crude and inexact terms "one".'[25]

Somewhere in the mix between Athanasius and the Cappadocians, in
that fourth-century struggle with Arians, semi-Arians, and neo-Arians,
the church learned that a simple God ('without body, parts, or passions',
as this doctrine has been put) who sends his eternal Son and Spirit simply
has to be triune in eternity, or triune all the way back. Divine simplicity
is central to all this, and I found Holmes's account of it compelling. 'God
is, and is ineffable. God is triune: Father, Son, and Holy Spirit. The church
believes, adores, and worships the one simple divine essence, which
exists three times over, as Father, Son, and Holy Spirit, inseparably united
in life and in action, one in everything save in their relations of origin.'[26]
If a return to the doctrine of divine simplicity is possible in our time, its

greatest opponents and defenders will alike be from the analytic philo-sophical field. Though the cultural and methodological divide between continental and analytic philosophy is not absolute, there is a recogniz-able difference at work, and perhaps it is not too much to say that the recent revival of Trinitarianism has been carried out almost exclusively in dialogue with continental philosophy. A change of dialogue partners, and a change of conceptual styles of exposition, might get the movement out of its dead ends, not to mention its ruts.

Handling Historical Theology

Much could be said about Holmes's admonition to deal more fairly with the primary texts and major theological figures from the history of this doctrine. He of course models for us the right way of handling the historical deposit, chiefly by rejecting overly simplified and stereotyped distinctions. He discards the East-versus-West schema that has come to be known as the de Régnon hypothesis, and wisely does not replace it with another equally simple one. Holmes prefers to seek complexity in the historical account, and to let the historical figures have their say without squeezing them into summarizing schemas. If we were to continue the geographic denotation of the de Régnon approach, we would have to break things down into much smaller regions than East and West: we would have to consider north Africa, Rome, Palestine, Asia Minor, Constantinople, Antioch, etc. And above all we would have to deal with the actual texts, not seeking in them instances of 'starting with the one and moving to the three', or 'starting with the three and moving to the one'. This trick may have helped in the classroom at some point, but it has never helped in the reading of a single text.

How much is at stake in straightening out falsified historiographies? Much every way. Consider a parallel discipline. When C.S. Lewis departed from Oxford to take up his chair at Cambridge, he took the title of 'Professor of Medieval and Renaissance Literature'. In his inau-gural lecture in that chair, he argued at length that the 'and' had the force of signifying real unity: medieval and Renaissance literature belonged together as one field of study. Most of his lecture is devoted to relativ-izing and problematizing the distinction between the two, which he iden-tifies as a 'figment of humanist propaganda' designed to cast the Middle Ages as the dark ages of baneful Christian influence, and to congratulate the Renaissance for being a new birth of wisdom. Lewis demolished this false division by examining the details of the actual record.[27]

The parallel to the deconstruction of the de Régnon hypothesis is striking. What we need, at least in the patristic period down to about the sixth century, is the elaboration of an Eastern and Western Trinitarianism, with the 'and' signifying real unity. It is also instructive that Lewis realized he could not simply abolish all periodization. While recognizing the provisional and heuristic character of periodization, he took the step of proposing a new way of dividing the times and seasons. He proposed that we should think of everything from antiquity through the Middle Ages and the Renaissance as belonging to one major period, and mark the great transition at a bravura but idiosyncratic point: Jane Austen. Western literature could be divided between pre-Jane and post-Jane.[28] I think he was partly joking. The next wave of Trinitarian theology should offer its own provisional, heuristic account of the story of doctrinal development, but it should be a modest periodization, and probably one with many categories rather than merely two.

The Authority of Tradition

Holmes's book highlights the gap between the great tradition and the recent revival. It thus implicitly raises the question of the authority of the central doctrinal tradition for contemporary constructive theology, especially evangelical theology that stands under the banner of *sola scriptura* and views the tradition of orthodoxy ministerially rather than magisterially.

For example, a major line of argument in the chapters on the fourth century is that the church fathers recognized that the Son is begotten by the Father, and the Spirit proceeds from him. These relations of origin are non-negotiable for any modern Trinitarian theology that wants to position itself as continuous with the traditional theology. 'The three divine hypostases are distinguished by eternal relations of origin – begetting and proceeding – and not otherwise.'[29] Both simplicity and relations of origin are considered controversial in some advocates of the modern Trinitarian revival. But that is why Holmes argues that the revival is so drastically out of touch with all that has gone before. It is really less of a revival and more of a revolution, as some of its advocates in fact boast. In a perceptive review of Holmes's book, Scott Swain said it was 'renewal without retrieval'. For theology since the late nineteenth century, 'the path to Trinitarian renewal required bypassing rather than retrieving the classical Trinitarian consensus'.[30]

One way would be to follow the lead of the classic tradition of Trinitarianism, carrying out the lines of investigation suggested by it as if they were a research program generated by a community of inquiry. Let us say that the church fathers are right about the Son and Spirit being related to the Father by hypostatic relations of origin, and that they are right because it is the correct interpretation of Scripture. To make further progress along those lines would not mean finding more relations of origin (that would be nonsense in so many ways), but might set us up to name other relationships among the three persons. Those relationships would be economic events that image immanent states. And perhaps they would be different aspects or threads of interpersonal relationships that we would recognize as more multifaceted than relations of origin. Wolfhart Pannenberg refers to the 'richly structured nexus of relationships' (*reichbar struktierten Bezeihungsgeflecht*) which 'constitute the different distinctions of the persons'.[31] I think those could use some closer attention.

These biblically witnessed relationships include things like resting on, glorifying, shining forth from, giving and receiving, and so on. I do think they may also include something like 'relations of destination', though that would take us into some pretty difficult territory. But even there, it may be possible to move forward without contradicting the great tradition. Near the end of his treatise on the triune God in the *Summa Theologiae*, Aquinas explains that if a divine person proceeds from another, his 'internal going-forth' has a conceptual starting point and also an end point, a terminus. The Son, it seems, comes from the Father and terminates in the divine being. The more perfectly he proceeds, in fact, the more perfectly unified he is with the Father. In the economy of salvation, he takes to himself an additional terminus, the human nature. But he does so in an extension of the fact that he has a terminus point in God, as God, already.[32] Might it not be the case that, just as missions reveal processions, returning to the Father may reveal or give an image of the Son's hypostatic terminus point in the immanent Trinity?

We might be in a position to do more of what the fathers did, and do it with different exegetical tools than we have had before. If we were to do that, I think we should take the patristic consensus as a normative baseline for getting Scripture right, and then take up and read the Bible with a retrieved and revived doctrine of God. Holmes has cleared the decks for action, I think, and whether that action is along the lines I have sketched here is somewhat beside the point. This is a barnstormer of a book, and I hope it succeeds in changing the direction of the conversation.

Bibliography

Aquinas, *Thomas. Summa Theologiae*
  http://www.newadvent.org/summa.

Ayres, Lewis. *Nicaea and Its Legacy: An Approach to Fourth-Century Trinitarian Theology* (Oxford: Oxford University Press, 2006).

Dale, R.W. *Christian Doctrine: A Series of Discourses* (London: Hodder & Stoughton, 1894).

Emery, Gilles OP. *The Trinity: An Introduction to Catholic Doctrine on the Triune God* (Washington, DC: Catholic University of America Press, 2011).

Irenaeus. *On the Apostolic Preaching* (New York: St Vladimir's Seminary Press, 1997).

Jenson, Robert. W. *Systematic Theology* (2 vols; New York: Oxford University Press, 1997–9).

LaCugna, Catherine Mowry. *God For Us: The Trinity and Christian Life* (London: HarperOne, 1993).

Levering, Matthew and Gilles Emery OP, eds. *The Oxford Handbook on the Trinity* (Oxford: Oxford University Press, 2012).

Lewis, C.S. 'De Descriptione Temporum.' Pages 1–14 in *Selected Literary Essays* (Cambridge: Cambridge University Press, 1969).

Lonergan, Bernard. *The Triune God: Systematics* (trans. Michael G. Shields; ed. Robert M. Doran and H. Daniel Monsour; Toronto: University of Toronto Press, 2007).

Marshall, Bruce D. 'The Unity of the Triune God: Reviving an Ancient Question'. *Thomist* 74 (2010): pp. 1–32.

Moltmann, Jürgen. *The Trinity and the Kingdom of God* (trans. M. Kohl; London: SCM Press, 1981).

Pannenberg, Wolfhart. *Systematic Theology*, vol. 1 (trans. G.W. Bromiley; Grand Rapids: Eerdmans, 1991).

Rowe, C. Kavin. 'Biblical Pressure and Trinitarian Hermeneutics'. *Pro Ecclesia* 11 (2002): pp. 295–312.

Swain, Scott R.
http://thegospelcoalition.org/book-reviews/review/the_quest_for_the_trinity (accessed 21 April 2014).

Torrance, T.F. *The Christian Doctrine of God: One Being Three Persons* (Edinburgh: T&T Clark, 1996).

Warfield, Benjamin B. 'Trinity.' Pages 3012–22 in *The International Standard Bible Cyclopedia*, vol. 5 (ed. James Orr; Chicago: Howard-Severance Company, 1915).

2.

Old and New, East and West, and a Missing Horse

Robert Letham

In his significant contribution to Trinitarian debate, Stephen Holmes argues that the trumpeted revival of Trinitarian theology over the last decades, far from being a positive development, represents a departure from the classic doctrine.

Positive Elements

There are many positive elements to Holmes's case. Much, if not most, recent writing has identified God with history. In so doing it has effectively eroded or removed the immanent Trinity or led towards intra-Trinitarian relations that verge on tritheism. Holmes's strong commitment to classic Trinitarian theology is to be welcomed. The book is thought provoking, the discussion it has aroused indicative of that. Holmes provides a very effective assessment of the frequent and negative misuse of Rahner's axiom.[1] Here he follows Paul Molnar's incisive and trenchant critique of these developments.[2]

Holmes summarizes his criticisms at the end of the book.[3] First, recent Trinitarianism has consisted of a focus on the gospels to the exclusion of other parts of the Bible, including the Old Testament (OT). A large part of the patristic debate centred on exegesis of the OT. It seems to me that this new focus has much in common with classic liberal theology. Second, there is a belief in the full personality of the three in the modern psychological sense, as akin to human persons. In this the Father, the Son, and the Holy Spirit are understood to be separate centres of consciousness. This is the basis of the idea of the social Trinity, where the persons are like members of a family. Third, there is a commitment to univocal language when talking of the divine, which misses the central point of the incomprehensibility of

God. It also allows for the other elements Holmes rejects by enabling an equating of God's internal life with human social relationships. Fourth, flowing from the previous commitments, recent writing has frequently sought to entwine God's life with the world. This trend is in many ways an outflow of the philosophy of Hegel and is seen strikingly in Moltmann and others influenced by him, and in Robert Jenson. These tendencies are all foreign to the Trinitarianism of the fathers and of the ongoing tradition.

Holmes is to be thanked for this stimulus to further thought. Naturally, there are some points for debate, among which I will address a few. Notwithstanding, given the central thrust of Holmes's argument, these caveats are made in the context of a broad appreciation of the book's achievement.

A Trinitarian Revival?

First, Holmes argues that a revival of Trinitarian doctrine was not needed and is not needed. He suggests that the widespread assumption that the doctrine of the Trinity has been revived is misplaced, should be dismissed, and ought never to have been countenanced. The church in East and West has held to the Trinity throughout; there was no need to revive it. Moreover, the vaunted revival is a misnomer. The proposed revived doctrine is a distortion of the historic Christian belief. It is not a revival of classic Trinitarianism but a departure from it. Indeed, the social doctrine of the Trinity, developed from Moltmann onwards, with its talk of a divine community, is an abandonment of the entire theological tradition.

I am in broad agreement with Holmes at this point. His criticism of the bulk of writing on the Trinity since Barth is fully justified. As I read his book, the argument of Paul Molnar was ringing in my ears that the abandonment of the doctrine of the immanent Trinity by many who follow Rahner's axiom compromises the freedom of God. Elsewhere, I have made strong criticisms of Rahner, Moltmann, and, to a lesser extent, Pannenberg.[4] Despite his sometimes interesting and intriguing suggestions, I was almost scathing about Moltmann's constructions, for his increasing move to a form of panentheism, and for his irresponsible exegesis of Scripture, which at times flies in the face of all intelligent textual criticism. Moltmann's idea of a Trinity void of power bears little resemblance to the historic position of the church.[5]

Holmes also strongly criticizes Moltmann's disciple, Miroslav Volf, as my former doctoral student Kevin Bidwell has done in forthright terms.[6] Beyond these, Robert Jenson, Catherine Mowry LaCugna, and Elizabeth Johnson exhibit a similar trajectory. As one instance, the patristic doctrine of *perichoresis* referred to the mutual indwelling of the three in the indivisible Trinity, each exhaustively God and occupying the same infinite divine space. However, in recent discussion it has been used to describe a dance of equals, without power or authority, frequently in pursuit of agendas that focus elsewhere: radical feminist, ecological, political.

However, may I make an important caveat? My own concern, as a pastor for twenty-five years, has been with the grass roots, with pulpit and pew. In my experience of sixty years of hearing sermons and prayers, I recall no Trinitarian sermons – not so much as a single one – other than those I or colleagues have preached. Nor have I heard prayers specifically invoking the Trinity from outside the Book of Common Prayer or the Orthodox liturgy. This includes a year – while working on my doctorate – spent in a pastorless church in Cambridge, while the then gamut of leading conservative evangelical preachers in England and Wales paraded through, from Martyn Lloyd-Jones downwards. Not only were almost all the sermons directed to sanctification and personal responsibility, but the prayers were uniformly devoid in any explicit sense of a distinctively Christian invocation of the triune God. From this angle a Trinitarian revival was needed and is needed still. As a test of this claim, I suggest asking a random sample of members of your congregation what the Trinity means to them in practical everyday life and see what answers you get, if indeed you get any. Better still, ask your minister when he last preached on the Trinity.

Even attempts to explain the Trinity often end up in a morass. Elsewhere, I have cited the example of the well-known evangelical Anglican, David Prior:

> In a letter to the editor of The Times (London) in June 1992, the well-known evangelical Anglican, David Prior, remarked how he had looked for an appropriate illustration for a sermon on the Trinity for Trinity Sunday. He found it watching cricket on television, the Second Test Match between England and Pakistan. Ian Salisbury, the England leg-spinner, bowled in quick succession a leg-break, a googly, and a top spinner. There, Prior exclaimed, was the illustration he needed – one person expressing himself in three different ways! We give full marks to Prior for spotting the importance of cricket – a pity about the theology. A perceptive correspondent wrote in reply that the letter should be signalled 'wide.'[7]

As for hymnology or chorusology, references to the Trinity, while welcome and necessary, frequently are garbled. For instance, the hymn 'There Is a Redeemer' has the refrain:

Thank you, O our Father,
for giving us your Son,
and *leaving your Spirit*
till the work on earth is done.[8]

Yet the Trinity is the common denominator of all Christians, for all are baptized into the name of the Father, and the Son, and the Holy Spirit (Matt. 28:19). The Trinity is the new-covenant name of God. At every stage of the outworking of God's covenant he names himself. Matthew demonstrates that Jesus has inaugurated the new covenant in his blood, extending to all nations. In this climactic covenant, disciples are baptized into *the one name* of the Father, the Son, and the Holy Spirit.[9] This is the context of prayer and worship – in the Holy Spirit and the truth incarnate (John 4:21–24) – for it is by the Spirit in Christ the Son that we have access to the Father (Eph. 2:18). The Trinity is the 'circumambient atmosphere', as Vos would say,[10] in which the church lives, moves, and has its being.

So while I agree with Holmes that the broad swathe of writing on the Trinity in the past half century has been largely retrograde and can hardly be termed a revival of Trinitarian doctrine, I cannot support his claim that such a renewed focus is not needed. However, such a focus will and must appropriate, rather than deconstruct, the classic Trinitarian doctrine, a conservative rather than a constructive task. With this Holmes is clearly in full agreement.

Eastern and Western Doctrines of the Trinity?

Holmes correctly agrees with Ayres that Augustine expresses concord with the Cappadocians and the Constantinopolitan settlement.[11] With this I have no problem. As Studer wrote, Augustine's starting point and governing direction was the traditional understanding of the biblical teaching expressed in the Nicene faith.[12] Yet this should not obscure a different nuance in Augustine when compared with, say, Gregory of Nazianzus. While Augustine never intended his famous psychological illustrations to represent the Trinity, only seeking to indicate how three things, exhibited separately, could operate indivisibly,[13] the latter firmly eschewed looking for any correspondence to the Trinity in creation.[14]

However, from this Holmes maintains that there is no substantive division of East and West on Trinitarian doctrine.[15] As has become commonplace recently, Holmes attributes the East–West model to the arguments of Theodore de Régnon.[16] This scholarship portrays de Régnon arguing for a significant distinction between Eastern and Western Trinitarianism, a position widely accepted since but which has come under criticism in recent years, spearheaded by M.R. Barnes.[17] In fact, de Régnon's main thrust was a temporal distinction between what he called patristic and scholastic Trinitarianism, categories encompassing both Greeks and Latins. Those influenced by the paradigm of East and West developed it to a far greater extent than he did.[18] How far is such a distinction valid? Ayres argues that it is inapplicable to the fourth century, stresses continuity between Augustine and the Cappadocians, and strongly questions its application to later developments.[19]

These questions can be debated by theologians, but the acid test with the Eastern church is the liturgy, which more than anything else is at the heart of Orthodox belief and practice. The writings of individual theologians are considered simply as *theologoumena*, theological opinions. In contrast to the West, for which originality refers to something new, in the East originality means faithfulness to the originals.[20]

The Eastern liturgy – whether of St Basil or St Chrysostom – contrasts widely with its Western counterparts. There is a profusion of Trinitarianism; prayers and doxologies abound, saturated in a repeated recognition of the three persons in indivisible union. Worship and theology are inseparable; the liturgy is the heart of its belief, exemplified in actions as well as words, with the movement of the priest into and out of the sanctuary laden with theological meaning.[21] While to Eastern Christians Trinitarian worship is axiomatic, to the vast majority of Westerners the Trinity is almost an abstruse mathematical conundrum.

We can add that Eastern apophatic theology differs significantly from its Western counterpart, being largely a negation of rational thought and an exercise in prayer and mystical contemplation, rather than a cognitive positing of qualities in God differing from those in humanity.[22]

Moreover, the claim that East and West diverged was not new with de Régnon or the paradigm that bears his name. It was firmly held over a millennium earlier by the Patriarch of Constantinople, Photios. In his treatise on the Holy Spirit he denounced Augustine and his Latin followers as effective heretics for – *inter alia* – their modalistic blurring of the distinctions between the Father and the Son.[23] Later developments that arose with Gregory Palamas, particularly the distinction between God's essence and energies, were not shared in the West.[24] One has only to recall the uniform hostility in the East to the capitulation of the Greeks at the Council of Lyons in 1274. Due to the pressing need to obtain assistance in their dire struggle against Charles of Anjou, the Greek bishops signed an agreement to the *filioque* clause. To this day, the West sees this as an indication of concurrence. However, in the midst of violent scenes, the council was overwhelmingly repudiated in the East and has never been recognized.[25] Even more, similar conclusions reached at the Council of Florence in 1439, when faced by imminent Muslim invasion, were rejected even by the Eastern signatories. Church bells rang in the West; the accord was not even made public in the East until the eve of the fall of Constantinople fourteen years later.

Certainly, this distinction can be overplayed. The West has had a strong focus on the simplicity of God – in a very strong form in Aquinas – but the Cappadocians also maintained it. Augustine may have proposed psychological illustrations to help in grasping aspects of the Trinity – while Gregory of Nazianzus ruled out attempts to seek created analogies – but his purpose was to affirm his agreement with the Trinitarian settlement, not to distance himself from it.

The *filioque*

Holmes states that Photios, the ninth-century Patriarch of Constantinople, in fulminating against Augustine and the double procession, generated more heat than light. His treatise, the *Mystagogy of the Holy Spirit*, composed in exile and without access to his books, contained 'more invective and mockery than theology'.[26] But underlying the polemic was a matter of substance; Ware comments that Photios spoke his mind since he considered the addition to be heretical.[27] Photios's lack of books explains the relative lack of substantive detail, but the invective reveals the depth of feeling that the *filioque* aroused. However, he was able to charge the West with blurring the distinction between the Father and the Son, subordinating the Holy Spirit, threatening the monarchy of the Father and also the divine simplicity.[28] Moreover, that his book was not an intemperate outburst is evident in his attempts to achieve reconciliation.

In contrast to Holmes, Bishop Timothy Ware Kallistos writes, 'From the viewpoint of traditional Orthodox theology . . . technical and obscure [the *filioque* controversy] undoubtedly is, like most questions of Trinitarian theology; but it is not trivial. Since belief in the Trinity lies at the very heart of the Christian faith, a tiny difference in Trinitarian theology is bound to have repercussions upon every aspect of Christian life and thought.'[29] These differences did not arise out of thin air; there was an underlying disagreement. The controversy over the *filioque* was hardly a chimera. Converts from Rome, Lutheranism, and Reformed churches are normally required to renounce it before chrismation.[30]

That this was and is a real issue is evident in wider ways. The Eastern rejection of the *filioque* allows a more prominent place to the Holy Spirit.

Western theology has been preoccupied with the cross, with sin, atonement, and justification; the East has focused on the resurrection and *theosis*. From this has arisen a piety more pneumatocentric than christocentric. Throughout the Orthodox liturgy, especially at crucial points in the sacramental prayers, the Holy Spirit is invoked. From the West, Gerald Bray has written that 'without a living appreciation of the *Filioque* clause within the context of a personal as opposed to a natural theology, Evangelical faith becomes incomprehensible.'[31] The question of the *filioque* clause is hardly a minor sideshow, eclipsed by the main item of the claims of the Church of Rome, as Holmes thinks. Rather, as Ware pointed out, the Western addition has been regarded as heretical, confusing the persons of the Father and the Son, subordinating the Spirit, and encouraging a false doctrine of the church.[32]

Holmes describes the *filioque* as a narrow issue.[33] The primacy of Rome, not the *filioque*, divided the church.[34] So it turns out that medieval Trinitarianism was united 'with the exception of a debate over the . . . *filioque*'. On that basis we could almost say that Europe was united during the Cold War except over communism. Holmes says so by asserting the classic Western doctrine, without reference to any substantial body of Eastern theology, nor with reference to the Divine Liturgy.

In support, Holmes cites Gregory Palamas, in his *Capita 150* (c.34–8), where he seems to adopt a psychological analogy similar to that of Augustine in *De trinitate*.[35] Holmes says Palamas considers this 'at some length' (in reality four or five short sections of around one paragraph each) and he considers it 'an acute embarrassment' to those who suppose there to be a difference between the East and the West on the Trinity.

It is true that this passage in Palamas has aroused a good deal of interest. The degree to which he adopts the Augustinian model here is open to debate. Yet the thrust of Palamite theology, and particularly its Trinitarianism, was noticeably different. Hussey considers that a correspondence with Augustine here and there does not mean that Palamas and the Latins were at one. The Greeks, due to their apophaticism, used many models, considering them all equal, whereas the West tended to build a theology out of Augustine's construction.[36]

Wilkins goes further.[37] He states that the exegesis of these passages is underdetermined, so no interpretation will be more than probable, possibly no more than plausible.[38] He thinks that 'this thunderbolt from the Augustinian sky seems but a passing squall in the total pattern of Gregory's thought.'[39] Gregory does not exploit this in any way, for 'his theology of mission and *theosis* is more tightly bound up with the essence-energies distinction'[40] and 'while in these chapters Gregory develops a doctrine of the Trinity with remarkable affinities to both

Augustine and Thomas Aquinas, it is far more peripheral to his theological project, and its virtualities for thinking about the divine missions and deification remain unexplored.'[41] It seems to me that Holmes's argument requires more justification than he can give in the book.

Even if we suppose, for the sake of argument, that Palamas deliberately borrowed from Augustine this would be hardly surprising, still less 'an acute embarrassment'. Both were Christian theologians writing about the Trinity. There is bound to be considerable overlap. On a purely personal level, I have used some extracts from Greek theologians, and some of their ideas, in material I have written. Does that mean there is no significant difference between Orthodox theologians and myself? Agreeing with and following the suggestions of another writer, even one from another tradition, does not of itself establish an accord on a wider basis. We often adopt ideas and patterns of thought from elsewhere while remaining aloof from the broader entailments of the source. Closer to our own day, Dumitru Staniloae 'while repudiating the *Filioque* . . . finds a place for the Augustinian notion of the Spirit as the bond and communion between Father and Son.'[42]

Such overlap does not require us to conclude that Augustine and Palamas were approaching this immense subject from the same perspective. This question of perspective is, of course, important in the interpretation of any text, ancient or modern. In north-west Scotland, there is a remarkable mountain, Suilven, an abrupt and bulbous protrusion when viewed from the south-west, an elongated ridge from the south, a jagged, nightmarish apparition out of Tolkein from the east. The contours are the same but the appearance differs radically. Any single object in relation to which human agents can be placed can appear different depending on the location of the observer.

Holmes opposes a position that assumes 'a fundamentally different tradition' in the East.[43] It depends what is meant by 'fundamentally different'. Both East and West believe and maintain the doctrine of the Trinity attested at Nicaea and Constantinople I. It is not surprising that there are wide areas of agreement between Latin and Greek theologians down the centuries. They both are Christian and Trinitarian; it would be remarkable if there was not a broad consensus.

In fact, there is inconsistency in Holmes's treatment of this issue. While he asserts that there is fundamental agreement between East and West, he also refers to Aquinas's *Contra errores Graecorum*, 'a controversial work . . . in favour of the Roman positions.'[44] Later, he writes of 'the irrevocable split' between East and West[45] and of the West's rejection of Palamas's formulation of the essence–energies division on the grounds that it violated principles laid down in the fourth-century controversies.[46] So, as much as Holmes wishes to dismiss talk of an East–West difference over the Trinity, he cannot quite manage it. The matter is not as elementary as Holmes might think. Timothy Ware – now Bishop Kallistos Ware – sums up the difference. 'Christians, in the West, both Roman and Reformed, generally start by asking the same questions, although they may disagree about the answers. In Orthodoxy, however, it is not merely the answers that are different – the questions themselves are not the same as in the West.'[47]

It is surprising in view of his assertions that Holmes hardly refers to Eastern and Orthodox representatives. Lossky, Meyendorff, Staniloae, Cabasilas, Florovsky, and Bobrinskoy are not mentioned. On the monarchy of the Father in Gregory of Nazianzus he does not refer to T.A. Noble's important discussion dealing with an apparent ambiguity in Gregory, where he attributes the monarchy at one time to the Father and elsewhere to the whole Trinity.[48]

Holmes overlooks the point that if he were to convert to Orthodoxy, before his chrismation he would be called on at some point, in common with converts from Rome and Protestantism, to renounce, *inter alia*, the *filioque*.[49] Seminar papers, journal articles, and theological treatises may seem to set the agenda, but for Orthodoxy the unchanging liturgy and the life of the church in creed, councils, and living worship is where the action is. Here de Régnon is at most a recent, remote, and largely irrelevant footnote.

Holmes and the Mystery of the Missing Theologian

In Arthur Conan Doyle's short story, 'Silver Blaze', there is a well-known exchange between Sherlock Holmes and the local detective, Inspector Gregory. Silver Blaze, a famous racehorse, has disappeared shortly before the Wessex Cup, the big race for which it is the favourite, its trainer murdered. Holmes is called to Devon to investigate, the local constabulary floundering. Holmes gives the local man a small clue to help him, if he has the wit to pursue it:

'[Inspector Gregory] Is there any point to which you would wish to draw my attention?'
'[Holmes] To the curious incident of the dog in the night-time.'
'The dog did nothing in the night-time.'
'That was the curious incident', remarked Sherlock Holmes.[50]

The point is that if the culprit were an intruder from outside, the guard dog would have barked. Since this was not the case, the dog must have known the kidnapper and murderer, whose presence at night would not have been unexpected. It was an inside job.

In the case of Holmes and the mystery of the Trinity there is also an incident surprising by its curious absence. There is a figure one would expect to earn more than a passing mention but who is unexpectedly ignored, save for a mere footnote on a tangential topic. Holmes's omission, similar to the one to which Holmes alludes in the story, is of T.F. Torrance. To my mind, Torrance is pre-eminent in recent Trinitarian theology. Where does he fit into Holmes's analysis, one wonders? Was his contribution unnecessary? Was he too a distorter of classic Trinitarianism? Or is his absence an indication that Holmes sees himself as in the same camp? Or does he see Torrance's contribution as less significant than I and others do? Perhaps Holmes has spotted clues, elementary no doubt, to which I have been blind.

Holmes's Understanding of the Trinity

Finally, I have some concerns with Holmes's understanding of the classic Trinitarianism as he expresses it in his final chapter. Perhaps due to his justifiable opposition to the social Trinity, he seems to go just a touch in the opposite direction.

Holmes opposes a relational and personal model. However, as Papanikolaou argues, if the core of the Christian faith is communion with the Father, in the person of Christ, by the power of the Holy Spirit, relational and personal language is difficult to avoid.[51]

Holmes's warnings about univocal predication about God seen in recent social Trinitarianism are well made. However, throughout the Trinitarian crisis it was held that the language relating to the hypostases entailed relationality. The Father is Father in relation to the Son, and vice versa. These are relational categories. Moreover, the incarnation entails a connection of some kind between the hypostasis of the Son and what is involved in being human. Human personhood shares a certain mystery and incomprehensibility that comes from its creaturely reflection of the God who created it for himself. Attempts to define it fall short of its reality, a reality that is constantly elusive, better understood through recognition and communion than logical abstraction.

This raises a question that I find the book does not clearly address. How does Holmes relate his Trinitarianism to the incarnation? There human nature was taken into union by the Son. Whatever human nature is, it is compatible on a finite level with whatever the divine hypostases are, since the hypostasis of the Son now has a full human nature. In short, not only is the hypostasis of the Son capable of uniting to itself human nature, but that nature, elsewhere in all other instantiations existent as human persons, is also in this instance perfectly existent (quintessentially existent) as the humanity of the divine hypostasis of the Son. While the incarnate Son is not a human person, I would have thought that there is consequently an affinity between the divine, eternal hypostasis of the Son and whatever human personhood is on the creaturely level. If this were not so, the incarnation could not be.

I mention this, granting that, as Staniloae remarks, 'relations among the divine persons transcend paternal and human relations among human beings to an incomparable degree.'[52] Yet Staniloae refers to Dionysius the Areopagite, who affirms 'the centrality of irreducible distinction among the three divine persons within the unity of being just as powerfully as he asserts the character of the divine being as a mystery inaccessible to our understanding.'[53]

Does this not justify thinking in relational and personal terms? Put another way, if we do not think in such terms can we lay claim to an orthodox Christology? If deity is forever hidden from human nature, and if there is no compatibility between the hypostasis of the Son and humanity, it would be interesting to see how Nestorianism can be avoided.

Holmes makes three related statements in his concluding summary. He says, 'The three hypostases are distinguished by eternal relations of origin – begetting and proceeding – and not otherwise.' Again, 'All that is spoken of God, with the single and very limited exception of that language which refers to the relations of origin of the three *hypostases*, is spoken of the one life the three share, and so is indivisibly spoken of all three.' Shortly afterwards he adds, 'The relationships of origin express/ establish relational distinctions between the three existent hypostases; no other distinctions are permissible.'[54]

As a statement of the immanent Trinity this is of course unexceptionable. It is, as he says, expressed in similar terms by John of Damascus.[55] However, if it were to be taken without nuance or qualification, as the language seems to suggest, it raises issues as serious as the ones Holmes has addressed. Do not the missions – the incarnation of the Son and the sending of the Holy Spirit – disclose something? In becoming incarnate the Son has taken into permanent union human nature. This is something neither the Father nor the Holy Spirit has done. Certainly, the incarnation – as all the works of God – entailed the united and indivisible operation of all three. Yet it was not the divine nature as such that became flesh but the *Logos*, the eternal Son of the Father. Similarly it was the Holy Spirit who came at Pentecost, not the Son or the Father. Again, the Spirit proceeds from the Father and was sent by the Father and the Son, so much so that Jesus is reported as affirming that in his coming the entire Trinity takes up permanent residence in the faithful (John 14:23). However, the coming of the Spirit is not a manner of speaking, nor was it the divine nature as such which came at that time, but the hypostasis of the Spirit came in reality. In this he is distinguished from the Son; the Son unites human nature hypostatically with himself, whereas the Spirit pervades the church and its members. These are two quite distinct actions, with equally distinct results.

This brings us close to the relationship between the Son in eternity and in human history, between his relation to the Father in the indivisible Trinity and his mission here for us and our salvation. Gilles Emery comments:

> The patristic and medieval tradition will be especially attentive to the correspondence between the sending of the Son into the world and his eternal origin: in the same way that the Son is sent by the Father, he has his existence from the Father. In other words, when Trinitarian doctrine speaks of the divine person in terms of 'relation of origin', it is not a speculation detached from the economy of salvation, but rather it proposes a doctrine grounded on the teaching of the Gospels about Jesus, whose existence is always relative to his Father. The *mystery* of the Father and the Son is present and revealed in the *economy*.[56]

So, Emery adds:

> This teaching makes manifest a profound correspondence between, on the one hand, the eternal property of the Son and the Holy Spirit, and, on the other hand, their 'visible mission.' The Son is begotten from all eternity by the Father. As Son, he receives from the Father his being the principle of the Holy Spirit, along with the Father: with the Father, the Son spirates the Holy Spirit. It therefore pertains to the Son, in his very quality as Son, to be sent by the Father as *Author of sanctification* – that is to say, as *Giver of the Holy Spirit*. This is a dimension of the 'fittingness' of the Son's incarnation that we discover here.[57]

The point I am making is that the clear distinctions in the missions of the Son and the Holy Spirit respectively indicate eternal distinctions within the indivisibility of God. As Staniloae again remarks, 'for this reason the Fathers take all their proofs for the Holy Trinity from the work of salvation accomplished in Christ.'[58] At root God is love; love entails relationality and an analogical correspondence between intra-Trinitarian relations and human personhood. Staniloae corroborates this thought when he says, 'In order to maintain the definition of love as the essential divine act . . . we must see the divine being at one and the same time as unity and as relation, as relation in the very heart of unity. Unity must not be destroyed for the sake of relation, nor relation abolished in favor of unity.'[59]

I am sure Holmes agrees with this; it is that in his rejection of recent trends it does not come across clearly, as far as I can see it. It may be that I have misunderstood what Holmes is saying, or have read too much into it; this has happened enough times with comments on what I have written for it to be a real possibility in this instance. If so, I will be glad to know that it is so.

I find the penultimate sentence rather puzzling. 'We thought about Father, Son, and Holy Spirit, but chose (with Sabellius, Arius, and Euno-mius) to affirm true personality of each, rather than following Augustine and John of Damascus in believing in one divine personality.'[60] Since, as far as we know, Sabellius considered that the three were simply modes in which the one God appeared, it is hard to work out how he could be associated with those who threaten the unity of the Trinity by their social programme. For their part, Arius and Eunomius placed the Son and the Spirit on the side of creation. Is Holmes confessing that he has not, until recently, been a Trinitarian?

Despite such caveats, Holmes is to be congratulated on writing an accessible book worth reading and pondering deeply.

Bibliography

Augustine. *Letter* 169.

Ayres, Lewis. *Augustine and the Trinity* (Cambridge: Cambridge University Press, 2010).

— *Nicaea and Its Legacy: An Approach to Fourth-Century Trinitarian Theology* (Oxford: Oxford University Press, 2004).

Barnes, Michel René. 'De Régnon Reconsidered'. *Augustinian Studies* 26 (1995): pp. 51–79.

— 'Rereading Augustine on the Trinity.' Pages 145–76 in *The Trinity: An Interdisciplinary Symposium on the Trinity* (ed. Stephen T. Davis, Daniel Kendall, and Gerald O'Collins; Oxford: Oxford University Press, 1999).

Bidwell, Kevin J. *The Church as the Image of the Trinity: A Critical Evaluation of Miroslav Volf's Ecclesial Model*. WEST Theological Monograph Series (Eugene, OR: Wipf & Stock, 2011).

Bray, Gerald. 'The Filioque Clause in History and Theology'. *Tyndale Bulletin* 34 (1983): pp. 91–144.

Conan Doyle, Sir Arthur. *The Complete Sherlock Holmes* (Garden City, NY: Doubleday, 1927).

De Régnon, Theodore. *Études de théologie positive sur la Sainte Trinité* (3 vols; Paris: Retaux, 1892–8).

Geanakoplos, Deno John. *Byzantium: Church, Society, and Civilization Seen through Contemporary Eyes* (Chicago: University of Chicago Press, 1984).

Emery, Gilles. *The Trinity: An Introduction to Catholic Doctrine of the Triune God* (ed. Matthew Levering; Washington, DC: Catholic University of America Press, 2011).

Festal Menaion (trans. Mother Mary and Archimandrite Kallistos Ware; South Canaan, PN: St Tikhon's Seminary Press, 1998).

Gregory Nazianzen. *Oration* 31.

Gregory Palamas. *The Triads*.

Hennessy, Kristin. 'An Answer to De Régnon's Accusers: Why We Should Not Speak of "His" Paradigm'. *Harvard Theological Review* 100 (April 2007): pp. 179–97.

Hussey, M. Edmund. 'The Palamite Trinitarian Models'. *St Vladimir's Theological Quarterly* 16 (1972): pp. 83–9.

John of Damascus. *On the Orthodox Faith*.

Lenten Triadion (trans. Mother Mary and Archimandrite Kallistos Ware; South Canaan, PA: St Tikhon's Seminary Press, 2002).

Letham, Robert. *The Holy Trinity: In Scripture, History, Theology, and Worship* (Phillipsburg, NJ: Presbyterian & Reformed, 2004).

— *Through Western Eyes: Eastern Orthodoxy; A Reformed Perspective* (Fearn: Mentor, 2007).

— 'The Trinity between East and West'. *Journal of Reformed Theology* 3 (2009): pp. 42–56.

Louth, Andrew. *John Damascene: Tradition and Originality in Byzantine Theology* (Oxford: Oxford University Press, 2002).

Molnar, Paul D. *Divine Freedom and the Doctrine of the Immanent Trinity: In Dialogue with Karl Barth and Contemporary Theology* (Edinburgh: T&T Clark, 2002).

Noble, T.A. 'Paradox in Gregory Nazianzen's Doctrine of the Trinity'. *Studia Patristica* 27 (1993): pp. 94–9.

Papanikolaou, Aristotle. 'Is John Zizioulas an Existentialist in Disguise? Response to Lucian Turcescu.' *Modern Theology* 20 (October 2004): pp. 601–7.

Photios. *On the Mystagogy of the Holy Spirit*.

Saint Photios. *On the Mystagogy of the Holy Spirit* (n.p.: Studion, 1983).

Service Book of the Holy Orthodox-Catholic Apostolic Church (Brooklyn, NY: Syrian Antiochene Orthodox Archdiocese of New York and All North America, 3rd edn, 1956).

Staniloae, Dumitru. *The Experience of God: Orthodox Dogmatic Theology,* vol. 1: Revelation and Knowledge of the Triune God (Brookline, MA: Holy Cross Orthodox Press, 1994).

Studer, Basil. *The Grace of Christ and the Grace of God in Augustine of Hippo: Christocentrism or Theocentrism?* (Collegeville, MN: Liturgical Press, 1997).

Vos, Geerhardus. *The Pauline Eschatology* (Grand Rapids: Eerdmans, 1972).

Ware, Timothy. *The Orthodox Church* (London: Penguin, 1969).

Wilkins, Jeremy D. '"The Image of His Highest Love": The Trinitarian Analogy in Gregory Palamas's Capita 150'. *St Vladimir's Theological Quarterly* 47 (2003): pp. 383–412.

3.

A Personal Response to
Stephen R. Holmes's *The Holy Trinity*

Kevin Giles

I am delighted to be invited to make a personal response to Stephen Holmes's book on the Trinity. I liked it so much that when I saw on Amazon what I thought was a second book by him entitled, *The Quest for the Trinity: The Doctrine of God in Scripture, History and Modernity*, published by IVP Academic, I ordered a copy only to find it was the same book with another title! The book is very well written, the explanations of the key ideas of the great Trinitarian theologians are excellent, the breadth of reading is impressive, and the coverage of the two thousand years of thought on the Trinity is wonderful.

The primary thesis of the book is that much twentieth-century work on the Trinity has been in large measure a departure from the historical understanding of the Trinity, especially as enunciated by the Nicene fathers, including Augustine. Too many modern theologians writing on the Trinity, Stephen believes,[1] have not mastered the received doctrinal tradition, and so they misunderstand it or distort it unknowingly, and so their work raises more problems than answers. He writes to affirm the great treasures of the Nicene tradition, advocating its importance at this present time. For him, the huge volume of work done on the Trinity in the last fifty years does not indicate a 'recovery' of the historic doctrine of the Trinity, and a big step forward in understanding it; rather, much of it has been a big step backward.

My Response

Stephen's book is a very good introduction to the historical development of the doctrine of the Trinity. We find in it an excellent coverage of two thousand years of thought on the Trinity, deep and profound reflection on this difficult doctrine, and a strong reaffirmation of Nicene Trinitarian orthodoxy that allows for no confusing of the divine persons, nor the dividing of them by ordering them hierarchically, nor by depicting them almost as individuals, each with their own will and consciousness. I commend Stephen also for rejecting the commonly held contemporary thesis that the Trinity prescribes our social agenda.

If this is all I said in making a response to Stephen's book it would be a boring essay. It would raise nothing to think about. I therefore mention a few details in his book that I would question, and raise three very important issues that I personally think need more consideration.

Details I Would Question

In a book of this length and scope it is easy to miss something, poorly word what you are trying to say on occasions, or make a cosmetic mistake here or there. I am sure my writings on the Trinity would give innumerable examples of such slips. On the few examples I raise in Stephen's work, I do so with hesitation because I may be the one mistaken.

On page 87 Stephen says the AD 325 'Creed of Nicaea stops short of affirming eternal generation'. It is true that this creed does not explicitly speak of the Son's begetting as 'eternal' as does the AD 381 creed. However, I think the addition of the word 'eternal' only makes explicit what is implied in the AD 325 creed. This speaks of Jesus Christ as '*begotten* from the Father, uniquely (*monogenes*), that is, from the substance of the Father, God from God, light from light, true God from true God, *begotten* not made, of one being (*homoousios*) with the Father.' If the Son is uniquely begotten from the eternal being of the Father and he is 'God from God', 'not created', and is one in being with the Father, what more needs to be said? The Son is definitely not a creature created in time, as Arius taught. Why this creed has the Son begotten from the Father's *ousia*/ being, whereas the 381 text has him begotten 'of the Father', is debated and uncertain. Both ideas are perfectly acceptable.

On page 92 Stephen says Athanasius only differentiates the Father and the Son on the basis that one is Father and one is Son. He says that this is 'about as far as [he] will go in distinguishing Father and Son in the *Orations*.' I do not think this is correct. It seems to me that for Athanasius what primarily distinguishes the Father and the Son is that one is unbegotten God and the other is begotten God. I give only one quote to substantiate my claim. He writes, 'one is Father, and the other Son; and one begets, and the other is begotten.'[2] The eternal generation of the Son is one of the most important theological doctrines that Athanasius develops in opposition to Arius who spoke of the Son as created in time. This doctrine was for Athanasius the linchpin that held together divine oneness in being and eternal self-differentiation. I note, however, that later in his book Stephen says that for all the Nicene fathers, 'the three *hypostases* are distinguished by eternal relations of origin, begetting and proceeding – and not otherwise.'[3]

One of the most important of the many breathtakingly innovative theological insights of the great Athanasius was his argument that to read the Bible rightly on the Son we must recognize that there is 'a double account of the Saviour' in Scripture: one as man in 'the form of a servant' and one as God in all might, majesty and power, a hermeneutical principle he found suggested in John 1:1–18 and Philippians 2:4–11.[4] Stephen does not mention this in his discussion of Athanasius[5] and would seem to suggest this hermeneutic was developed by Gregory of Nazianzus.[6]

I also thought that in discussing the *filioque*[7] not to mention the Orthodox–Reformed agreed statement on the Trinity in general and on the *filioque* clause in particular, negotiated by T.F. Torrance, was a significant omission.[8]

But it is not only that Stephen does not mention the solution to the *filioque* that Torrance negotiated with Eastern theologians; he does not mention Torrance's very important work on the Trinity at all. What is distinctive and exciting about Torrance's writings on the Trinity is that his thorough exploration of the Greek patristic tradition uncovers jewels that enrich and deepen the contemporary articulation of this doctrine.

Finally, I thought that Stephen's outline of Charles Hodge's exposition of the Trinity was over-generous. For Hodge, three 'essential facts' sum up the doctrine of the Trinity: 'unity of essence, distinction of persons, and subordination.'[9] At least thirteen times Hodge speaks of 'the principle of subordination of the Son to the Father, and the Spirit to the Father and the Son'[10] – hierarchical ordering in the Trinity. This subordination, for Hodge, is not in the economy alone as in the Nicene tradition, but in 'the mode of subsistence and operation of the persons.'[11] He even speaks of the Son as 'inferior in rank.'[12]

Now to Three Bigger Issues

Stephen's book is wide ranging but I was disappointed not to find (1) a more positive evaluation of the Nicene fathers' exegetical work, (2) any concession that some twentieth-century Trinitarian theology has enriched and added to the Nicene faith, and (3) no mention at all of the many books by evangelicals that argue for the eternal subordination of the Son and for the abandonment of the doctrine of the eternal generation of the Son, in direct opposition to the Nicene faith.

1. The Nicene fathers and Scripture

In chapter 2 of his book, Stephen criticizes the Nicene fathers' exegetical work and explores what in Scripture led to the Nicene doctrine of the Trinity. I commend him for both the breadth of his reading on biblical interpretation and his brief summary of the New Testament data that is the ground and basis for the doctrine of the Trinity. I must admit, however, I was disappointed with this chapter. To begin with I find his argument somewhat convoluted. Stephen argues both that the exegesis of the church fathers is 'unconvincing, obscure, or seemingly arbitrary to the modern reader',[13] even 'contradictory',[14] and that 'there is a remarkable level of continuity in the exegetical appeals made by developers and defenders of Trinitarian doctrine from the patristic period down to (conservative) defenders of the doctrine of the Trinity today.'[15] Can we affirm both conclusions?

More importantly, I think that, in focusing on the limitations of the Nicene fathers' exegesis, Stephen fails to note the great inheritance they bequeathed to the church in their pioneering work of showing how the Scriptures are to be read in the 'doing' of theology. We need to thank Athanasius most of all for this bequest, but Augustine's contribution is also important. Athanasius's great challenge was that the Arians had one proof text that seemed to endorse exactly what they were teaching, Proverbs 8:22, 'The LORD created [*ktizo* in the LXX] me at the beginning of his work' (NRSV), and numerous texts that spoke of the Son as 'sent' by the Father, praying to the Father, doing the will of the Father, confessing his ignorance of some things and getting tired, all of which for them suggested that the Son was not God in the same way as God the Father. He was God in second degree, created God. Much of Athanasius's *Discourses against the Arians* are given to offering an alternative interpretation of the texts of Scripture that Arius quoted in support of his theology.

Athanasius did not dispute Arius's appeal to Old Testament texts that the New Testament authors read christologically; he only disputed his interpretation of them. Arius and Athanasius assumed that the Old Testament speaks prophetically of Christ. Paul and the other New Testament writers also believed this!

Athanasius saw clearly that there must be something wrong with how Arius was interpreting the Bible, despite all the texts he quoted in support of his views, because what he concluded undermined the full divinity of Christ, something clearly taught in and fundamental to Scripture. In answer to Arius's 'proof-texting' approach, Athanasius put forward three principles or rules on how to do theology by appeal to Scripture that have been endorsed virtually by all theologians after him, until they were forgotten in modern times when the critical and historical reading of Scripture eclipsed them. When the Scriptures can only be interpreted critically and historically, which emphasizes diversity in Scripture, how one does theology becomes very problematic, especially for evangelicals. We contemporary evangelicals have much to learn from Athanasius on how to do theology by appeal to Scripture.

First, Athanasius was convinced that Arius's reading of Scripture could not be right because his conclusions were contrary to what 'the bishops who preceded us and our first catechising' had taught on the full divinity of Jesus Christ. This he calls 'the tradition of the fathers.'[16] After the Council of Nicaea in 325, this 'tradition' was summed up in the Creed of Nicaea. Athanasius was firmly convinced that the right starting point for the theological interpretation of Scripture was what the church had come to believe the Scriptures taught, read holistically. Weinandy says, 'Athanasius opposed Arius, and those who later held similar positions, precisely because he was convinced that they interpreted scripture apart from the ecclesial tradition. Theirs was a private and personal, and thus idiosyncratic, interpretation of scripture.'[17]

Athanasius's appeal to 'the tradition of the fathers' was not an appeal to a body of teaching separate to Scripture, but to how others he highly respected before him had interpreted Scripture. For him, this kind of tradition prescribing how to rightly read Scripture was authoritative. This he contrasted with 'the traditions of men',[18] teaching without scriptural support or worse, contrary to Scripture, which he denigrated.

Second, Athanasius recognized that in Scripture there is much diversity of teaching and there are isolated texts that seem to contradict what the rest of Scripture affirms. To grasp the right meaning of any individual text, he argued, the whole 'scope' of Scripture had to be kept in view.[19] He argued in effect that no one text or even two or three should ever be interpreted to contradict what was plain in all of Scripture.

Third, Athanasius argued that in seeking theological coherence in the diverse teaching of Scripture, often a hermeneutical rule suggested by Scripture itself is demanded. This he argued was certainly the case with what the Bible says about Jesus Christ, the Son of God. In Holy Scripture there is 'a double account of the Saviour; that he was ever God and is the Son, being the Father's *Logos* and Radiance and Wisdom; and that afterwards for us he took the flesh of a virgin.'[20] This 'double account' of the Saviour is most clearly enunciated in John 1:1–18 and Philippians

2:4–11. Once this 'double account' hermeneutic is embraced, Athanasius concluded, the Scriptures can be seen to be giving consistent teaching on the Son. The texts that speak of the Son in all might, majesty and power speak of him as God. The texts that speak of him as praying to the Father, doing the will of the Father, obeying the Father and as ignorant of some things speak of him as God in the 'form of a servant', in his earthly ministry for our salvation.

Augustine follows Athanasius closely, calling such hermeneutical guidelines 'canonical rules'.

Where the exegesis of texts by the Nicene fathers is inadequate, we can and should do better. The critical and historical study of Scripture definitely helps us to grasp more accurately what the authors were trying to say. My argument is that to focus on the inadequacies of some of their exegesis is to miss the point that they pioneered a way of reading Scripture theologically that is needed today as much as it was in the fourth century.

2. A more positive evaluation of some developments in twentieth-century Trinitarian theology

I thoroughly agree with Stephen that the Nicene doctrine of the Trinity is definitive and should not be undermined, but this is not to say that it cannot be reworded, refined, and even conceptually improved subsequently, especially in a changed cultural and historical context. I accept Stephen's very trenchant criticism of a number of innovative twentieth-century formulations of the Trinity, but I nevertheless think some positive advances have been made. The way the Nicene fathers conceived the Trinity undeniably reflects in some measure a fourth-century world in which Greek philosophy and terminology prevailed and other cultural norms foreign to us were assumed. Must our modern, even postmodern, articulation of the Trinity be limited to what was articulated in the fourth century? I think not. I believe in fact that we may be able to speak of the Trinity in ways today that are more in line with biblical thinking than the Greek and Latin fathers.

Stephen acknowledges the 'massive and influential' contribution Barth made to twentieth-century theology, and nowhere is this truer than with his work on the Trinity.[21] Barth did not simply reiterate the Nicene tradition, but sought to advance it with his own creative contribution. So important is his work on the Trinity that much of what has followed can be seen either as a development of some of his ideas or a rejection of them.

I have already mentioned that I was disappointed not to see mention by Stephen of the very significant work on the Trinity by T.F. Torrance.

Torrance definitely wanted to stand within the Nicene tradition, but at the same time he developed certain strands within it in order to exclude any hint whatsoever of subordinationism, and to open a door for rapprochement with the Eastern tradition on the *filioque* clause. I think it would be hard to deny that he too made objective advances on the received Nicene tradition.

Then we have the modern redefinition of what constitutes a 'person'. From the time of Augustine it has been recognized that to speak of the divine three as 'persons' is problematic. Stephen notes that both Barth and Rahner avoided this term. The use of the word 'person' in Trinitarian grammar is questioned because we tend to think of a person as an individual with their own mind, will and consciousness. This is how radical social Trinitarians often speak of the divine persons and so border on tritheism. In modern times, the case has been put that what constitutes one as a person is one's relation to other persons. Self-identity is found in these relations. This understanding of what constitutes personhood is wonderfully evocative in thinking about the divine persons. They are the one God in threefold relationship, each finding their personal identity by and in their threefold relationship. I for one think this is a better way to think of a divine person. It is a positive step forward in Trinitarian theology.

Closely allied with this development is the argument that rather than thinking of divine unity in philosophical terms as a *oneness in being*, it is better to think of divine unity in terms of *being in community*. This images divine unity as dynamic, interpersonal and communal. I think this too is an objective improvement in how we may understand divine life.

I do, however, agree with Stephen that social Trinitarianism is a departure from the Nicene tradition which should not be uncritically endorsed. This construal of the Trinity is novel and borders on tritheism. Three divine persons each with their own will and consciousness would seem to imply three separate individuals. I also agree with him that the thesis that the Trinity prescribes a social agenda on earth is novel and untenable. Before modern times when hierarchical social ordering prevailed no one thought that a Trinity 'where none is before or after, greater or lesser, all are co-equal' (the Athanasian Creed) called into question aristocracy. However, I think that we need to make a distinction between social Trinitarianism, of which we are both critical, and communal Trinitarianism. Today there are three competing ways of trying to explain what constitutes divine unity. First, we have the classic Nicene model that grounds divine unity in *oneness of being*. Second, we have the social model which grounds divine unity in the doctrine of *perichoresis*, mutual indwelling. And third, we have communal models of divine unity such as those spelt out by Zizioulas and more helpfully by T.F. Torrance. This grounds divine unity in a communion of being, as we noted above.

3. *The omission of any comment on the rejection of Nicene orthodoxy by some of the most widely read contemporary evangelical theologians*

I now come to my own hobby horse. I am continually on the lookout for a book by a competent Trinitarian scholar that comments on and discusses the now popular evangelical hierarchical construal of the doctrine of the Trinity, which is made the ground for the hierarchical ordering of the sexes, and which is often associated with a rejection of the doctrine of the eternal generation of the Son. Again I was disappointed. Stephen is silent on this matter. This is the starkest contemporary example of a departure from the Nicene Trinitarian faith by those who have not mastered it or understood it and as a consequence distort it unknowingly.

This widespread evangelical departure from the Nicene faith may be my hobby horse, but it is also a matter of huge importance. It is a tragedy that hardly any theologian, especially among evangelicals, wants to mention the issue, let alone discuss it. Wayne Grudem's *Systematic Theology*[22] has sold more than 350,000 copies, and this is only one of many books by leading conservative evangelical theologians that promulgate this non-Nicene doctrine of the Trinity. Grudem's large tome is mainly bought by clergy, and almost every evangelical, charismatic, and Pentecostal theological student has a copy of this book. The readership of most of the books Stephen mentions pale into insignificance when compared with the sales of Grudem's *Theology*, which he does not mention at all.

The best theologians in the church today need to address this dangerous development that now pervades evangelical circles. Evangelicals who promulgate this doctrine say they are only endorsing the eternal subordination in 'role' or 'function', not the ontological subordination of the Son. They claim that they are teaching historic orthodoxy. The problem is that this role or functional subordination of the Son, which in plain speech always speaks of the Son's *subordination in authority* to the Father and nothing else, is that it is eternal, necessary, and immutably person-defining. It is thus ontological. It speaks of who the Son is, not just how he functions in the economy. This doctrine of the Trinity is undeniably a hierarchical one, and this term is often used in this literature. The Father has the commanding 'role' and the Son the obeying 'role' and this can never change. Most discussions on fourth-century Arianism in its differing expression conclude that hierarchical ordering or ranking in divine life was the essence of this error, and most of the definitions of the modern term 'subordinationism', in dictionaries of theology and in theological texts, say hierarchical ordering or ranking in divine life is the essence of this error. Thus to argue that the divine three persons are ranked or ordered hierarchically in any way is a denial of the Nicene faith. The Athanasian Creed says, 'in this Trinity none is before or after; none is greater or less than another', the three persons are 'co-equal'.

What is more, to make the doctrine of the Trinity the basis and ground for a social agenda is also a departure from Nicene orthodoxy. Stephen is right to criticize Catholic and mainline Protestant social Trinitarians for arguing that three co-equal divine persons prescribe social equality on earth and *mutatis mutandis* this criticism must apply to the evangelicals who argue that a hierarchically ordered Trinity prescribes hierarchical ordering on earth, especially for the male–female relationship. In Nicene orthodoxy the Trinity is our Christian doctrine of God, not our social agenda. What is needed is for those like Stephen who believe that the Nicene faith prescribes orthodoxy to call for a moratorium on appeals to the Trinity for the hierarchal ordering of the sexes. Here it is to be carefully noted that rarely have egalitarian evangelicals appealed to a co-equal Trinity for their agenda. I personally have never done so. The appeal to the Trinity was first made by George Knight in his highly influential 1977 book, *New Testament Teaching on the Role Relationship of Men and Women*,[23] and it has been popularized by Wayne Grudem and Bruce Ware, all of whom are 'complementarians'.

And third, to advocate the abandonment of the doctrine of the eternal generation of the Son, as Grudem, Ware and many other evangelical theologians do, is without question a blatant breach with the Nicene faith. To ask that two lines from the Nicene Creed that undergird the full divinity of the Son and his distinction from the Father be deleted is to part company with the catholic faith. It is to deny a doctrine clearly taught in both the Nicene and Athanasian creeds and all the Reformation and post-Reformation confessions of faith, and supported by almost every theologian of note, including Athanasius, the Cappadocian fathers, Augustine, Aquinas, Luther, Calvin, Barth, and Torrance. The reply that our authority as evangelicals is the Bible, not the creeds or confessions, is particularly worrying. These documents are what the church has agreed to be what the Bible teaches.

I certainly think to omit any discussion at all of this widespread evangelical belief in a hierarchical, ordered Trinity and the rejection of the doctrine of the eternal generation of the Son is a worrying omission. It certainly is a departure from the Nicene faith.

I conclude, Stephen Holmes's book, *The Holy Trinity*, is a very good read, and part of its strength is that it opens up many questions for discussion and comment. I look forward to hearing what Stephen says to me in reply.

Bibliography

Giles, Kevin. *Jesus and the Father: Modern Evangelicals Reinvent the Doctrine of the Trinity* (Grand Rapids: Zondervan, 2006).

Giles, Kevin. *The Eternal Generation of the Son: Maintaining Orthodoxy in Trinitarian Theology* (Downers Grove, Il.: InterVarsity Press, 2012).

Grudem, Wayne A. *Systematic Theology: An Introduction to Biblical Doctrine* (Grand Rapids: Zondervan, rev. edn, 2000).

Hodge, Charles. *Systematic Theology* (3 vols; Grand Rapids: Eerdmans, 1960).

Jowers, Dennis W. and H. Wayne House, eds. *The New Evangelical Subordinationism?* (Eugene, OR: Pickwick, 2012).

Knight, George W., III. *New Testament Teaching on the Role Relationship of Men and Women* (Grand Rapids: Baker, 1977).

Nicene and Post-Nicene Fathers (ed. Philip Schaff and Henry Wace; New York: Christian Literature Company, 1892).

Torrance, T.F. *Trinitarian Perspectives: Toward Doctrinal Agreement* (Edinburgh: T&T Clark, 1994).

Weinandy, Thomas G. *Athanasius: A Theological Introduction* (Aldershot: Ashgate, 2007).

4.

A Double-Headed Luther? A Lutheran Response to *The Holy Trinity* by Stephen R. Holmes

Jon Mackenzie

The Double-Headed Luther, or Are Two Heads Really Better than One?

In his book, *The Holy Trinity*,[1] Stephen R. Holmes produces a bold reading of the development of the doctrine of the Trinity from its earliest beginnings as it materialized from within the doxological practices of the early church, tracing its decline and fall through the seismic upheavals that followed in the wake of the Enlightenment, before documenting the attempted recovery of a Trinitarian form within the theology of the twentieth century up until the present day. His thesis is clear: 'In brief, I argue that the explosion of theological work claiming to recapture the doctrine of the Trinity that we have witnessed in recent decades in fact misunderstands and distorts the traditional doctrine so badly that it is unrecognizable.'[2]

More precisely, his contention is that a paradigmatic instance of the doctrine was formalized within the fourth century, and that this paradigm was maintained with 'only very minor disagreement or development, by all strands of the church – West and East, Protestant and Catholic – until the modern period.'[3] Around the turn of the twentieth century, Holmes detects an aporetic movement in the theological tradition in which various thinkers professed a return to a presumed 'orthodoxy' with respect to Trinitarian theology but which actually introduced 'concepts and ideas that cannot be found in patristic, medieval, or Reformation accounts of the doctrine of the Trinity.'[4] He goes so far as to claim that, 'In some cases, indeed, [these concepts] are points explicitly and energetically repudiated as erroneous – even occasionally as formally heretical – by the earlier tradition.'[5] What results is a two-stage reading of the history: a period of Trinitarian orthodoxy encompassing 'West and East, Protestant and Catholic', 'patristic, medieval, or Reformation', over against a period of presumed Trinitarian recovery in which the protagonists adopt a novel approach to the tradition, more often than not distorting the orthodoxy beyond any form of recognition.

And what of the great Reformer, Martin Luther? How does he fit into this two-stage narrative depicting the rise and fall of Trinitarian theology? Unsurprisingly perhaps, Holmes interpolates him into the first period, interspersing him among those other theologians who found themselves committed to what Holmes labels 'the historic doctrine of the Trinity'.[6] In the end, Holmes devotes two paragraphs of text to Luther, noting his unstinting orthodoxy despite his frequent tendencies to baulk against the more arcane concepts conveyed to him from within the preserve of the scholastic tradition.[7] Overall, Holmes finds Luther himself to be untroubled regarding the acceptance of the Trinitarian theology of the fourth century, deeming it to be easily traced to the scriptural accounts of the divine life. He writes: 'Luther's distinctive exegetical procedure centred on a belief that the meaning of the text was "whatever most exalted Christ"; with this commitment in view, instinctively Trinitarian readings, whether borrowed from the tradition or novel, are not a surprise.'[8] In this way, Luther is allowed to join in the great cloud of witnesses to the traditional doctrine of the Trinity that Holmes has presented in the pages preceding his exegesis of Luther's Trinitarianism.

This brevity of treatment with regard to Luther's articulation of the doctrine of the Trinity should not prove in any way extraordinary on a *prima facie* reading of the text (indeed, it does not). After all, even the famous *Lutherschüler*, Paul Althaus, only devoted a two-page chapter to the doctrine of the Trinity in his book-length exposition of Luther's theology as a whole.[9] In the remaining, albeit scant, allusions to Luther's Trinitarianism within the scholarship,[10] it has become mandatory to underscore the unobtrusive nature of Luther's renditions of the doctrine as it appears in his writings before moving on to more innovative *loci* such as the law/gospel distinction, the doctrine of justification, or the machinations of *Anfechtungen*, to name but a few. On a cursory reading, therefore, Luther's theology of the Trinity is unremarkable, adopting the paradigm that Holmes has delineated in the first part of the book, and ultimately defensible from a position of orthodoxy – an attractive arrangement for a Baptist theologian writing from within a self-consciously Reformed context with a view to defending a fourth-century orthodoxy.

Were this the full story, however, then my task as a respondent would seem to be over before it was even begun. On Holmes's version of events,

Luther has been saved against those purveyors of a modern unorthodoxy, and the only line of attack available to the critic would be a mini-
malist disagreement (at least in terms of the wider argument of the book)
concerning Holmes's reading of Luther's Trinitarian theology which
would achieve very little at any rate, considering the brevity of Holmes's
treatment of Luther, and would devolve very rapidly into *esoteria*, only
interesting to those well-versed in Lutheran terminology and theological
divergences.

That such an approach might be fruitful, despite its almost certain
tendency towards tedium and the consideration of abstract *theologoumena*, is not beyond reasonable conjecture. However, there is, I suspect, a
far more fascinating Luther lurking behind the surface of Holmes's book
who offers himself as a more attractive topic of discussion. For in spite of
Holmes's insistence that Luther be read into the paradigmatic Trinitarianism of the fourth century, the troublesome Reformer seems to protrude
beyond the neat flow of the narrative, finding his way at various junctures
within the subsequent period of Trinitarian theology, the period of the
twentieth-century unorthodoxy. While Holmes clearly wants to overstate
the first Luther's interpolation into the period of Trinitarian orthodoxy,
the Luther of the second period remains a shadowy figure, often lying
undetected beneath the surface of the text or, at times, being absorbed
into the ideas of subsequent theologians or, although Holmes admittedly
attempts to avoid resorting to this line of reasoning, wrapped within the
pejorative mantle of a so-called 'Hegelianism' and, thus, passed off as
heterodox.

As a result, through the course of *The Holy Trinity*, a doubling occurs
in which two Luthers appear: on the one hand, Holmes offers a Luther
who steps confidently within the fourth-century paradigm of Trinitarian
theology, who is happy to adopt the formulations of Nicaea and Chalcedon with little modification; on the other, a more mysterious Luther
emerges who entices modern theologians beyond the bounds of the
fourth-century paradigm and into the ambit of an innovative unorthodoxy. While Holmes's Luther is not quite the seven-headed Luther of
Johannes Cochlaeus, a double-headed figure can be seen to emerge from
within the text of his book, leading to the inquiry as to the feasibility of
his presentation of Luther.

In effect, this double-headed Luther can be seen to inveigle Holmes
into opposing trajectories within the flow of the argument of the book as
a whole. As a theologian consciously writing from within the Reformed
tradition, Holmes is keen to associate his post-Reformation theology
to the archetypal fourth-century Trinitarianism that he sees as being
normative for a properly 'Christian' theology. Luther offers this linkage

between the two traditions so that Holmes can state with confidence that 'All the mainline Reformers were committed to the historic doctrine of the Trinity, believing it to be clearly taught in Scripture.'[11] Being at the head of the Reform movement, Luther's backing of the traditional paradigm of Trinitarian theology is undoubtedly a coup for Holmes's broader project, allowing him the ability to speak of a Trinitarian tradition despite the historical antagonisms between the Protestant and Catholic churches.

Yet much of the narrative of Holmes's depiction of Trinitarian unorthodoxy draws him off along a second trajectory corresponding to a more enigmatic reading of Luther's theology in which the main protagonists are either self-identifying Lutherans or draw strongly from Luther's theological legacy in order to make their claims. For instance, in the first chapter of the book, Holmes traces the genesis of the innovative Trinitarianism to the theology of Karl Barth as the *point de départ* for the renaissance of the doctrine of the Trinity in the modern period. Barth's introduction of a theology of the Word into the liberal traditions of twentieth-century German Christianity, a move which subsequently allowed him to speak of the triune God who reveals himself in his threefold distinction and laid the groundwork for Rahner's insistence that 'the "economic" Trinity is the "immanent" Trinity and the "immanent" Trinity is the "economic" Trinity',[12] can be convincingly connected to the great influence that Luther's theology had on the young Swiss theologian.[13] The first volume of the *Church Dogmatics*, in which the doctrine of the Word is linked to the doctrine of the Trinity, can be viewed, on more careful inspection, as Barth's own attempt to come to terms with Luther's *theologia crucis*. Indeed, on even a cursory glance through the index of volume I/1 of the *Church Dogmatics*, Luther is clearly Barth's primary interlocutor throughout the text. Barth's emphasis upon the incarnational movement of the divine into the world, as God 'takes up a place' among his people as Barth puts it,[14] bears all the marks of a theologian coming to terms with Luther's theological methodology articulated as it is in the maxim *Crux probat omnia*. By linking this crucified man with the triune God, Barth is clearly offering a reading of the doctrine of the Trinity from the outside in, propounding an approach to Trinitarian theology which would become normative within the ensuing tradition. While not necessarily collapsing the distinction between 'economic' and 'immanent' Trinities, Barth is clearly setting a precedent in terms of their hermeneutical ordering: regardless of any logical priority of the immanent Trinity *in se*, our access as human subjects to the triune nature of the divine is always by means of the economic Trinity. In this sense, Barth's approach to the Trinity can be read as a palpable restatement of Luther's *theologia crucis* in a modern setting.

Yet despite lighting upon Barth's Trinitarian project in the *Church Dogmatics* as the efficient cause for the subsequent period of unorthodoxy, Holmes himself, rightly in my opinion, finds Barth to retain 'conservative tendencies' within his account of the doctrine of the Trinity. Accordingly, he references Robert Jenson's observation that 'it is Barth who taught twentieth-century theology – or the lively parts of it – the importance and point of Trinitarian discourse . . . But his contribution to required new Trinitarian *analysis* is not so great as might be expected, nor does he carry us to full liberation from a past-determined interpretation of God. There is room for further reflection.'[15] Needless to say, his retention of the traditional doctrine of the Trinity notwithstanding, Barth's catalytic account of divine revelation, which Holmes invokes as the point at which this period of Trinitarian unorthodoxy is initiated, can be construed as the introduction of a Lutheran account of the word of God within the twentieth-century theological milieu.

From this point onwards, Holmes's account of the heterodox traditions of post-twentieth-century theology diverges, as he distinguishes between a tendency towards 'social Trinitarianism', in which the concepts of divine personhood and human personhood become homogenized, and a tendency towards what Holmes terms 'historical entanglement' in which 'God chooses to be God with, not without, the created order, and its history is his story.'[16] Within this latter strand, which will form the domain within which the remaining discourse is located, Holmes presents a number of theologians who can all, to varying degrees, be located within some kind of Lutheran framework: Pannenberg, baptized Lutheran, and developing a theology of revelation strongly influenced by Barth's theology of the word in conjunction with a philosophy indebted to the thinking of G.W.F. Hegel;[17] Moltmann, who ranked Bonhoeffer, Hegel, and Luther himself among his earliest influences, as he came to react against a perceived anti-historicism in the theology of Barth;[18] Jenson, the American Lutheran theologian, who melded together elements of Barth and the Lutheran tradition into a stunning pastiche in his two-volume *Systematic Theology*;[19] Dorner, the *professor extraordinarius* in theology at the university of Tübingen, who attempted a synthesis of Lutheran and Reformed theologies in the latter stages of the nineteenth century;[20] Schleiermacher, whose doctrine of creation which underpinned his account of the 'Feeling of Absolute Dependence' consisted of an extended commentary on Luther's account of divine creation in his *Genesisvorlesung*;[21] and the litany goes on. Before long, a shadowy version of Luther starts to loom large in the background, coming into sharper relief against the backdrop afforded by Holmes's interlocutors in this second strand of his criticism. In the end, the question becomes:

what is the relationship between the Luther of the first period, the age of Trinitarian orthodoxy, and the second, the age of Trinitarian heterodoxy? At what point does Luther's theology move beyond the limits described by the fourth-century debates and impel the doctrine of Trinity into dangerous new surroundings?

There can be little doubt that an exploration of the pervasive influence of Hegel upon broad swathes of post-Enlightenment theology would offer an initial path towards a solution to this question. However, admirably, Holmes wants to avoid this sort of reductive account of the history. In a footnote he remarks astutely that, 'generic accusations of "Hegelianism", unless supported by close textual evidence, are not helpful to the task of understanding theological development.'[22] This is, of course, completely correct, and yet Holmes makes a subsequent claim insisting that 'there is sufficient motivation and resource in the history of theology's own development to explain the turn to history'.[23] On the one hand, regardless of Holmes's perhaps rhetorically motivated insinuation that there are easy boundaries to be drawn between the spheres of the theological and philosophical, which is nowhere more debatable than in the face of Hegel's writings, the initial sentiment remains true: the solution to this problem cannot be as simple as an introduction of a nonspecific Hegel as a 'vanishing mediator' (to borrow Frederic Jameson's helpful term)[24] between old and new accounts of the Trinity. Nevertheless, despite emphasizing the relative unhelpfulness of appeals to a generic Hegelianism, this does not mean that Hegel should fall out of the picture entirely.[25] Indeed, attempting to divine the 'sufficient motivation and resource in the history of theology's own development to explain the turn to history' may have everything to do with the philosophy of Hegel, although not in terms of the efficient causality that Holmes seems to want to avoid, but rather in terms of the leeching of the theological into the philosophical that provides the conditions for Hegel's philosophical ideas in the first place.[26] For, as we have seen, lying behind the perceived 'Hegelianism' of Holmes's crowd of heretic interlocutors is a far deeper engagement with the theology of Luther than Holmes might like to admit. In essence, the motivating factor behind this movement towards the historical is not simply a *prima facie* Hegelianism but appears to be motivated by some latent facet of Luther's theology that compels Hegel and subsequent theologians to make the claims that they do. A startling thought presents itself: what if the 'vanishing mediator' between orthodox and heterodox Trinities is actually Luther himself? What if the impulsion to move the doctrine of the Trinity into a new frame comes from within the affiliates of Holmes's own perceived orthodoxy? What then?

In his treatise, *The Papacy at Rome*, Luther made a pointed comment about the tendency of his detractors in the Vatican to 'treat the Scriptures artfully and make out of them what they like, as if they were a nose of wax to be pulled around at will.'[27] Within the pages of *The Holy Trinity*, the same criticism could be levelled against Holmes and his treatment of Luther; the Luther who emerges through the course of the discussion appears to have been carefully moulded so as to accommodate Holmes's rendering of the genesis of Trinitarian unorthodoxy – the conducive aspects being augmented and the less favourable aspects being smoothed over so that the twofold periodization can be easily maintained throughout the text.

In what follows, the discussion will attempt to clarify the particularly Lutheran theological developments that pushed the doctrine of the Trinity beyond the comfortable setting of the fourth-century paradigm. Initially, the work of Christine Helmer will be examined as it offers a historical rendition of the occlusion of the orthodox doctrine of the Trinity in the *Lutherforschung* that Holmes himself would find attractive.[28] Through the course of this narrative, Helmer argues that Luther's orthodox account of the doctrine of the Trinity is passed over in light of the neo-Kantian approaches to Luther which sprang up as a result of the Luther renaissance, emphasizing the divine economy as the starting point for Trinitarian discussion and disposing with a need for an account of the immanent Trinity altogether. However, despite the great benefit to the subject that her study affords, I will suggest that she ultimately drives a wedge between Luther's Trinitarian theology and his innovative Christology, a wedge that may be palpable within the theology of Luther himself and which the subsequent theological traditions have attempted to remedy. If this is the case, then the source for the doubled-headed Luther lies not within the ensuing tradition *per se* but within the ambit of Luther's theology itself, offering a subtle criticism of Holmes's narrative account of Luther's place within Trinitarian development. In the end, the periodization ceases to follow an easy two-stage division but, in fact, overlaps, with Luther at the centre, calling into question the ease with which Holmes might want to portion out the traditions of Trinitarian theology and necessitating a return to Luther's theology in order to determine its place within the genetic development of the doctrine of the Trinity.

In light of Helmer's reading of the narrative, therefore, Holmes's version of the tradition can be seen to rely on the implementation of a rift between Luther's conservative Trinitarianism on the one hand, and his innovative Christology on the other, with its introduction of the concept of the *communicatio idiomatum*. For no sooner than Luther's Christology is brought alongside his Trinitarianism, questions arise as to the feasibility of the fourth-century paradigm (at least in the stringent form that Holmes delineates) as a framework for this novel approach to the person of Christ. Accordingly, by relocating the 'doubled Luther' from the ambit of the neo-Kantians into the realm of Luther's theology itself, the need for an enquiry into the precise location of Luther within the Christian tradition is generated. Does Luther's Christology operate against his conservative Trinitarianism? If it does, should his Christology be jettisoned as unorthodox or his Trinitarian paradigm modified to suit this christological development?

Following Helmer, Holmes's approach to these questions is to trump the doctrine of Christology with the doctrine of the Trinity, allowing the Christology to reside behind the scenes of the discussion while simultaneously extolling the virtues of Luther's Trinitarianism. However, in light of his criticisms of the later Trinitarian approaches, whose approach follows along the opposite trajectory (viz. modify the Trinitarian doctrine in light of the Christology), Holmes will not afford their 'Luther' the same privileges, criticizing their accounts of the divine entanglement with the created order. Yet if they are in danger of divine entanglement in their Trinitarian theology, then is not the same true of Luther in his christological innovation? Is the protection afforded the divine substance in the fourth-century paradigm in danger of collapsing in the light of Luther's christological innovation? This question of the historical entanglement of the divine will be covered in conclusion and will raise a final question as to the place of Luther within Holmes's retelling of the history in *The Holy Trinity*.

Luther's Elusive Trinity: A Question of Immanence or Economy?

Christine Helmer's study of Luther's doctrine of the Trinity as it emerges through his later writings is a *tour de force* in the scholarship. Exploring the doctrine through a number of different genres through the latter stages of the Reformer's career, she goes on to show the extensive overlap between Luther's Trinitarian thought and the preceding traditions in their variously patristic, scholastic, and nominalist forms. Helmer's broader argument is framed by her attentiveness to a perceived misreading in the *Lutherforschung* in which the hermeneutical approach to Luther's doctrine of the Trinity underwent a shift from a traditional starting point in the immanent Trinity to a novel methodology which privileged the economic Trinity as the key to Luther's Trinitarian method.[29] In this sense, she sees the contemporary approaches to Luther's theology as dichotomizing between the 'new' and the 'old' in his theological approach, with the 'new' coming to take precedence over the 'old', allowing a reassignment of the doctrine of the Trinity from immanent sphere to economic sphere to occur.[30]

The principal cause of this shift Helmer locates in the readiness of neo-Kantian-infused theologies to associate the *pro me* character of Luther's thinking with post-Kantian epistemological approaches to divine knowledge, which consequently reallocated discussions about the Trinity to within the economic sphere. She writes: 'The conceptual link between the "new" in Luther's theology and its assignment to the divine economy is, to a large extent, a function of neo-Kantian presuppositions . . . The turn in language towards the *pro nobis* reflects a theological shift towards privileging the epistemological accent of what [Risto] Saarinen has classified as neo-Protestant, Luther Renaissance and Barthian dialectical theology.'[31] Her argument is simple enough: Luther's traditional account of the doctrine of the Trinity which prioritized the immanent Trinity over the economic becomes occluded by a neo-Kantian emphasis on epistemology which prioritizes the economic Trinity over the immanent. The post-Kantian allergy towards speaking about *Dinge an sich selbst* instigated a shift in emphasis away from any language of immanence with respect to the divine being and towards language of divine economy, towards the realm within which the human subject could be said to have genuine knowledge of the divine. Accordingly, the repositioning of the site of the threefold distinction to within the economy led to various assumptions being made of the divine being and its relation to the created order. In this manner, the question as to the divine entanglement with human history finds its fulcrum in the chosen point of departure for the discussion of the doctrine of the Trinity, be it in the immanent relating of the divine being or the *oikonomia* in which God comes in the person of Jesus Christ.

Helmer's narrative closely mirrors Holmes's with its interpolation of Luther into the period of Trinitarian orthodoxy and consignment of the later interpreters of Luther into the folds of heterodoxy. However, a number of fault lines appear in the smooth surface of the analysis which suggest that there is more to the *prima facie* reading of the history than meets the eye. For example, principal among Helmer's authorities in her reading of the development of Luther scholarship is Risto Saarinen, a member of the Finnish School of Luther Studies.[32] While there may be an element of truth in Helmer's claim that contemporary enquiry into Luther's thinking has been unduly concerned with amplifying the 'new' in his writings to the detriment of the 'old', the Finnish School offers a premier example of an approach to Luther which advocates the opposite extreme, with the innovative aspects of Luther's ideas being pushed into the background in a veiled attempt to unify the theologies of the East and West. The fact of the matter is that the question of the 'new' and 'old' in Luther's theology is not to be presented in such a way as to suggest some kind of 'concluded' Luther – a chimeric figure without any internal contradiction or inconsistency – which the historical theologian should attempt to reconstruct as the 'authentic' Luther. It may be the case, especially with regards to the theological writings of Martin Luther, that irregularities do arise within the broader compass of his theology which should not be smoothed over by the historian.

Yet throughout the course of her framing narrative, there is a suspicion that Helmer is endeavouring to do just this. By laying the blame for the shift in emphasis from the immanent to the economic in the prevailing discussions of Luther's doctrine of the Trinity at the feet of the neo-Kantian presuppositions that make their way into the *Lutherforschung* in the nineteenth and twentieth centuries, she deflects discussion of the matter at hand away from those problematic aspects internal to Luther's theology, and into the realm of the history of ideas, implying that the causes for this modification in Trinitarian thought exist beyond the remit of Luther's own ideas. But as Holmes himself averred of generic appeals to Hegelianism, these sorts of arguments, 'unless supported by close textual evidence, are not helpful to the task of understanding theological development.'[33] What is more interesting from our perspective is the enquiry into the correspondence that arises between the philosophical ideas of the twentieth century (be they neo-Kantian or Hegelian or whatever) and the theology of Martin Luther itself. That is to say: what are the nodal points within Luther's theology that drew these contemporary theologians into the sphere of Lutheran theology in the first place? What is it about Luther's theology that makes it so conducive to a post-Enlightenment intellectual milieu? On this appraisal, the focus should not turn away from Luther to seek after the formal conditions for this shift in the broader intellectual history, but rather should return to Luther in an attempt to assess his part in the transferral. In this way, rather than assuming that the later interpreters are simply erroneous in their engagement with Luther, what results is an appreciation that these scholars may find themselves drawn towards different facets of Luther's theology as inhabitants of a different intellectual climate.

By posing the problem in this form, a provisional solution to the *aporia* of the 'double-headed' Luther presents itself with particular regard to the issue as to the precise starting point for the Trinitarian analysis of Luther's theology. As we have seen, Helmer's historiography suggests a movement towards the divine economy as the site for the discussion of the divine being in its threefold distinction primarily on epistemological grounds. In the post-Kantian morass, access to the divine had been more carefully delineated in terms of the phenomenal sphere within which human experience was located. As a result, any claim to genuine knowledge of God outside of this phenomenal realm was treated with suspicion by post-Enlightenment thinkers, necessarily leading to the onset of suspicion with regards to any self-standing account of an 'immanent' Trinity beyond the bounds of any tangible human experience. However, this shift in attention from the internal operations of the divine towards the tangible activities of the divine within the economy as the starting point for Trinitarian theology is not, as Helmer would have it, entirely antagonistic to Luther's own approach, but finds a correlate in the *theologia crucis* developed by Luther within the period of his earlier theology.

In this famously anti-speculative theological methodology, Luther reacted against a perceived late-medieval tendency towards abstraction and proposed a return of the focus of attention to the person of Christ Crucified, God himself come among human persons. The *theologia crucis* is summed up in a famous passage from the *Commentary on Galatians*, where Luther entreats the theologian to:

> Begin where Christ began – in the Virgin's womb, in the manger, and at his mother's breast. For this purpose he came down, was born, lived amongst men, suffered, was crucified, and died, so that in every possible way He might present Himself to our sight. He wanted us to fix the gaze of our hearts upon Himself and thus prevent us from clambering up into heaven and speculating about the Divine Majesty.[34]

In this sense, the project of the *theologia crucis* can be viewed as one of divine placement in which the fullness of the Godhead came to be indistinguishable from the human person, Jesus of Nazareth. By entering into the world as a man, God chose to relate to his creation from within the economy that it provided rather than remaining distant from it, neither revealing himself to human persons obliquely nor simply maintaining it dispassionately as a sort of ontological regulator lying behind the scenes. As a consequence, the concept of divine placement can be seen as an important impetus behind many of Luther's theological writings, impelling him to accentuate the self-presencing of the divine within the created world as the starting point for a Christian theology. This tendency can be observed throughout his career, even through to the composition of the *Genesisvorlesung*, the final lecture series of his academic life. In the pages of the *Genesisvorlesung*, Luther's primary concern is to explicate the interaction of God with his people in the place of human existence as the domain within which he makes himself available to them. In this way, the perceived emphasis upon the divine economy as a starting point for theology in the contemporary renditions of Luther's thought cannot be simply attributed to 'neo-Kantian presuppositions' on the part of the interpreters but can be seen as reflective of something internal to Luther's own thinking.

Yet as to the precise character of this significant concept of divine placement, Luther's concern in its formulation is not simply epistemological in a narrow post-Kantian sense of the term.[35] Instead, he attempts to go beyond the merely experiential aspect of the divine presence to offer some account of the ontological structuring of this divine incarnation within the world which gave credence to the divine revelation through the *Logos*. Luther's eucharistic articulations, with their introduction of the notion of *communicatio idiomatum*, the communication of idioms, as the mechanism regulating the interaction between divine and human natures in the hypostatic union, go beyond a mere epistemological interest and highlight Luther's attempts to give an ontological underpinning to his concept of divine presence. In effect, on Luther's account, God can only be present to us as human subjects if God *really* is present in an ontological sense in the person of Jesus Christ; there can be no buffering between the natures in the hypostasis by which a hypothetical Arianism might obtain within the Son with the result that, in speaking of the hypostatic union, there may be a compromise on the *unity* of the natures. In the person of Jesus Christ, the fullness of the Godhead *is* present in such a way that he can be said to be one of those three whose mutuality is the divine life.[36]

In light of this fact, the *communicatio idiomatum* becomes the fulcrum around which Luther's theological pendulum swings.[37] The hotly debated concept of the ubiquity of Christ's body should, therefore, not be read as a piece of arcane theologoumenon but rather finds itself located within Luther's desire to encompass Jesus of Nazareth in his full humanity within the perfect divinity of the triune life.[38] The Reformed attitude towards the natures, the ascription of activities to the nature to which they are proper, ran the risk of holding the divine and the created apart in such a way as to call into question the efficacy of the incarnation to obtain any soteriological purchase at all, both ontologically and epistemologically. If God can be said to die through the humanity of the Son, then does he also save through the divinity of the Son? Does this approach not suggest that the hypostatic union is no union at all? And what of the *Extra Calvinisticum*, that vestigial remainder of the divine *Logos* which protruded beyond the humanity of Christ? Was this elusive part of the divinity of Christ not available to human persons with the subsequent result that Jesus of Nazareth was not fully revelatory of the divine? The possibility of the relationship between the divine and human persons stands or falls, both ontologically and epistemologically, on the capacity for a correct rendering of the relationship between divinity and humanity in the person of Jesus Christ. The *theologia crucis* requires that the human person dying in frailty on the cross is indistinguishable from the second person of the Trinity, and it is at this point that the theologian begins.

Read along these lines, the Lutheran formulation of the relationship of the two natures in the person of Jesus Christ can be seen to take a logical priority over the precise arrangement of the Trinitarian formulation. For, were it not the case that the *communicatio idiomatum* held true, there could be no human access to the doctrine of the Trinity in the first place (both in terms of ontology and epistemology). As a result, any articulation of the doctrine which allowed a rift to obtain between the divinity and humanity in Christ would operate at variance to the *theologia crucis*, causing Luther's whole project to collapse in on itself.[39] At this juncture, two options present themselves to the impartial observer. In light of the ordering of Luther's theological methodology through the *theologia crucis*, the presence of a traditional doctrine of the Trinity in Luther must either mean that Luther himself saw no contradictions arising between his innovative Christology and the doctrine of the Trinity he received from the earlier theological tradition; or that there exists an internal inconsistency within Luther's theology between his Christology and his doctrine of the Trinity which he himself overlooked. On the one hand, the doctrine of *communicatio idiomatum* may be compatible with the fourth-century paradigmatic instance of the doctrine of the Trinity; on the other, it may require that the traditional doctrine of the Trinity requires modifying, and the distinction between immanent and economic Trinities needs collapsing.

To return to our problematic 'doubled-headed' Luther, we now begin to see where a division might appear between the earlier and later periods in Helmer's (and also Holmes's) historiographical approach. Where Helmer (and Holmes) are consciously beginning with Luther's Trinitarian formulation, which is unavoidably orthodox, the later theologies of historical entanglement find their genesis in the christological innovation of the *theologia crucis*, working back to a doctrine of the Trinity which corresponds to this prior logic. In the case of the former, the doctrine of the *communicatio idiomatum* is able to be bracketed off in their discussion of Luther's Trinitarianism either by dint of an interpretation of the *communicatio* which is congruent with the fourth-century model of the triune relations or by overlooking Luther's own mistaken supposition that his doctrines of Christology and Trinity were entirely consistent. The result is an exploration of the conditions of the heterodox Trinitarianism beyond the scope of Luther's writings.

Compare this approach with that taken by the advocates of historical entanglement: by beginning with the Christology arising from the *theologia crucis*, they posit that the fourth-century account of the doctrine of the Trinity is unsatisfactory as a framework for an account of the God who is indistinguishable from the man dying on a cross in the Middle East, and recommend a return to the question of the concept of God in light of this phenomenon. Consider, for example, the Lutheran theologian Eberhard Jüngel, who asks: 'How can the divine essence be thought of together with the event of death without destroying the concept of God – that was the question raised anew and radically by the Reformation, and theology should have dealt with it. But it did not. It did not happen until the philosopher Hegel took up the question in its radicality and sought to resolve it.'[40] In this way, the theological conditions that allow Holmes to construct his two-stage narrative are not to be found, as Helmer would have it, in the introduction of 'neo-Kantian presuppositions' within the late modern theological milieu, or, as Holmes might suggest, in the wake of a burgeoning Hegelianism which, although undoubtedly a major influence in the emergence of the theologies of divine entanglement, cannot be considered the prime mover in the development. In fact, these conditions can actually be perceived as inherent within the theology of Luther himself, the Reformer whom Holmes places squarely within the orthodox renderings of the doctrine of the Trinity. As to the rightness or wrongness of either reading of Luther's theology, time does not allow us the privilege of exploring in any great depth. Needless to say, whichever way you read it, the neat historiography of *The Holy Trinity* is rendered more complex by the figure of Martin Luther who forms the hinge around which the entire narrative can be seen to turn.

Conclusion

Where does this leave us? The double-headed Luther who emerges within the pages of *The Holy Trinity* presents Holmes with an uncomfortable choice to make regarding his placement of Luther in the flow of the argument of his book. He has two options: in the first instance, he can maintain his present taxonomy and argue that Luther's accounts of Christology and Trinity are compatible and that the later readings of Luther's Trinitarian thought go too far in suggesting a collapse between economic and immanent Trinities. This is, no doubt, the direction he would naturally want to take. However, this leaves him with the need to develop an account of *communicatio idiomatum* which would require more careful argumentation for the narrative as it is to hold tight, and would, almost certainly, end up looking more like a Reformed Christology than a Lutheran one. Were such a rendering of the *communicatio* to prove impossible, therefore, it would require that Holmes adopt a different approach in which he would have to concede that the scholars of the later period of Trinitarian heterodoxy were justified in modifying Luther's account of the doctrine in order to make space for the innovative Christology that he developed in response to his *theologia crucis*. Yet such a course would problematize Luther's relationship to the fourth-century paradigm, suggesting that his inclusion among the orthodox be little more than a historical inaccuracy instigated by his own incapacity to appreciate the full extent of his radical Christology. In either case, Luther ceases to be worth a mere two paragraphs, and emerges as the efficient cause of an entire strand within the recent development in Trinitarian theology.

Bibliography

Althaus, Paul. *The Theology of Martin Luther* (trans. R.C. Schultz; Philadelphia: Fortress Press, 1966).

Asendorf, Ulrich. *Luther und Hegel: Untersuchung zur Grundlegung einer neuen systematischen Theologie* (Wiesbaden: Franz Steiner Verlag, 1982).

Barth, Karl. *Church Dogmatics*, vol. I/1. (Edinburgh: T&T Clark, 1936).

Bayer, Oswald. *Martin Luther's Theology: A Contemporary Interpretation* (trans. Thomas H. Trapp; Grand Rapids: Eerdmans, 2008).

Dalferth, Ingolf U. *Becoming Present: An Inquiry into the Christian Sense of the Presence of God* (Leuven: Peeters, 2006).

Eckardt, Burnell F., Jr. 'Luther and Moltmann: The Theology of the Cross'. *Concordia Theological Quarterly* 49 (1985): pp. 19–28.

Gerrish, Brian A. *A Prince of the Church: Schleiermacher and the Beginnings of Modern Theology* (Eugene, OR: Wipf & Stock, 1988).

Helmer, Christine. *The Trinity and Martin Luther: A Study on the Relationship between Genre, Language, and the Trinity in Luther's Works (1523–1546)*. Veröffenlichungen des Institutes für europäische Geschichte/ Abteilung abendländische Religionsgeschichte 174 (Mainz: Verlag Philipp von Zabern, 1999).

Hunsinger, George 'What Karl Barth Learned from Martin Luther'. *Lutheran Quarterly* 13 (1999): pp. 125–55.

Jameson, Frederic. 'The Vanishing Mediator: Narrative Structure in Max Weber'. *New German Critique* 1 (1973): pp. 52–89.

Jenson, Robert W. 'Luther's Contemporary Theological Significance.' Pages 272–88 in *The Cambridge Companion to Martin Luther* (ed. Donald K. McKim; Cambridge: Cambridge University Press, 2003).

— *Systematic Theology* (2 vols; Oxford: Oxford University Press, 1997, 1999).

— *The Triune Identity: God According to the Gospel* (Philadelphia: Fortress Press, 1982).

Jüngel, Eberhard. *God as the Mystery of the World* (Edinburgh: T&T Clark, 1983).

Lohse, Bernhard. *Martin Luther's Theology: Its Historical and Systematic Development* (trans. Roy A. Harrisville; Edinburgh: T&T Clark, 1999).

Luther, Martin. *Dr Martin Luthers Werke* [WA] (Weimar: Böhlau, 1883–1993).

— *Luther's Works* [LW] (ed. Jaroslav Pelikan and Helmut T. Lehmann; St Louis: Concordia and Philadelphia: Fortress Press, 1955–86).

Małysz, Piotr J. 'Hegel's Conception of God, and Its Application by Isaak Dorner to the Problem of Divine Immutability'. *Pro Ecclesia* 15 (2006): pp. 448–71.

— 'Storming Heaven with Karl Barth? Barth's Unwitting Appropriation of the Genus Maiestaticum and what Lutherans Can Learn from It'. *Modern Theology* 9 (2007): pp. 73–92.

McGrath, Alister E. *Luther's Theology of the Cross* (Oxford: Blackwell, 1985).

Min, Anselm K. 'The Dialectic of Divine Love: Pannenberg's Hegelian Trinitarianism'. *International Journal of Systematic Theology* 6 (2004): pp. 252–69.

Ngien, Dennis. *The Suffering of God According to Martin Luther's 'Theologia Crucis'* (New York: Peter Lang, 1995).

Norgate, Jonathan. *Isaak A. Dorner: The Triune God and the Gospel of Salvation* (Edinburgh: T&T Clark, 2009).

O'Regan, Cyril. *The Heterodox Hegel* (New York: State University of New York, 1994).

Pannenberg, Wolfhart. 'Luther's Contribution to Christian Spirituality'. *Dialog* 40 (2001): pp. 284–9.

Rahner, Karl. *The Trinity* (trans. Joseph Donceel; Tunbridge Wells: Burns & Oates, 1970).

5.

T.F. Torrance and the Patristic Consensus on the Doctrine of the Trinity

Jason Radcliff

Introduction

Colin Gunton states that T.F. Torrance provides 'a reopening of a major historical conversation'[1] and George Dragas elucidates: 'few contemporary theologians in [Torrance's] tradition have so thoroughly and consistently appropriated the spiritual wealth of Greek Patristic Theology'.[2] Indeed, standing in the midst of the late twentieth-century *ressourcement* of the fathers and revival of Trinitarian theology, Torrance sees himself as returning to the patristic consensus on, among other central dogmas of the church, the doctrine of the Trinity.[3]

In *The Holy Trinity*, Stephen Holmes has called into question these so-called Trinitarian 'revivals' of which Torrance was a part, arguing that, while ostensibly patristic, they in fact had more to do with the preconceptions and commitments of the twentieth-century figures leading the revival and less to do with the classical Trinitarian theology to which they claimed to be returning.[4] Embedded within this is Holmes's critique of the tendency towards a strong bifurcation of East and West on the doctrine of the Trinity as popularized by the 'de Régnon thesis' and Holmes's assertion of a seamless garment of the patristic tradition on the doctrine of the Trinity spanning East and West, Greek and Latin.[5]

Standing within the revival which Holmes critiques in his book, Torrance sees himself as following the fathers in nearly every element of his theology, not least on his doctrine of the Trinity. In *Trinitarian Faith*, Torrance traces the 'inner theological connections that gave coherent structure to the classical theology of the ancient Catholic Church'[6] and in *Christian Doctrine of God*, Torrance offers a doctrine of the Trinity he calls 'heavily influenced' by Greek patristic theology.[7] Torrance says that the Greek fathers shaped his work from the beginning of his theological development.[8] However, is Torrance actually returning to the fathers or is he presenting his readers more with a twentieth-century theology, alongside his fellow Trinitarian revivalists?

In order to answer these questions, this essay will first introduce Torrance's overall reading of the fathers in light of Holmes's critique. This essay will argue that Torrance's reading is a creative attempt to produce a Reformed and evangelical version of the patristic tradition on the doctrine of the Trinity involving significant changes to both standard readings of the fathers and Torrance's own tradition. Second, this essay will explore some key differences between Torrance and Holmes such as their somewhat different visions of the patristic era, Torrance's close identification of the immanent and economic Trinity (in a fashion similar to Karl Rahner), and Torrance's emphasis on epistemology (in a fashion similar to Karl Barth), arguing that these arise from Torrance's dynamic and theologically constructive approach to the fathers on the doctrine of the Trinity. Third, this essay will explore the points where Torrance's vision is highly relevant for the current conversation of which Holmes is a part by means of examination of Torrance's work in the Reformed–Orthodox Dialogue. The overall argument will be that Torrance's reconstruction of the fathers on the doctrine of the Trinity offers a dogmatic-theological approach, complementing Holmes's book and his more historical-exegetical approach.

Torrance's Reconstruction of the Fathers

Holmes states: 'We could have returned to careful readings of the fathers and the classical tradition, but we chose to see the doctrine taught by the fathers as the problem, not a potential solution'.[9] Torrance as well urges a return to the fathers, especially the 'Athanasius-Cyril axis'.[10] His 'Foreword' to *Theology in Reconciliation*[11] is a plea to all Christian traditions to return to this core and leave behind their cultural additions (while at the same time keeping their distinctive pietistic differences) and to embrace the 'patristic foundation' of their common faith.[12] Indeed, Torrance, with Holmes, believes the fathers are the answer, not the problem.

In a letter written in 1988, the then Eastern Orthodox Archbishop Methodios of Aksum writes to Torrance: 'I admire your patristic expressions and your use of catholic terms'.[13] Methodios's language captures Torrance's approach to the fathers well: Torrance does not simply return to the fathers attempting to offer a narrow representation of their concepts. Rather, he constructs (or to use his language, 'reconstructs')[14] the fathers around ecumenical themes and figures.[15] As Dragas puts it,

Torrance 'seeks to build up his theology on the one, historical common ground of all three traditions and . . . he is prepared at the same time to confess in full modesty and sincerity their historical particularities and fortify himself only with their positive forces.'[16] Torrance extrapolates what he sees as the best of the patristic, Reformation, and modern eras of the theological tradition, dynamically combining them, re-centring them upon Jesus Christ. This combination makes Torrance a theological figure of ecumenical import inasmuch as his reconstruction has points of contact with many different Christian traditions.

Torrance's reading of the fathers is a creative attempt to produce a Reformed and evangelical version of the patristic consensus involving significant changes to both the standard interpretations of the fathers and Torrance's own tradition. This Torrancian consensus has a plethora of constructive achievements that have been overlooked by many on account of his being evaluated simply as an historian. When Torrance is viewed rather as a *theologian* constructing a Reformed and evangelical version of the patristic consensus, his many contributions emerge.

Torrance approaches the fathers as a dogmatician and not as a patrologist, and he reads the fathers christologically rather than historically. As such, Torrance's reading and use of the fathers neither resembles traditional patrology nor traditional Reformed dogmatic theology but is rather a truly unique Reformed and evangelical reconstruction of patristic theology involving reform to his own tradition. Throughout the many texts where he appropriates the fathers, Torrance remains consistently centred on this reconstructive approach to the fathers, allowing him fresh insight into them by means of his creative connections, rereading, and re-situation of them.

The Nicene doctrine of ὁμοούσιον τῷ Πατρί ('one being with the Father') serves as the cornerstone of Torrance's creative reconstruction of the fathers. Torrance's ὁμοούσιον is taken from Nicene theology and it is a patristic reconstruction of the Reformation principle of *solus Christus* (Christ alone). As such, it exemplifies Torrance's approach to a truly Greek patristic theme, the ὁμοούσιον, from a Reformed and evangelical perspective, Word-centredness. Torrance sees the flowering of the evangelical theology of the fathers in the Nicene doctrine of ὁμοούσιον, which, for him, means that 'God Himself is the actual content of his revelation and God Himself is really in Jesus Christ reconciling the world to Himself.'[17] The core of Torrance's patristic consensus is ὁμοούσιον and for Torrance all theology must be centred upon it. In this way it acts as a linchpin for theology.[18] The ὁμοούσιον is the centre of the Torrancian patristic consensus and his creative reading of the fathers is done on the basis of it and through it and he reconstructs everything around it.[19] For him, everything in theology rests upon this Father–Son relationship.

For Torrance, the ὁμοούσιον contains key epistemological and evangelical/soteriological implications. Primarily the ὁμοούσιον means, 'God is really like Jesus.'[20] Accordingly, this means that due to the ὁμοούσιον God can be known internally *in himself*.[21] Due to Jesus' and the Holy Spirit's ὁμοούσιον with the Father on the one hand and Jesus' ὁμοούσιον with humankind on the other, God is now knowable as he is in himself by means of Christ and the indwelling of the Holy Spirit.[22] Torrance sees the ὁμοούσιον implying epistemologically that God is knowable as he is *in himself* by means of the Son and the Spirit who are ὁμοούσιον with the Father. For, the only reason that anything can be said about God is because of the ὁμοούσιον, the objective reality of God in Christ. The ὁμοούσιον also has key soteriological/evangelical implications. At the core it means that the acts of Jesus are the acts of God. Thus, God is really in Jesus reconciling the world to himself.[23]

Torrance reconstructs the patristic tradition around the ὁμοούσιον into streams or threads in theological history. In Torrance's vision there is one overarching stream running throughout the church's history: the evangelical stream. Torrance believes that certain eras of theological history capture the inner structure of the gospel best.[24] Torrance sees these eras connected to one another as a sort of 'golden thread' running throughout theological history. According to Torrance, the three instances that best captured this inner structure are Nicaea (particularly Athanasius), the Reformation (particularly John Calvin), and contemporary evangelical theology (particularly Barth).[25] Herein, Torrance sees the Reformation emphasis on grace as complementary to the Nicene emphasis on the ὁμοούσιον,[26] creatively connecting Nicene theology and his Reformed evangelical tradition, seeing the two as better understood in light of each other.[27] The Reformation, therefore, complements the patristic tradition for Torrance.[28] Ultimately, Torrance sees Barth as inheriting these two parts of the evangelical stream, combining them dynamically. As such, Barth is the funnel through which the Nicene theology of the ὁμοούσιον of Christ and the Reformation theology of the ὁμοούσιον of grace are dynamically combined and filtered into contemporary theology as the evangelical stream.

Torrance connects Barth and Athanasius directly as well. He does this primarily on the doctrine of the Trinity and the emphasis on the dynamic nature of the being of God. He consistently maintains that both Barth and Athanasius asserted a doctrine of the Trinity that affirms *God to us* is *God in himself*. He believes Barth was doing this in order to preserve the conception that the gift of grace and the Giver are identical.[29] Torrance states this in a number of ways, including his argument that for both theologians God is 'Being in Person'. Elsewhere, he elaborates upon this in more detail when he connects the Athanasian concepts of ἐνούσιος λόγος ('word intrinsic to essence')[30] and ἐνούσιος ἐνέργια ('energy intrinsic to essence') directly to the Barthian conception of 'Being-in-Act and Act-in-Being'.[31] Torrance sees these two concepts as not only mutually informing but as asserting the same basic theology, namely that there is no epistemological disconnection between the *ontological Trinity* and the *economic Trinity*.[32]

Torrance understands this evangelical stream to have run from the Athanasius–Cyril axis through Anselm,[33] Kierkegaard,[34] certain figures in Scottish theology, and finally to its climax in Barth (and H.R. Mackintosh who was a conduit of Barthian theology into Scotland). The fount of this evangelical stream is the Nicene stream (and its best exponent, Athanasius) and the themes (especially the ὁμοούσιον).[35] Torrance also sees other, diverging, streams of theological history. He contends that the dualist elements of Reformed theology were inherited from Augustinian thought[36] and is critical of the Augustinian stream (leading into Latin Scholasticism).[37] He is also critical of the Cappadocian distinction[38] which he believes led to the dualist Byzantine tradition.[39]

Torrance's positive appraisal of Barth and his intimate connection of the immanent and economic Trinity might raise some suspicion for the reader of Holmes's book. Holmes is, on the one hand, appreciative of both Barth and Rahner's starting point: 'Insisting that revelation, divine identity, and the narrative of redemption demand a doctrine of the Trinity' for Barth and 'insisting that accounts of the immanent Trinity must be somehow responsible to the economy of salvation' for Rahner.[40] However, on the other hand, Holmes accuses Barth of the semi-collapsing of the Trinity into his doctrine of revelation and his novel Trinitarian terminology[41] and Rahner of a too-intimate ontological identification of the immanent and economic Trinity.[42]

Torrance sees 'obvious connections' between Barth and Athanasius[43] on the important connection between the doctrine of the Trinity and revelation, and he sees a broad tradition in the church following in this stream.[44] However, despite Torrance's language occasionally sounding as if he considers the fathers to have been saying essentially the same thing as Barth, it is clear he does not really intend this. Rather, he simply sees Barth insisting upon truthful theological concepts complementary to the Reformation and the patristic era.[45]

In his article on Rahner's Trinitarian theology published in *Trinitarian Perspectives*,[46] Torrance raves about the import and relevance of Rahner's intimate connection of the economic and immanent Trinity. He states:

'what [Rahner] seems to be intending in his own way is basically in agreement with St Athanasius on the one hand and Karl Barth on the other hand'.[47] Throughout this important article, Torrance is highly appreciative of Rahner's insistence on the centring of knowledge of God on God's self-communication rather than some sort of abstract knowledge.[48] Notably, his hesitation about Rahner is on precisely the same point where Holmes is critical, on the potentially ontological implications of Rahner's epistemological assertions.[49] Torrance states: 'There would appear to be some ambiguity, in the course of Rahner's exposition, between the doctrine of the Trinity and the Trinity'.[50] He criticizes Rahner in a substantially similar way to Holmes, pointing out that if 'Rahner's rule' is solely epistemological that is helpful but, if ontological, problems arise.

In his reading of the fathers on the doctrine of the Trinity Torrance is, however, up to something slightly different from Holmes; Holmes is attempting historical exposition of the fathers, critiquing contemporary theology for departing from the fathers, whereas Torrance is offering a dogmatic and theological reconstruction of the fathers. Torrance appreciates figures such as Barth and Rahner of whom Holmes is critical; however, Torrance is, as a dogmatician, taking what he sees as their positive qualities and offering a theologically constructive approach to the doctrine of the Trinity, utilizing positive elements (as he sees it) from the fathers, the Reformers, Barth, and contemporary theology. However, this leads to particular discrepancies between Torrance and Holmes on their reading of what the patristic era looked like as well as some Trinitarian specifics.

Torrance in the Light of Holmes

The theme that East and West spoke with 'one voice' runs throughout Holmes's book.[51] Holmes's section on the *filioque* debate[52] brings this view to its apex and he concludes that 'neither position on the *filioque* does violence to the received orthodox and catholic tradition.'[53]

Torrance also departs from the traditional Western emphasis on the *filioque* without simply returning to the Eastern rejection of the doctrine. Rather, his doctrine of the Trinity is a Reformed version of the classical Eastern patristic viewpoint and, as such, he offers a via media of ecumenical importance, as does Holmes.[54] According to Torrance, it is only through the Nicene ὁμοούσιον that one is able to approach the doctrine of the Trinity. He holds that for the Nicene fathers the ὁμοούσιον safeguards the key evangelical doctrine of the connection between the ontological and immanent Trinity. Torrance contends that the fathers did not adhere to a general/abstract notion of God's being (οὐσία); rather, the term has 'an intensely personal and concrete meaning.'[55] Torrance wants to preserve the dynamic nature of the οὐσία because he sees the term as personal as opposed to abstract and static. This he contends is Athanasian.[56] For Torrance, this means God is 'being in internal relations'.[57]

Once again, Torrance turns to Athanasius and the ὁμοούσιον to illustrate his point. Torrance argues that Athanasian triadology focused on the wholeness of the Godhead and viewed each person of the Trinity 'in terms of their coinherent and undivided wholeness, in which each person is "whole of the whole."'[58] Torrance believes this is rooted in Athanasius's method and starting point: the ὁμοούσιον.[59] Thus, he views Athanasius as rooting his doctrine of the Trinity in the oneness of the Godhead, rather than the threeness of the divine persons.[60] For Torrance this came out most clearly in Athanasius's understanding of the procession of the Spirit: from the being of the Father (ἐκ τῆς οὐσίας τοῦ Πατρός).[61] For Torrance, this stands in contrast to the procession from the person of the Father (ὑπόστασις τοῦ Πατρός) as in the Cappadocians. Torrance argues that Athanasius rooted the three persons intrinsically in the one essence and therefore the unity is necessarily the starting point. Torrance sees this Athanasian emphasis to have derived from the doctrine of ὁμοούσιον and the implied dynamic nature of God's essence. As such, he sees Athanasius's triadology with the Son and Spirit rooted in the Father's οὐσία not in his ὑπόστασις.

According to Torrance, many of the other fathers such as Cyril of Alexandria,[62] Gregory Nazianzen,[63] Epiphanius of Salamis and Didymus the Blind,[64] and Hilary of Poitiers followed Athanasius in this approach. These figures are connected on the basis of the doctrine of the Trinity that arose from their shared methodological commitment. Torrance sees in this stream a focus on the dynamic nature of God's οὐσία, meaning emphasis on neither unity nor Trinity but unity in Trinity and Trinity in unity. He garners this Trinitarian emphasis from a focus on the ὁμοούσιον and argues that these figures focused upon a dynamic conception of the Trinity.

Holmes's connection of Eastern and Western patristic theology on the doctrine of the Trinity is, in some senses, a sentiment with which Torrance would agree. Despite the widespread assumption of the strict distinction between East and West on the Trinity, Torrance sees Augustine as basically Greek in his doctrine of the Trinity. Torrance asserts that Calvin adopted his doctrine of the Trinity from Augustine who was steeped in Greek patristic theology through Hilary of Poitiers.[65] Thus, according to Torrance, Hilary acted as a conduit bringing Greek patristic theology to the West. As such, Torrance was a pioneer in his time, portraying the Latin and Greek approaches to the doctrine of the Trinity as having substantial overlap.

However, Torrance finds a divergence from this consensus on the doctrine of the Trinity in certain aspects of the Cappadocian tradition; a divergence he sees magnified in the later Eastern Orthodox tradition. Any divergence means for Torrance a subtraction from the central patristic assertion that owing to the ὁμοούσιον humankind has knowledge of God *in himself* and is truly united to God and saved. In general, he sees these departures as falling into some sort of theological dualism which cuts off knowledge of and union with God *in himself* and thus is unfaithful to the meaning of the Nicene ὁμοούσιον.

Torrance's problem with the Cappadocian move to make οὐσία refer to the general and ὑπόστασις refer to the particular in God and the placing of the *monarchy* in the ὑπόστασις is that this seems to him to imply some level of subordination in the Trinity. For Torrance this move severs God's economy from God's ontology, which if true means that humankind cannot really know God as he is *in himself* and cannot really be united to God; two assertions that are for him core assertions of orthodoxy and the patristic tradition flowing from the inner meaning of the ὁμοούσιον.[66]

It is notable that Torrance's writings on the Cappadocians develop throughout his life. In the 1960s, he voices hesitation about the ascetical slant of Basil's pneumatology, desiring a more christological slant.[67] By the 1970s Torrance begins to discuss what he sees as a division between God's essence and energies in the Cappadocians and later Byzantine theology.[68] It is only by the 1980s in *The Trinitarian Faith* and with his work in the Reformed–Orthodox dialogue that his strong critique of the Cappadocian distinction emerges. As such, perhaps Torrance's aversion to the Cappadocians is more about the 1980s than the 380s and more about John Zizioulas than Basil the Great. By this time Torrance was deep in a debate going on 'behind the scenes' of Torrance's publications with his one-time assistant at New College, John Zizioulas, now the Metropolitan of Pergamon. Holmes as well is critical of Zizioulas in the first chapter of his book[69] and argues that Zizioulas's reading and presentation of the Cappadocians shows more about Zizioulas's own convictions than the approach of the Cappadocians themselves.[70] Accordingly, whereas at first glance Torrance's critique of the Cappadocians may look like a divergence from Holmes, if Torrance's critique of the Cappadocians is seen, rather, as a critique of John Zizioulas (or, John Zizioulas's reading of the Cappadocians), agreement between Torrance and Holmes becomes further apparent.

However, scholars might consider Torrance's overall reading of the Cappadocians out of date today. It is along the lines of the traditional

Protestant version of the fourth century as popularized by Adolf von Harnack nearly a century earlier.[71] Harnack and other Protestant, mostly liberal, scholars contend for a view of the fourth century consisting of the 'Old Nicenes' and 'New Nicenes'.[72] The Old Nicenes were faithful Athanasians emphasizing fluidity of theological terms and focused on God's presence with humankind. The New Nicenes became more theologically rigid and dogmatic, influenced by Origenist subordinationism in their theological content. Most scholars now contend that the fourth century was less simply categorized than this. The large majority of patristics scholars today consider the Harnackian division as far too simplistic. Many now conceive of the Cappadocians as faithful Athanasians.[73] The current scholarly trend, as seen in Holmes, tends to depart from these categories and view Nicene theology in a more synthetic and nuanced fashion than Torrance's broad categories and distinctions.[74] Here it seems Torrance assumes and works with the accepted categories of his time, which are now becoming out of fashion.

Points where Torrance Is Highly Relevant for Holmes and the Current Trajectory: The Reformed–Orthodox Dialogue

Torrance's approach is highly relevant for the current scholarly conversation. His work in the Reformed–Orthodox dialogue reveals Torrance's ecumenical relevance in his approach to the patristic consensus on the Trinity. The impetus for the dialogue came from 'deep theological rapport' between Torrance (on the Reformed side) and Methodios (on the Orthodox side) over the understanding of classical Alexandrian theology as represented by Athanasius and Cyril.[75]

Torrance believes that the best approach towards theological and ecumenical dialogue is on the basis of the Trinity, Christology, and pneumatology; and on that basis the Eucharist, the church, and the ministry.[76] This is the approach he proposes in the Reformed–Orthodox dialogue. He contends that the best method for discussion and the best approach for agreement is on the basis of Athanasian–Cyrilline theology.[77] Torrance reminisced that in the discussions following the papers presented, everyone 'kept returning to the need for a dynamic understanding of the living Triune God in the inseparability of his Being and Act', or, the ὁμοούσιον.[78] By means of this focus, Torrance thought the Reformed and Orthodox traditions would be able to return to their common fount and 'cut behind' the cosmological and epistemological dualism problematically informing later developments in the Byzantine East and Augustinian West.[79] Such an approach, he thinks, would bring about agreement between Chalcedonians and non-Chalcedonians, Orthodox and Reformed, and Roman Catholics and evangelicals.[80]

The outcome of the dialogue between Orthodox and Reformed churches was the *Agreed Statement on the Holy Trinity*[81] drafted by Torrance and his former student George Dragas (on the Orthodox side). Ultimately, the Reformed and Orthodox agreed they had differences of approach to the doctrine of the Trinity but 'they insisted that they agree on the content of the doctrine'.[82] The main points of the *Agreed Statement* have to do with: (1) the centrality of God's revelation of himself as Trinity; (2) the distinctiveness of the three Trinitarian *hypostaseis*; (3) the order of *hypostaseis* in the Trinity beginning with the Father who has *monarchia*; (4) yet the Godhead is undivided and One; (5) the *perichoretic* mutual indwelling of all members of the Trinity; (6) the affirmation of the formula *mia ousia, treis hypostaseis*; and (7) the doctrine of the Trinity is the core of the apostolic and catholic faith. A close comparative study of the *Agreed Statement* to Holmes's list of the key elements of the received doctrine of the Trinity in the patristic consensus reveals an essential similarity.

Conclusion

Torrance's many connections and reconstructions in exploration of the connections between Greek patristic and Reformed evangelical theology raise the question as to whether Torrance is fair to the fathers. One might reasonably ask whether Torrance's ὁμοούσιον is the same as the Nicene ὁμοούσιον. Georges Florovsky warns of the danger of a 'Western captivity' of the fathers when their theology is forced into categories foreign to them.[83] Is Torrance open to this accusation? Is the ὁμοούσιον which Torrance emphasizes really just Western (or even Barthian) theological concepts in the Greek language? Some critique him along these lines. Foremost in the critiques is that Torrance's reading of the fathers, primarily Athanasius and the ὁμοούσιον, sounds too Barthian.[84] Gunton puts a related critique forward. He argues that Torrance's reading of the ὁμοούσιον is Western and sounds more Augustinian than Athanasian.[85]

This essay has shown that Athanasius's use of the ὁμοούσιον is not exactly the same as Torrance's[86] and thus Holmes's critique of so-called Trinitarian 'revival' is, perhaps, applicable. However, this would not be an entirely fair critique. Torrance would have contended that he is able to synthetically combine the fathers with Barth and Reformed theology as a dogmatic theologian. Historically, this may be unhelpful, but theologically it is extremely insightful and constructive. The themes, while perhaps not explicitly from the pen of the fathers in the form Torrance presents them, are fair theological statements to make inasmuch as Torrance reads the fathers from a theological and Reformed evangelical perspective and unpacks the inner logic behind patristic concepts. In this sense it is not far-fetched to say that Torrance understands the theological implications of the fathers better from his point of view post-Reformation and post-Barth.

Ultimately, all interpreters of the patristic tradition have a lens through which they view the fathers; the key is to balance historical faithfulness with confessional commitment. Torrance does this successfully. His reading of the Nicene fathers on the doctrine of the Trinity is a creative Reformed evangelical rendering of the patristic consensus that is neither statically Reformed nor statically patristic; rather, it is dynamically Reformed and patristic.

Ultimately, Torrance's reading and imaginative reconstruction of the fathers around the ὁμοούσιον has much to offer. His emphasis on the ὁμοούσιον may be influenced by a Barthian commitment to God's self-giving in revelation and reconciliation, but if anything this allows Torrance fresh insight into Athanasius and the other fathers. Torrance sees in Athanasius and the other fathers on the ὁμοούσιον a commitment to Barthian views and thus uses this shared mindset to draw out what had not been drawn out before. Torrance's emphasis on the ὁμοούσιον and the inner meaning behind it, that revelation and reconciliation come from the side of God, provides fresh insight into the fathers by paring away patristic theology that did not focus on it and highlighting the classical theology that did.

So, Torrance does not fit within Holmes's critique of the twentieth-century Trinitarian revival inasmuch as Torrance is doing something entirely different. Torrance's approach is a reconstruction of the patristic consensus and, while this may be historically unsatisfactory for some, it is a viable theological reconstruction of the fathers on the Trinity. Torrance's reading of the fathers on the doctrine of the Trinity, particularly upon the *filioque* debate, is a fresh insight, and his ὁμοούσιον-centred reconstruction allows him this new reading. His connection of God's being and acts and emphasis on God's immediate presence in Christ sheds further insight in the *filioque* debate and debate on the doctrine of the Trinity. As Noble notes, Torrance offers a potential answer to the ongoing debate between social Trinitarians and those emphasizing the unity of God.[87] Here Torrance provides great insight into the question of the procession of the Holy Spirit. It is highly unfortunate that scholars writing on the subject today do not often discuss Torrance's significance.[88]

Holmes has shown that the long-held 'de Régnon thesis', which sharply distinguishes between Latin and Greek doctrines of the Trinity, is currently falling out of fashion with patristics scholars and current scholarship is moving forward, viewing Augustine and Latin triadology in line with Greek (both Athanasian and Cappadocian) triadology.[89] Torrance, though still falling into some now outdated categories (such as Cappadocian vs Nicene), is at the same time a pioneer in his time inasmuch as he sees Augustine in line with Greek Trinitarian thought.[90] Furthermore, Torrance helps to show the essential unity of East and West on the Trinity. As such Torrance's scholarship in this area has much to offer the current Trinitarian conversation and he is seriously under-utilized by patristic scholars and theologians alike on this topic. As Noble states: 'Torrance's Trinitarian theology holds out the best hope of combining the concerns for divine Unity with the concerns of the social Trinitarians.'[91]

In the final analysis, Holmes's *Holy Trinity* and Torrance's reconstruction of the patristic consensus are complementary. Holmes and Torrance share a commitment to the importance of the fathers on the doctrine of the Trinity. Holmes and Torrance share the view that the Eastern fathers and the Western fathers are, in substance, propagators of the same doctrine of the Trinity. In substance both Holmes and Torrance offer a much more dynamic conception of the doctrine, seeing God as three-in-one and one-in-three, starting neither with the Unity nor the Trinity and offer ecumenically relevant approaches to classic debates such as that of the *filioque*.

Torrance stands apart from Holmes inasmuch as Torrance offers a theologically constructive and christologically conditioned reconstruction of the fathers in light of the Reformed and evangelical tradition. Holmes stands apart from Torrance inasmuch as he offers a less reconstructive and more historical approach, while remaining theologically focused. As such, Holmes's approach is likely more palatable for the historically leaning approach popular in contemporary patristic scholarship today.[92] Holmes's book is a helpful addition to theological and patrological scholarship, balancing historical faithfulness with theological centeredness most admirably, and this essay has argued that Torrance's patristic consensus on the doctrine of the Trinity offers helpful insight into the current trajectory of patristic and theological scholarship of which Holmes is a part, adding a helpful theologically constructive approach.

Bibliography

Anatolios, Khaled. *Retrieving Nicaea: The Development and Meaning of Trinitarian Doctrine* (Grand Rapids: Baker, 2011).

Ayres, Lewis. *Augustine and the Trinity* (Cambridge: Cambridge University Press, 2010).

— *Nicaea and Its Legacy: An Approach to Fourth-Century Trinitarian Theology* (Oxford: Oxford University Press, 2004).

Barnes, Michel René. 'Rereading Augustine's Theology of the Trinity'. Pages 145–76 in *The Trinity: An Interdisciplinary Symposium on the Trinity* (ed. Stephen T. Davis, Daniel Kendall, and Gerald O'Collins; Oxford: Oxford University Press, 1999).

Behr, John. *The Mystery of Christ* (Crestwood, NY: St Vladimir's Seminary Press, 2006).

— *The Nicene Faith: Part I.* Crestwood, NY: St Vladimir's Seminary Press, 2004.

Colyer, Elmer. *How to Read T.F. Torrance: Understanding His Trinitarian and Scientific Theology* (Downers Grove, IL: InterVarsity Press, 2001).

Dragas, George Dion. 'The Significance for the Church of Professor Torrance's Election as Moderator of the General Assembly of the Church of Scotland'. *Ekklesiastikos Pharos* 58 (1976): pp. 214–31.

Ernest, James. *The Bible in Athanasius of Alexandria* (Boston: Brill, 2004).

Gunton, Colin E. *Father, Son, and Holy Spirit: Essays toward a Fully Trinitarian Theology* (London: T&T Clark, 2003).

Harnack, Adolf von. *History of Dogma*, vol. 4 (London: Williams & Norgate, 1894).

Kelly, J.N.D. *Early Christian Doctrines* (London: A&C Black, 1958).

Meyendorff, John. *Byzantine Theology: Historical Trends and Doctrinal Themes* (London: Mowbrays, 1974).

Molnar, Paul. *Thomas F. Torrance: Theologian of the Trinity* (Farnham: Ashgate, 2009).

Noble, T.A. *Holy Trinity: Holy People: The Theology of Christian Perfecting* (Eugene, OR: Wipf & Stock, 2013).

Radcliff, Jason. *Thomas F. Torrance and the Church Fathers* (Eugene, OR: Pickwick, 2014).

— 'Thomas F. Torrance's Conception of the Consensus Patrum on the Doctrine of Pneumatology'. *Studia Patristica* 69 (2013): pp. 417–34.

Reid, J.K.S. 'The Office of Christ in Predestination'. *Scottish Journal of Theology* 1 (1948): pp. 5–19.

Siecienski, Edward. *The Filioque: History of a Doctrinal Controversy* (Oxford: Oxford University Press, 2010).

Torrance, Thomas F. *The Christian Doctrine of God: One Being Three Persons* (Edinburgh: T&T Clark, 1996).

— *Gospel, Church, and Ministry* (ed. Jock Stein; Eugene, OR: Wipf & Stock, 2012).

— *Karl Barth: An Introduction to His Early Theology, 1910–1931* (Edinburgh: T&T Clark, 2000).

— 'Karl Barth and the Latin Heresy'. *Scottish Journal of Theology* 39 (1986): pp. 461–82.

— *The Mediation of Christ* (Colorado Springs: Helmers & Howard, 1992).

— *Preaching Christ Today: The Gospel and Scientific Thinking* (Grand Rapids: Eerdmans, 1994).

— *Reality and Evangelical Theology: The Realism of Christian Revelation* (Eugene, OR: Wipf & Stock, 1999).

— *Reality and Scientific Theology* (Eugene, OR: Wipf & Stock, 2001).

— *Theological Dialogue between Orthodox and Reformed Churches*, vol. 1 (Edinburgh: Scottish Academic Press, 1985).

— *Theological Dialogue between Orthodox and Reformed Churches*, vol. 2 (Edinburgh: Scottish Academic Press, 1993).

— *Theology in Reconciliation: Essays towards Evangelical and Catholic Unity in East and West* (Eugene, OR: Wipf & Stock, 1996).

— *Theology in Reconstruction* (Eugene, OR: Wipf & Stock, 1996).

— *The Trinitarian Faith: The Evangelical Theology of the Ancient Catholic Church* (Edinburgh: T&T Clark, 1988).

— *Trinitarian Perspectives: Toward Doctrinal Agreement* (Edinburgh: T&T Clark, 1994).

Wilken, Robert L. 'Review of Divine Meaning: Studies in Patristic Hermeneutics by T.F. Torrance'. *Theological Studies* 57 (1996): pp. 743–4.

6.

An Analytic Response to Stephen R. Holmes, with a Special Treatment of his Doctrine of Divine Simplicity

R.T. Mullins

Steve Holmes has taken us on a delightful romp through the history of Trinitarian doctrine. While he notes throughout that the political landscape had an important role to play in the development of creeds and the decisions of councils, Holmes does an excellent job at cutting straight to the theological arguments offered by Christian thinkers in the past. He traces out the classical doctrine of the Trinity through a lucid discussion of the types of arguments at play in each time period. Holmes believes that certain forms of contemporary Trinitarian theology have gone astray from the classical tradition, and in some cases completely misread the tradition. I find Holmes's arguments that certain contemporary Trinitarian retrievals have misread the tradition to be persuasive, and thank him for giving us a better reading of the classical doctrine. With the classical Trinitarian arguments clearly laid out on the table before us in Holmes's book, I ask that we contemporary Trinitarians consider the strengths and weaknesses of those arguments. I also ask some worrying questions. What do we do if the heretical arguments are stronger than the orthodox arguments? What do we do when orthodox theologians in the past have failed to rebut serious objections from the heretics? There are various ways to examine these questions, but I must limit myself to a brief discussion on the problem of subordinationism. In order to understand the heretical argument for subordination, and the failure of the orthodox to defeat this argument, I must first set the stage by discussing religious language, divine simplicity, and ineffability. Before delving straight into those topics, I feel obligated to make a few comments on Steve's discussion of analytic theology.

Analytic Theology, the Trinity, and Religious Language

I have been asked to write this chapter from the perspective of an analytic theologian, and as such, felt the need to comment on Holmes's discussion of contemporary analytic philosophy of religion and theology. I have little qualms with being called an analytic theologian, but I must stress that there is no such thing as *the* analytic perspective. Analytic theologians are divided on an array of issues just like any other subgroup of theologians. Holmes notes some of this diversity when he discusses the three main positions on the doctrine of the Trinity within contemporary analytic philosophy of religion and theology.[1] Those positions are social Trinitarianism, Latin Trinitarianism, and relative identity/constitutional Trinitarianism. I greatly appreciated Holmes including this in his discussion of contemporary Trinitarian theology. I found his discussion of analytic theology to be quite clear and fair for the most part. This was a pleasant surprise since, in many theological circles today, seldom is heard an encouraging word about analytic theology. There is only one complaint that I have about his discussion of analytic theology: religious language.

Holmes writes that:

> analytic discussions of the Trinity seem generally to proceed with a remarkable confidence about the success of language in referring to the divine. The theological question of analogy is, as far as I can observe, never raised, and the assumed answer would always seem to be that language refers univocally to the divine and the created. (If it does not, the core project of analysis would be impossible.)[2]

My complaint with this statement is twofold: (A) It is false that the theological question of analogy is never raised, and that univocity is assumed; (B) It is false that analytic philosophers of religion and theologians always hold to the doctrine of univocity.

With regard to (A), there is a plethora of discussion among analytic theologians over religious language.[3] The typical handbook or companion to philosophy of religion will contain a chapter on religious language. Two of the most famous analytic treatments of religious language are William Alston's *Divine Nature and Human Language* and Richard Swinburne's *Revelation: From Metaphor to Analogy*. Both give a careful consideration of the doctrine of analogy and offer a rigorous defence of univocity.[4] Many more discussions of analogy, and defences of univocity, can be found in the literature as well.[5] So it is simply false that the doctrine of analogy is never raised, and false that univocity is assumed. The doctrine of univocity is consistently argued for and defended against objections.

With regard to (B), not all analytic philosophers of religion and analytic theologians hold to the doctrine of univocity. It might well be the case that most analytic theologians do, but there is some dissent. In several recent papers, the doctrine of univocity has been called into question, and the doctrine of analogy has been defended.[6] Again, as noted above, there is no such thing as the analytic perspective. Analytic theology is more diverse than it is sometimes realized.

There is one remaining issue from the quote above that will be taken up further in the sections below. Holmes notes that analytic philosophy of religion seems to be highly confident in its ability to speak about God. This is something he later chides the Eunomian heretics for doing as well. It would be hard to deny this characterization of contemporary philosophy of religion. However, it is worth noting that there is debate and disagreement among analytics. For instance, John Hick and William Wainwright have offered defences of the doctrine of ineffability and the place of mystery in theology.[7] While it is true that some analytic theologians have little patience for ineffability, it is certainly not ruled out by all in the analytic camp.[8] The diversity among analytics needs to be recognized as this budding branch of theology continues to grow.

Divine Simplicity

The editors of this volume have requested that I analyse Holmes's discussion of divine simplicity. There is a startling oddity in Holmes's book, however. Throughout he thoroughly romances the doctrine of divine simplicity, yet there is little by way of an explanation for what divine simplicity is. Chapter 5 'The Godhead Is by Nature Simple' would seem to be the best place to find such an articulation, but instead the emphasis is on the doctrine of ineffability. As Holmes makes clear, many classical Christian theologians hold that ineffability follows from divine simplicity. This is an interesting point in the dialect between the orthodox and heterodox, and I shall discuss this below. Before doing so, however, it is important to put the doctrine of divine simplicity before us. Elsewhere I have given a thorough articulation of the doctrine of divine simplicity.[9] Due to space limitations, my articulation here must be brief.

What does it mean to say that God is simple? Peter Lombard offers the following definition of divine simplicity: 'The same substance alone is properly and truly simple in which there is no diversity or change or multiplicity of parts, or accidents, or of any other forms.'[10] Peter is here noting the connection between divine simplicity and immutability. Augustine explains that 'nothing simple is changeable.' Why is a simple God unchangeable?[11] A simple God has no properties, no diversity, and no distinctions. 'So there is no modification in God because there is nothing in him that can be changed or lost.'[12] Allow me to unpack some of the claims contained in Peter's definition.

What does it mean to say that a simple God has no diversity? The idea is that God does not have any physical or metaphysical complexity. The assumption is that in order to be spatial a thing must have physical parts. God is immaterial, so God does not have any physical parts. This much is fairly straightforward and uncontroversial.

What about metaphysical complexity? To start, there can be no real distinction in God's attributes because the attributes are all identical to each other and identical to God. In *The Trinity* 15.7 Augustine argues that God is genuinely immortal since he never began to exist, and can never cease to exist. So, genuine immortality, he says, is unchanging. 'But that is also genuine eternity by which God is unchangeable, without beginning, without end, and consequently incorruptible. Therefore one and the same thing is being said, whether you say God is eternal or immortal or incorruptible or unchangeable.' Whether you say that God is wise, powerful, living, understanding, or beautiful, 'the same thing is being said.'

Sometimes contemporary defenders of divine simplicity wish to shy away from this aspect of divine simplicity because it is too strong, but Augustine makes it clear that divine simplicity is committed to this strong identity claim. 'But for God it is the same thing to be as to be powerful or just or wise or anything else that can be said about his simple multiplicity or multiple simplicity to signify his substance.'[13] Elsewhere Augustine writes:

> God however is indeed called in multiple ways great, good, wise, blessed, true, and anything else that seems not to be unworthy of him; but his greatness is identical with his wisdom (he is not great in mass but in might), and his goodness is identical with his wisdom and greatness, and his truth is identical with them all; and with him being blessed is not one thing, and being great or wise or true or good, or just simply being, another.[14]

This is the way Christians throughout history have understood divine simplicity.[15]

Maximus the Confessor states that 'in the multiple there is diversity, unlikeness, and difference. But in God, who is eminently one and unique, there is only identity, simplicity, and sameness.'[16] John Duns Scotus agrees: 'There is nothing in the divine that is not the same thing as the divine essence and also the same as anything essential, so that considering such in the abstract, one can say simply "This is this".'[17] The seventeenth-century English theologian Richard Stock notes that:

> it appeares, that however these things are attributed to God, that he is love, mercy, favour, and anger, howsoever they are spoken, as though they were many and different, yet in God they are but one, and the same. True it is, that we are of a compounded understanding, they are as severall things to us; because we cannot conceive God as he is, yet by faith, we are brought to beleeve that there is no such difference between them in God: that which is the love of God, is the hatred of God; and that which is his wisdome, is his power also; because there is but one and the same Essence [sic].[18]

Stock, like so many others throughout church history, is following Augustine's moves in *The Trinity*.

Augustine continually argues throughout *The Trinity* that all of God's essential divine attributes are identical to each other. On divine simplicity, anything that one might predicate of God should be understood as signifying the divine substance. One could say that God is eternal, immortal, incorruptible, unchangeable, living, wise, powerful, beautiful, and so forth. Yet all of those terms signify the divine substance. They are not qualities or properties that God has because they are identical to God.[19] Creatures have properties by participating in goodness, wisdom, life, and so on. God, who is the greatest being, does not have goodness by participating in something else. Goodness is identical to his essence, and God is identical to his essence. So God is the Good.[20] Other things have an essence and subsist, or underlie, the properties they have. Not so with the simple God. '[I]t is impious to say that God subsists to and underlies his goodness, and that goodness is not his own substance.'[21] As Katherin Rogers points out, the traditional doctrine of divine simplicity denies that God has any properties. Echoing Peter Lombard, Rogers says, 'With God we do not hypothesize any unity underlying the diversity because there is no diversity.'[22]

The claim that God does not have any properties is a radical claim that does not merely apply to God's essential attributes. Theologians like Augustine, Boethius, Peter Lombard, and Thomas Aquinas all deny accidental properties of God as well. Standard examples are things like *Creator, Redeemer,* and *Lord.* James Arminius adds *Judge of all men* to the list as well. For these theologians God cannot have these accidental properties because accidental properties entail a modification in the thing that has them. In other words, possessing these accidental properties would entail that God came to, or began to, have them since creation and salvation history are not co-eternal with God.[22] Creation and salvation history began to be. If God came to have these accidental properties when creation began to be, that would involve a change in God. Thus, God would be mutable, temporal, and not simple. Classical theologians held that we can refer to God, but that we must realize that our accidental predicates only befall us and not God.[23] Further, these properties are relational properties, and classical theology denies that God stands in a real relation to creation. If God stands in a real relation to creation, God would depend upon creation for these properties. This might not seem like a problem, but classical theology is strongly committed to the notion that God in no way depends upon creation.[24]

The lack of complexity in God goes even further. There is no distinction between God's act and being. God is pure act.[25] God has no potential. As Aquinas explains, composite things have potential. They move from potential to actual. But God is simple, so he must lack potentiality and be pure act.[26] One example of this idea is that God just is his act of existence.[27] God is not something that underlies his properties because he does not have any properties. God does not go from potential to actual since he is pure act. God's act is identical to God, and not something distinct. 'His action is His being . . . God's action is His substance.'[28] '[T]he manifold actions ascribed to God, as intelligence, volition, the production of things, and the like, are not so many different things, since each of these actions in God is His own very being, which is one and the same thing.'[29]

Even this does not exhaust the extent to which classical theologians wish to deny all metaphysical complexity and diversity of God. Conceptual distinctions are also repugnant to divine simplicity. As Anselm explains, 'what either actually or conceptually has parts can be divided into parts, and this is altogether foreign to God.'[30] Compare a similar statement made by James Arminius in his *Twenty-Five Public Disputations*, *Disputation* 4.11. 'Simplicity is a pre-eminent mode of the Essence of God, by which he is void of all composition, and of component parts whether they belong to the senses or to the understanding.'[31]

Divine simplicity is a truly radical doctrine, and I am not quite sure why Holmes does not offer a full articulation. As noted above, in his chapter on divine simplicity he focuses primarily on the doctrine of ineffability. Perhaps Holmes does not discuss simplicity at length because he believes that the main difference between the orthodox and certain heterodox theologians over divine simplicity concerns divine ineffability.[32] He seems to suggest this in his discussion of Gregory of Nyssa and Eunomius.

Eunomius clearly believes that divine simplicity involves the claim that all of the attributes are identical to each other, and uses this to mount his subordinationist argument against the *homoousian* Trinitarian theologians (to be discussed below). Gregory, however, points out that the terms for the divine attributes are not synonymous with each other, so Eunomius must have gone wrong somewhere. Where did he go wrong? Not with divine simplicity since Gregory affirms this doctrine. Gregory says that Eunomius goes wrong in thinking that our terms name the divine essence. Gregory does not deny simplicity, but instead denies that our terms name God's essence because the divine essence is ineffable.[33]

Orthodoxy, Heresy, and Ineffability

One of the things I find troubling about the history of Christian theology is the role that the doctrine of ineffability has played in the defence of orthodox dogma. I am one of those pesky analytic theologians who have no patience for ineffability, or claims that God is completely unknowable. Part of this stems from my deep commitment to the belief that in Christ we know God. Christians do not worship an unknown God as the people of Athens do (Acts 17:23), but instead know God as he has revealed himself through Christ. In Jesus, God has made all the riches and glory of the knowledge of himself known to us, and we ought to pray that we will continue to increase in the knowledge of God (Col. 1 – 2). Christians worship a revelatory God, a God who has made himself known, and not an unknown and unknowable God.

The doctrine of ineffability seems like a cheap card to play in theological discussions – a dirty theological trick shrouded in a façade of piety, that one plays when one cannot answer a serious objection to one's own theology. Instead of answering an objection, it appears that many orthodox Christians invoked ineffability. This is unfortunate because it leaves the objection unanswered.

What is ineffability? It is a doctrine that states that God is completely unknowable, completely beyond all human comprehension, completely beyond all human language and conceptions. 'God is unknown and unknowable'.[34] 'The divine essence is fundamentally beyond our conceptions; all our language and thought, limited as it is by created categories, is inadequate to speak of what God is.'[35] It should be noted how strong this doctrine is. This is not the same thing as saying that we cannot fully grasp, or fully comprehend, the nature of God, but do have some partial grasp of the divine essence. Nor is it the same thing as saying that there are just some things about God that we will never know. Ineffability is a much stronger doctrine than the weaker doctrine of partial comprehension. The distinction between these two doctrines is important to note since many theologians will often start with the stronger doctrine of ineffability to refute an objection, and then sneak in the weaker 'partially, but not fully comprehend God' doctrine to work out their own theology, all while thinking that they are being consistent with ineffability. Partial, but not full, comprehension of God is not the same thing as saying that God is completely unknowable. One cannot have partial knowledge of an unknowable God.

What is wrong with ineffability? There are many things wrong with ineffability. First, it is self-referentially incoherent, and as such is necessarily false. There is no possible world in which it is true. Propositions that are self-referentially incoherent are propositions that contradict themselves or are self-defeating. Keith Yandell, in explaining the concept of self-referential incoherence, gives the following illustration. 'It is as if a bear, gifted with speech, assured us solemnly that bears cannot talk, and expected us to take it at its word.'[36] The talking bear's claim is simply incoherent. Yandell believes that ineffability is just as self-referentially incoherent as the talking bear's claim. It is not hard to demonstrate this either. Consider the following statement from Augustine:

> [I]f I have said anything [about God], it is not what I desired to say. How do I know this, except from the fact that God is unspeakable? But what I have said, if it had been unspeakable, could not have been spoken. And so God is not even to be called 'unspeakable,' because to say even this is to speak of Him. Thus there arises a curious contradiction of words, because if the unspeakable is what cannot be spoken of, it is not unspeakable if it can be called unspeakable. And this opposition of words is rather to be avoided by silence than to be explained away by speech. And yet God, although nothing worthy of His greatness can be said of Him, has condescended to accept the worship of men's mouths, and has desired us through the medium of our own words to rejoice in His praise.[37]

This sort of statement from Augustine is common throughout the early church. He recognizes that he has contradicted himself, and yet continues to claim that God is ineffable. This makes no sense. It would be better if theologians got rid of incoherent doctrines, and ineffability is certainly an incoherent doctrine. To say that God is unspeakable is to say something about God. To say that God is unknowable is to know something about God. To say that God is beyond all human language is to say something about God in human language. Ineffability is simply incoherent.

Second, if one is not convinced that ineffability should be got rid of because it is self-referentially incoherent, one should get rid of it because it is incoherent with the rest of Christian theology and anything theologians wish to say. One of the things I find utterly baffling about proponents of ineffability is their knowledge of God. These theologians seem to know an awful lot about the unknowable God. Consider this summary of John of Damascus's view offered by Holmes: 'God is unknown and unknowable . . . The divine names – goodness, power, omniscience, eternity, etc. – demonstrate the unknowability of God, because we can only speak of God's nature partially and severally, and yet God's nature is one, simple, and uncompounded.'[38] It is not at all clear to me why these attributes of God demonstrate that God is unknowable. It seems that these are things that John knows about God to such an extent that he is willing to argue from what he knows about God (i.e. divine simplicity) to the claim that God is unknowable. That is incoherent. One cannot argue that God is unknowable from the basis of knowing certain things about God. Throughout *On the Orthodox Faith*, he really seems to believe that he knows that God is simple, good, immutable, all-knowing, all-powerful, and triune. If God were truly unknowable, John could not know any of this.

One might try to reply by saying, 'Yes, but the divine attributes only speak of God's nature partially, not fully. They gesture towards the ineffable essence of God.' This response fails. To say that a divine attribute gives one partial knowledge of God demonstrates that God is not unknowable. One cannot have a partial knowledge of a God who is unknown and unknowable. If one knows something about God, then it is false that God is unknowable. Further, one cannot know that a particular attribute gestures towards the ineffable essence without knowing something about the essence of God. If one does not know anything at all about the essence of God, one could certainly not know that a particular attribute like goodness somehow pointed towards the essence of God.

Another rejoinder might be to say, 'We know the perfections or attributes of God as displayed through his various acts, but we do not know the essence of God. Only the essence of God is ineffable and unknowable.' This is an odd rejoinder, but very much in line with patristic thought.[39] The problem with this rejoinder is that it rests on some deep confusion. An essence or nature is a set of essential properties or attributes that a thing must have to be the kind of thing that it is.[40] In this instance, it would be the set of attributes that a being must have in order to be divine. Typically, the set of attributes for being divine will include something like necessary existence, eternality, omniscience, and omnipotence. So, if we know that God has these attributes, we know the essence of God.

If one wishes to deny that this is knowledge of the divine essence, one will have to face another difficulty – divine revelation. Christian theology is based on divine revelatory action. The basic claim is that God, in the former days, revealed himself through prophets, but in these last days he has revealed himself to us through his Son (Heb. 1:1). This is obviously in conflict with ineffability. An unknown and unknowable God cannot reveal himself to human persons and continue to be unknown and unknowable. But ignore that for the moment, and focus on the claim that one can know the attributes and actions of God, but not know the essence of God. Ineffability says that we cannot know 'what God is'.[41] If the divine essence is ineffable, one cannot know that God is the sort of being who can act. To know that God is capable of acting is to know something about what God is. So one cannot know that God is capable of acting if God's essence is truly ineffable. The problem gets worse. Christians wish to say that the resurrection of Jesus was a divine action that revealed God's goodness. If God is ineffable, one could not know that God performed this action because that would be to know enough about the essence of God to accurately attribute this action to him. If the essence of God is truly ineffable, one cannot know that God would perform good or evil actions, nor any sort of action at all. To know that God would perform good or evil actions is to know something about his essence, to know something about what he is. If the essence of God is truly ineffable, one would not be able to identify any particular action as coming from God because such an identification would depend upon having some sort of knowledge about what God is.

Divine ineffability is a disaster for Christian thought for all of these reasons and more. Yet, as Holmes shows in his book, it played a decisive role in responding to heretical objections to orthodox dogma. Continually throughout his book, Holmes makes a point of saying that the difference between the heretics and the orthodox is that the orthodox believed that the divine essence was ineffable. Heretics like Eunomius and Socinus believed that they 'could reason adequately about the divine essence, instead of following Basil, Gregory of Nyssa, Augustine, Thomas Aquinas, and John Calvin in asserting divine unknowability.'[42]. Ineffability is supposed to be the doctrine that preserves orthodox dogma, and refutes the objections of subordinationist heresies. However, since ineffability is (A) self-referentially incoherent so not possibly true, and (B) completely in conflict with revealed Christian theology, it cannot serve as a sound refutation of any objection to Christian thought.

Subordinationism Left Unrefuted

Since ineffability is necessarily false it cannot be used to refute subordinationism. Where does that leave Christian theology? It leaves us in the position of having to give real answers to serious and ancient objections to our faith. Elsewhere I have offered a suggestion for how to deal with subordinationism, and I shall briefly sketch a possible strategy in the conclusion. For now, I wish to lay out exactly what the problem is so that others might rise to the challenge. Here is one Eunomian-style subordinationist challenge that must be met.

First, assume the orthodox Creator/creature distinction. God is a necessary and eternal being, whereas creatures are contingent and time-bound beings.[44] A necessary being does not have a cause for its existence and does not depend upon anything for its existence, whereas a contingent being does. Contingent beings only exist by the free and gracious volition of God.

Next, assume the orthodox doctrine of the eternal generation of the Son by the Father. Eternal generation, or eternal begetting, is a causal notion. It posits a timeless cause with a timeless effect. The Father does not have a cause for his existence, but the Father causes the Son to exist.[45] As Gregory of Nyssa puts it in *On Not Three Gods*, 'The principle of causality distinguishes, then, the Persons of the holy Trinity. It affirms that the one is uncaused, while the other depends on the cause.' Further, as Holmes makes clear, the 'act of begetting . . . is personal and volitional, not some sort of involuntary overflowing.'[46] The Father freely causes the Son to exist.

With these two assumptions we can begin to understand one form of the Eunomian-style subordinationist argument. I say one form because the original form of the argument assumes divine simplicity. Contrary to what Holmes suggests,[47] one does not need divine simplicity to get the argument up and running. To be God is to be a necessary being. A necessary being does not have a cause for its existence. It thus exists *a se*. A being exists *a se* if and only if that being does not have a cause for its existence. That being's existence is not derived from, nor dependent upon, something outside of itself. The Father is a necessary being, and so does not have a cause for his existence. The Father exists *a se*. The Son, however, does have a cause for his existence. The Son is caused to exist by a free volitional act of the Father. Thus, the Son is a contingent being and does not exist *a se*. To be a creature is to be a contingent being. The Son is a contingent being, and thus a creature.

How are orthodox theologians to respond? They cannot invoke ineffability since ineffability is self-referentially incoherent. They must come up with a different strategy. It should be noted that trying to draw a distinction between *begotten* and *made* will be of no use. Both are causal notions. To be made is to have a cause for one's existence such that one begins to exist. To be begotten is to have a cause for one's existence such that one does not begin to exist.[48] Perhaps this distinction helps with the earlier Arian objection which argued that there was a time when the Son was not, but this distinction will not help with the Eunomian-style subordinationist objection. The Eunomian-style objection rests on the causal claim. All that is needed for the argument to go through is the claim that the Son has a cause for his existence since that is sufficient to make the Son a contingent being. But the claim that the Son is caused to exist by the Father is part of the orthodox doctrine of the Trinity.

Consider also that the orthodox theologian cannot appeal to the doctrine of *homoousios* since that would be question begging. The claim that the Father and the Son are *homoousios* is what is being called into question with the Eunomian-style objection. Orthodox theologians need to explain how the Father and the Son can be *homoousios* in the face of this objection. They cannot simply assert it.

One possible orthodox rejoinder would be to remove the claim that the Father volitionally causes the Son to exist. Perhaps one might say that the Father necessarily causes the Son to exist. After all, isn't that a stronger doctrine of the Trinity? If the existence of the Son rests upon the free volitional act of the Father, then it is possible for the Son not to exist. The Father need not have acted to cause the Son to exist. So God being triune is a contingent state of affairs on the orthodox doctrine of the Trinity![49] Surely a contemporary Trinitarian will want a stronger doctrine than that such that God is necessarily triune.

But does making the Father's begetting of the Son a necessary act remove the threat of subordination? I cannot see how it does. It doesn't remove the problem because the Son is caused to exist, and thus is not a necessary being. A necessary being does not depend for its existence on anything outside of itself. The Son does depend for his existence on the person of the Father, so the Son is not a necessary being.[50] What is needed to remove the problem is a way to make the Son a necessary being as well, but it is difficult to see how the Son could be a necessary being if the Son is caused to exist. Perhaps one might say that since the Father necessarily causes the Son to exist, the Son has a kind of necessary existence. However, it is not clear how the Father and the Son would have the same kind of necessary existence since the Son is causally dependent upon the Father. Different kinds of necessary existence would entail that the Father and the Son are not *homoousion*. Further, the fact that the Son's existence is from the Father entails that the Son is not *a se*. The Father and the Son do not share the same essence. This is just another form of subordinationism.

Given space restrictions, I cannot go any further into this issue here.[51] I will simply end with this question. How do we contemporary theologians defeat subordinationism without resorting to self-referentially incoherent doctrines, and doctrines that conflict with the basic Christian claim that God has truly revealed himself to us? As Kevin Giles points out in his chapter, many contemporary evangelical theologians are abandoning the doctrine of eternal generation on theological and biblical grounds. This is a move that I endorse. I maintain that the Bible does not explicitly or implicitly teach the doctrine of eternal generation.[52] Given the conceptual difficulties surrounding the doctrine of eternal generation, an evangelical Christian should not be too worried about abandoning a doctrine that is not explicitly or implicitly taught in Scripture. Further, there is some precedent within the tradition for denying the claim that the Father causes the Son to exist. For example, Thomas Aquinas makes this suggestion.[53] Yet I doubt that Steve will wish to follow this path. Perhaps he can suggest another way forward.[54]

Bibliography

Alston, William P. *Divine Nature and Human Language: Essays in Philosophical Theology* (Ithaca: Cornell University Press, 1989).

Aquinas, Thomas. *The Collected Works of St. Thomas Aquinas*, electronic edition (ed. J.N. Deely; Charlottesville, VA: InteLex Corporation, 1993).

Arminius, J. *The Works of James Arminius*, vol. 2 (trans. J. Nichols. London: Baker, 1986).

Augustine, S. *The Trinity* (trans. Edmund Hill; Hyde Park, NY: New City Press, 1991).

Barnes, Michel René and D.H. Williams. *Arianism After Arius: Essays on the Development of the Fourth-Century Trinitarian Conflicts* (Edinburgh: T&T Clark, 1993).

Berthold, G.C., ed. *Maximus Confessor: Selected Writings* (London: SPCK, 1985).

Bettenson, H., ed. *The Later Christian Fathers: A Selection from the Writings of the Fathers from St. Cyril of Jerusalem to St. Leo the Great* (Oxford: Oxford University Press, 1970).

Blowers, P.M. *Drama of the Divine Economy: Creator and Creation in Early Christian Theology and Piety* (Oxford: Oxford University Press, 2012).

Boethius. *Trinity Is One God Not Three Gods* (n.p., n.d).

Bradshaw, D. 'The Divine Glory and the Divine Energies'. *Faith and Philosophy* 23 (2006): pp. 279–98.

Burleigh, J., ed. *Augustine: Earlier Writings* (Philadelphia: Westminster Press, 1953).

Burnaby, J., ed. *Augustine: Later Works* (Philadelphia: Westminster Press, 1955).

Church, H. *Miscellanea Philo-Theologica* (London: I.N. for John Rothwell, 1638).

Clark, David K. *To Know and Love God: Method for Theology* (Wheaton, IL: Crossway, 2003).

Cross, R. 'Idolatry and Religious Language'. *Faith and Philosophy* 24 (2008): pp. 190–96.

Dolezal, James E. *God without Parts: Divine Simplicity and the Metaphysics of God's Absoluteness* (Eugene, OR: Wipf & Stock, 2011).

Duby, Steve J. 'Divine Simplicity, Divine Freedom, and the Contingency of Creation: Dogmatic Responses to Some Analytic Questions'. *Journal of Reformed Theology* 2 (2012): pp. 115–42.

Eunomius: The Extant Works (trans. R.P. Vaggione; New York: Oxford University Press, 1987).

Flint, T.P. and Michael C. Rea, eds. *The Oxford Handbook of Philosophical Theology* (New York: Oxford University Press, 2009).

Giles, Kevin. *The Eternal Generation of the Son: Maintaining Orthodoxy in Trinitarian Theology* (Downers Grove, IL: InterVarsity Press, 2012).

Hackett, J., and J. Wallulis, eds. *Philosophy of Religion for a New Century: Essays in Honor of Eugene Thomas Long* (Dordrecht: Kluwer Academic, 2004).

Hardy, E.R., ed. *Christology of the Later Fathers* (Philadelphia: Westminster Press, 1954).

Hick, John. 'Ineffability'. *Religious Studies* 36 (2000): pp. 35–46.

John of Scythopolis and the Dionysian Corpus: Annotating the Areopagite (trans. P. Rorem and J.C. Lamoreaux; Oxford: Oxford University Press, 1998).

Kelly, J.N.D. *Early Christian Doctrines* (London: Black, 1958).

Kvanvig, J., ed. *Oxford Studies in Philosophy of Religion* (4 vols; Oxford: Oxford University Press, 2012).

Lincoln, A.T., and A. Paddison, eds. *Christology and Scripture: Interdisciplinary Perspectives* (London: T&T Clark, 2008).

Lombard, Peter. *The Sentences, book 1: The Mystery of the Trinity* (trans. G. Silano; Toronto: Pontifical Institute of Mediaeval Studies, 2007).

Mann, W.E., ed. *The Blackwell Guide to the Philosophy of Religion* (Oxford: Blackwell, 2005).

Marenbon, J., ed. *The Cambridge Companion to Boethius* (Cambridge: Cambridge University Press, 2009).

McGuckin, J.A. *The Westminster Handbook to Patristic Theology* (Louisville, KY: Westminster John Knox Press, 2004).

Mullins, R.T. 'Simply Impossible: A Case against Divine Simplicity'. *Journal of Reformed Theology* 7 (2013): pp. 181–203.

Norris, R.A., Jr, ed. *The Christological Controversy* (Philadelphia: Fortress Press, 1990).

Oppy, G. and N. Trakakis, eds. *The History of Western Philosophy of Religion, vol. 2: Medieval Philosophy of Religion* (Durham: Acumen, 2009).

Paasch, J. 'Arius and Athanasius on the Production of God's Son'. *Faith and Philosophy* 27 (2010): pp. 382–404.

Quinn, P.L. and C. Taliaferro, eds. *A Companion to Philosophy of Religion* (Malden: Blackwell, 1999).

Richards, J.W. *The Untamed God: A Philosophical Exploration of Divine Perfection, Simplicity and Immutability* (Downers Grove, IL: InterVarsity Press, 2003).

Rogers, K.A. *The Anselmian Approach to God and Creation* (Lewiston: Mellen, 1997).

— *Perfect Being Theology* (Edinburgh: Edinburgh University Press, 2000).

Scotus, J.D. *God and Creatures: The Quodlibetal Questions* (trans. F. Alluntis and A.B. Wolter; Princeton: Princeton University Press, 1975).

Stock, R. *A Stock of Divine Knowledge, being a lively description of the divine nature, or, The divine essence, attributes, and Trinity particularly explaned and profitably applied:the first, shewing us what God is: the second, what we ought to be* (London: T.H. for Philip Nevil, 1641).

Swinburne, Richard. *Revelation: From Metaphor to Analogy* (Oxford: Oxford University Press, 2nd edn, 2007).

Torrance, T.F., ed. *The Incarnation: Ecumenical Studies in the Nicene-Constantinopolitan Creed A.D. 381* (Edinburgh: Handsel, 1981).

Trakakis, N. 'Does Univocity Entail Idolatry?' *Sophia* 49 (2010): pp. 535–55.

Wainwright, W.J., ed. *The Oxford Handbook of Philosophy of Religion* (Oxford: Oxford University Press, 2005).

Werther, D. and M.D. Linville, eds. *Philosophy and the Christian Worldview: Analysis, Assessment and Development* (New York: Continuum, 2012).

Williams, T. 'The Doctrine of Univocity is True and Salutary'. *Modern Theology* 21 (2005): pp. 575–85.

Wolterstorff, Nicholas. *Inquiring about God: Selected Essays*, vol. 1 (ed. T. Cuneo; New York: Cambridge University Press, 2010).

Yandell, K.E. *The Epistemology of Religious Experience* (Cambridge: Cambridge University Press, 1993).

— 'The Ineffability Theme'. *International Journal for Philosophy of Religion* 10 (1979): pp. 209–31.

— 'Some Varieties of Ineffability'. *International Journal for Philosophy of Religion* 6 (1975): pp. 167–79.

7

A Conversation Overheard: Reflecting on the Trinitarian Grammar of Intimacy and Substance

John Colwell

> After Jesus said this, he looked towards heaven and prayed: 'Father, the time has come. Glorify your Son, that your Son may glorify you' (John 17:1).

A search of personal records reveals that, in almost forty years of ordained ministry, I have preached on this seventeenth chapter of John's gospel more than any other single passage. If we are allowed favourite passages of Scripture then this, for me, is unrivalled. Unrivalled because, as Robert Jenson observes, we are allowed to eavesdrop on a most intimate conversation between the Father and the Son,[1] an intimate conversation which, one suspects, is not merely testimony to how Jesus prayed on earth once, but more profoundly is indicative of his eternal intercession: as our High Priest he constantly is praying that we will be kept, that we will be holy, that we will be one, that we will be with him. And this suspicion of an overhearing of an eternal conversation is both crucial and programmatic: a doctrine of revelation stands or falls here, stands or falls on the conviction that the gospel story is not a divine deception, that the 'glory' of the Father that the Son has revealed on earth is truly the eternal glory of the Father, that the intimacy that characterizes this conversation is truly and eternally the intimacy of the true God, that the glory of the Son on earth – that is, the glory of his cross and resurrection – is truly a reiteration of the glory he has with the Father before the world began (v. 5). In overhearing this conversation we are standing on the holiest of ground.

Of course, we do not understand that which we are hearing. Were it not for such overhearing which is the witness of Holy Scripture we would be wholly ignorant of the true God, our theological musings would be no more than the wishful yet specious philosophical speculations of the terminally ignorant. But even with such overhearing our grasp of its significance is minimal: we recognize the words – the language of Father and Son is our own human language – but we cannot possibly know the significance of these familiar and familial words in this entirely unfamiliar context: in classic apophatic fashion we are more comfortable in asserting what should not be inferred from the terms than in venturing what might be inferred – whatever Father and Son language here might signify it surely is not significant of a biological relationship; God is Spirit (John 4:24); he cannot be comprehended biologically. Or, as a friend of mine once put it, in the light of our overhearing of this conversation we know who God is, but we cannot possibly know what it is to be God.[2] It is in this respect that Thomas Aquinas's discussion of analogy is much misunderstood and misappropriated: his discussion of the 'Names of God' is not an attempt to speak of the being of God in analogy with the being of the world – as Laurence Hemming observes, Thomas Aquinas never (here or anywhere else) speaks of an analogy of being (*analogia entis*)[3] – his primary concern rather is to discuss the manner in which we should try to understand the names used of God in his self-disclosure, names witnessed in Holy Scripture, and, thereafter, names we attribute to God (such as 'person' or 'relation') in response to this self-naming.[4] And, in this respect, we must also accept that whatever terms we employ in response to this self-naming of God as Father and Son, all talk of nature, essence, and substance, all talk of identity, subsistence, and person, will inevitably fall short of what needs to be said; as analogous terms their usage here can never be univocal; God is unique and no term can be applied to God merely with respect to its creaturely employment.[5] We are not reduced to silence here, but we are constrained to a humble hesitancy.

But while we might not fully comprehend the language we overhear, and while we must recognize all such overheard language of intimacy as analogous, this overheard language must remain the control for our language of theological response. Or, to put the matter more straightforwardly, our Trinitarian language must continually be tested against this Father and Son language of intimacy to which it seeks to respond and which it seeks to explicate. And here we arrive at the specific question for our attention, the question of whether Cappadocian accounts of the Holy Trinity and more recent 'social' analogies or Aurelius Augustine's so-called 'psychological' analogy are faithful and helpful responses to the overheard language witnessed in Scripture. And without in any degree mitigating the controlling function of this overheard language we must acknowledge an immediate and troubling problem, a problem surfacing in the reflections of Basil and both Gregories as also in the musings of Augustine and subsequent Trinitarian explorations: there is no explicit reference to the Holy Spirit in this most intimate and detailed prayer, nor yet in Jesus' praying in Gethsemane, nor yet in the prayer in which he invites his disciples to share. I will return to this difficulty of explicit absence and to the consequent temptations to effective binitarianism at the conclusion of this chapter.

In beginning to address the specific question of distinct (if not rival) Trinitarian analogies I am aware of at least three procedural problems. In the first place (and not wishing to appear a grumpy old cynic) one must beware of the inevitable tendency of historical research, and thereby of historical theology, to identify evidence for that which it is seeking to establish, to find that which it is seeking.[6] It really is not difficult to find passages in the Cappadocians and in Augustine that give evidence of their similarity of thought, nor is it that difficult to cite passages that highlight possible distinctions. Second, and in relation to this first sceptical observation, the various 'social' analogies that increasingly emerged during the second half of the twentieth century (and seem to have been increasingly challenged through these early years of the twenty-first) were not infrequently the guise for other (distinctly twentieth-century) challenges to the tradition, specifically challenges to doctrines of divine simplicity and impassibility which, with my friend Steve Holmes, I would find it almost impossible to believe were challenged by the Cappadocians any more than by Augustine.[7] I admit, of course, that there are valid questions here, that the doctrine of the Trinity itself gives particular shape to the affirmation of divine simplicity, that the suffering of Christ as one who is both truly God and truly human challenges abstracted notions of divine impassibility – but, with Steve Holmes and others,[8] I note that such questions were addressed with significant subtlety and care within the early tradition – perhaps with rather more subtlety and care than some of their more recent treatments[9] – that it is simply simplistic and wrong to suggest that this early tradition comprehensively capitulated to Hellenistic notions of abstracted absolute substance. Indeed, there is ground to suspect that the Cappadocians would have repudiated even the ascription 'social analogy' with its implicitly more commonplace analogical strategy of conceiving God according to the pattern of human socialities. It may be the case, as is argued by Colin Gunton and others,[10] that what it means to be a human person is identified (in part at least) by relatedness to other persons, but such human-defining relatedness can be but a shadowy reflection of the defining relatedness of Father, Son, and Spirit, and certainly I will never come to comprehend this divine-defining relatedness by reflecting on the potentialities of human relatedness. For Basil of Caesarea, Gregory Nazianzen, and Gregory of Nyssa the defining relations of Father, Son, and Spirit, of the Unbegotten, the Begotten, and the 'Breathed-out' One, are unique: they are unique precisely because they are divine, the relations of the Creator rather than the relations of the creature. Neither here nor anywhere else can there be any possibility of an analogy of being between creature and Creator, the human and the divine.

But I am running ahead of myself – and we will return to this crucial question of analogy later in this chapter – for the third (and most disabling) procedural problem is that, while we know (at least in part) of Augustine's response to the Cappadocians (and to Basil in particular), we have no way of knowing of how the Cappadocians might have responded to Augustine's *De trinitate* since they died between twenty-four and forty years before its completion. We can compare and contrast (bearing in mind the dangers of the first procedural difficulty), but it would be presumptuous to construct a later response from these earlier writings given that, in several respects, the debate was continuing.

We can, of course, take note of what the Cappadocians said in their own context, aware already of how their terms of expression, if not their understanding, differed in particular from the Latin West. In his oration on the death of Athanasius, Gregory Nazianzen attributes the Italians' introduction of the term 'person' (*persona*) to the 'scantiness of their vocabulary, and its poverty of terms . . . they are unable to distinguish between Essence and Hypostases, and therefore introduce the term Persons, to avoid being understood to assert three Essences'.[11] But perhaps more interestingly, in his regretful but gracious resignation oration at the Council of Constantinople, Gregory muses both on the comparability and on the potential dangers of these two forms of expression:

> let not those who are contentious on these points utter their scandalous taunts, as if our faith depended on terms and not on realities. For what do you mean who assert the three Hypostases? Do you imply three Essences by the term? I am assured that you would loudly shout against those who do so. For you teach that the Essence of the Three is One and the same. What do you mean, who assert the Three Persons? Do you imagine a single compound sort of being, with three faces, or of an entirely human form? Perish the thought! You too will loudly reply that he who thinks thus, will never see the face of God, whatever it may be. What is the meaning of the Hypostases of the one party, of the Persons of the other, to ask this further question? That They are three, Who are distinguished not by natures but by properties.[12]

That the hypostases of the Father, the Son, and the Spirit were distinguished by their distinctive property (ἰδιότης) or relation (σχέσις) is crucial for each of the Cappadocians, albeit differently expressed.

Though Nazianzen distinguishes the Father both by his 'unbegottenness' (ἀγεννησία) and as 'unoriginate' (ἄναρχος) inasmuch as the Son, distinguished by 'begottenness' (γέννησις), and the Spirit, distinguished by 'procession' (ἐκπόρευσις), find their 'cause' in the hypostasis of the Father,[13] he remains cautious concerning this manner of distinction lest it be misappropriated as signifying any distinction of essence.[14] For Gregory Nazianzen then, as for Basil and Gregory of Nyssa, there can be no question of inferring from the language of three hypostases the suggestion of three essences; the essence of the Godhead is undivided, subsisting identically in the Father, the Son, and the Spirit. So (famously) Basil:

> The distinction between οὐσία and ὑπόστασις is the same as that between the general and the particular; as, for instance, between the animal and the particular man. Wherefore, in the case of the Godhead, we confess one essence or substance so as not to give a variant definition of existence, but we confess a particular hypostasis, in order that our conception of Father, Son and Holy Spirit may be without confusion and clear. If we have no distinct perception of the separate characteristics, namely, fatherhood, sonship, and sanctification, but form our conception of God from the general idea of existence, we cannot possibly give a sound account of our faith. We must, therefore, confess the faith by adding the particular to the common. The Godhead is common; the fatherhood particular.[15]

Turning, then, to Augustine, it is perhaps not so much this subtle yet clear and careful distinction between essence and subsistence that eludes him (though it appears to do so[16]) as a broader disquiet with the notion of substance and its common implications:[17]

> If, I say, God subsists so that He can be properly called a substance, then there is something in Him as it were a subject, and He is not simple . . . But it is an impiety to say that God subsists, and is a subject in relation to His own goodness, and that this goodness is not a substance or rather essence, and that God Himself is not His own goodness, but that it is in Him as in a subject . . . whence to be God is the same thing as to subsist; and so the Trinity, if one essence, is also one substance. Perhaps therefore they are more conveniently called three persons than three substances.[18]

This is far from being an easy passage to comprehend (and I shamefully acknowledge my competence in Latin to be at least as frail as Augustine's competence in Greek), but I suspect that, if there is validity in the dominant criticisms of Augustine by Robert Jenson and others, this passage is crucial. Nonetheless, for the most part Augustine is content to admit that the Cappadocians simply employ different terms, according to the possibilities of the Greek language, to signify that which he wishes to signify by the terms essence and person (and in this context Augustine graciously admits his own limitations in grasping these subtleties[19]).[20]

Moreover, Augustine similarly distinguishes Father, Son, and Spirit on the basis of their distinctive relations with one another: 'although to be the Father and to be the Son is different, yet their substance is not different; because they are so called, not according to substance, but according to relation, which relation, however, is not accident, because it is not changeable.'[21]

But while so much can and should be said positively; while (as one would expect given a similar starting point with the text of Holy Scripture) there are certain similarities and parallels to be drawn between these authors, there remain significant differences and, herein, justification for at least some of the criticisms of Augustine that emerged in the latter part of the twentieth century only (as mentioned previously) themselves to be challenged in these first years of the twenty-first century. In a playful (yet serious) response to recent 'bashers' of the 'Augustine bashers' Robert Jenson catalogues the persisting difficulties of his account:

> What is *not* done by those who bash us Augustine-bashers is to face up to the truly disastrous propositions Augustine did in fact emphatically and insistently lay down, propositions that became maxims of subsequent Western theology. He *did* in fact say that the Cappadocian distinction of *ousia/hypostasis* – the very distinction that enabled the creedal doctrine of the Trinity – could be no more than a purely linguistic device, that it could tell us nothing about the reality of God. He did treat the works of God in the economy, in the history of God's saving work, as 'indivisible', in the sense that any of them *could* have been done by any of the three, thereby destroying the whole basis on which an immanent triunity could be affirmed in the first place. He did say that it is absurd, as violating the divine simplicity, to think that the Father could not be what he is apart from the Son, and vice versa – thereby rejecting a foundational proposition of trinitarian thought and worship from Tertullian on. Augustine, alas, did in fact say these things, and they have been a curse on Western theology ever since.[22]

It is true, of course, that Gregory of Nyssa also asserts that the Father, the Son, and the Spirit are indivisible in their external works, but they are indivisible in their relational distinctions: 'every operation which extends from God to Creation, and is named according to our variable conceptions of it, has its origin from the Father, and proceeds through the Son, and is perfected in the Holy Spirit'.[23] It is similarly true that Nyssa, like those before him, assumes divine simplicity, but it is a changeless simplicity in which the naming of the Father implies the Son just as the naming of the Son implies the Father.[24] It is certainly true, as Jenson goes on to say, that Augustine has been far more of a blessing than a curse, and that, as he has previously acknowledged as the common theme of the 'bashers' of 'Augustine bashers', Trinitarian language shaped his teaching, his pastoral practice, and his personal piety. But the indictment remains; I haven't found it at all adequately answered[25] – and, in this particular indictment Jenson has not even made mention of the disastrous predilection for seeking a reflection of the eternal Trinity in the single human person,[26] not least when his reasons for seeking this divine image in the individual man rest on a (now) questionable conflation of the creation accounts in Genesis 1.1 – 2.3 and Genesis 2.4–25 and an explicitly androcentric reading of both accounts.[27]

If we heed Gregory Nazianzen's warning in his farewell oration, that the language of persons, as distinct from hypostases, could be taken as signifying a single compound being with three faces, it is difficult not to stumble at the series of reflected Trinities Augustine considers in the final books of De trinitate. Here, if not previously, it surely is hard to maintain that by the reflected image of memory, understanding, and love (or will),[28] or any other such reflected image, Augustine is implying the same form of identity distinction as is implied by the notion of hypostasia. Let it be granted that, in this discussion, Augustine moves from a static image of God in the single human person to a dynamic and reflective image,[29] let it similarly be granted that the whole discussion is enclosed in prayer,[30] and let it be granted that the tone throughout is often marked by commendable humility and hesitancy, but can it really be so surprising that the various forms of Western monism should spring from such a source?

It should be acknowledged in this context that both Gregory of Nyssa and, previously, Gregory Nazianzen ponder the sun and its rays or the light emanating from a lamp as an analogy of the relation between the Father and the Son but, in Nyssa's case, the analogy is clearly not that between the Father and the sun (or lamp) and between the Son and the rays issuing from the sun (or lamp) but rather the analogy is between the relation of the Father to the Son and the relation of the sun (or lamp) to its rays; an analogy of relation rather than an analogy of being.[31] Nazianzen had previously dismissed precisely this analogy as impersonal:[32] 'it seems best to me to let the images and the shadows go, as being deceitful and very far short of the truth'.[33]

The suspicion, however, is that Augustine is not so much intending to offer an analogy, whether an analogy of being or an analogy of relation, as he is intending to explore the possibilities of tracing an image of God's triunity in the individual human person, albeit an individual human person worshipfully and prayerfully contemplating the triune God: might not these latter books of the *De trinitate* be more concerned with a doctrine of humanity in response to a doctrine of the Trinity than with the doctrine of the Trinity itself? This may well be the case – and if it is the case it surely falls to the criticisms offered by Karl Barth of any form of a *vestigium Trinitatis*[34] – but this is not our focus of attention here: whatever Augustine's intentions in this discussion (whether a continuing focus on the Trinity or a corresponding focus on the human person as the image of God), that he elects to trace a triunity within a single human person is sufficient root for subsequent Western monism and, whether or not it fails Gregory Nazianzen's test of Trinitarian orthodoxy, it would certainly seem to offend the control of the gospel narratives: as it has so often been objected, is Jesus in Gethsemane talking to himself?

And here I would continue to agree with Colin Gunton and others that the legacy of this irredeemably monadic oneness is disastrous, certainly (as Gunton suggests) in the various manifestations of a Western predisposition to individualism, but more primarily and simply in a conception (or misconception) of a Christian doctrine of God – and this in both academic reflection and popular piety. Within the development of Western doctrine this resolving of God's triunity in terms of monadic oneness issues inevitably (again as Gunton, Jüngel, and others have shown) either in the effective deism of God's supposed absolute otherness to creation or, and in response and reaction to this, in the effective deification of creation as a means of reasserting his (monadic) presence: abandon a thorough Trinitarianism and issues of transcendence and immanence are rendered irresolvable. It should not surprise us that accounts of the Trinity play such a minor part in so much Western theology. It should not surprise us that *in extremis*, Father, Son, and Spirit cease to be considered as persons in any meaningful sense. It should not surprise us that, for all he did to bring a Trinitarian doctrine of God to the fore, and notwithstanding his criticisms of Augustine, Karl Barth (at least in the first volume of his *Church Dogmatics*) speaks of Father, Son, and Spirit, as three 'modes of God's existence'.[35] Though I do admit surprise when my friend Paul Fiddes seems surprised that some contemporary theologians, following the lead of Gregory Nazianzen, view the divine persons as constituted by their mutual relations.[36] And I'm simply staggered when Prof. Fiddes continues, following a possible reading of Thomas Aquinas's discussion of divine relations, by reducing the terms Father, Son, and Spirit to the naming of movements in the one God: '"Father" is the name for a fatherly movement in God, and "Son" for a filial movement. Moreover, we can speak of the Father, Son and Spirit in this sense as "persons", if by person we mean a "hypostasis" or distinct reality, rather than a subjective agent.'[37]

But it is within popular piety that we encounter this legacy at its most damaging. Visit almost any church in the UK dedicated to the Holy Trinity and you will probably find a prominent stained-glass window, continuing the form of frescos throughout Western Europe, where the Father is depicted enthroned (often in the image of all too human imperial power), the Son (usually a much smaller figure) is held out on his cross by the Father, and the Spirit is depicted as a dove, hovering between Father and Son. Ask any schoolchild, and probably ask any adult member of the congregation, to point to God in that portrayal and they will invariably and inevitably identify the Father – this is, of course, in poignant contrast to Eastern icons of the Trinity in the image of Abraham's angelic visitors where distinguishing the Father, Son, and Spirit necessitates the following of less than obvious clues.[38] As a Christian pastor I frequently encounter those, even in the congregation, who believe in God but see Jesus as simply a great moral and spiritual teacher – I cannot but ponder the identity of this God in whom such profess to believe.

Do I blame Augustine for all this? Of course not: but it might have proved harder for the Western church to have developed in these ways had he not laid such an uneven foundation. Neither am I simplistically claiming all that is Western as bad and all that is Eastern as good. On the one hand, as Robert Jenson opines, Gregory Palamas may be responsible for introducing similar confusion to the Eastern tradition,[39] but more basically, there are aspects of the Cappadocians' thought that merit similar critical scrutiny.

In the first place we should remember that the Cappadocians, like Augustine, were thinking and writing before the Council of Chalcedon and, in the former case at least, before the questions addressed by that council had been brought to sharp focus. One wonders whether, in this later context, the Cappadocians any more than Augustine could have quite so simply distinguished what Jesus does as human and what Jesus does as God. Nor, of course, did Chalcedon resolve such issues: stemming from here is perhaps the first major division of the church, and it is one thing to declare Christ's two natures to be without division, confusion, etc.; it is something else entirely to maintain his humanity without prejudice to his divinity and his divinity without prejudice to his humanity. The starting point for this chapter – and surely for all authentically Christian theology – is that God is in the gospel story who he is eternally in himself. Any distinction between the immanent and economic Trinity, then, concerns the freedom of God to be immanent in this particular way. Consequently, the sadly acrimonious debate between Bruce McCormack and Paul Molnar is of far greater interest and significance than a mere dispute concerning possible readings of Karl Barth.[40]

But more immediately, and as indicated earlier in this chapter, the Cappadocians' discussion of the Holy Spirit is hardly more satisfactory than that of Augustine: to identify the Spirit as sanctifying power is no more indicative of personal agency and relatedness than is the outcome of identifying the Spirit as love; to speak of the Spirit as the breathed-out-one, just as to speak of the Spirit as the proceeding one, merely identifies the Spirit in distinction to the Father and the Son. Indeed, Gregory of Nyssa is quite explicit in resolving to define the Spirit negatively.[41]

The identity of the Holy Spirit in fully personal terms has persisted as a problem in both Eastern and Western traditions from the beginning and can be grounded precisely in the prayer of Jesus with which this chapter began. Here, as in Gethsemane, in the praying of the Son we catch a glimpse of his eternal intimacy with the Father. The doctrine of the Trinity is the church's response to this revelation of eternal intimacy – but the Spirit, here as elsewhere, remains invisible and silent. As a simplistic response to what is visible and audible in this praying, the church could have settled on a binitarian account of God with no personal account of the Spirit whatsoever. But the church did not respond to such overheard conversations simplistically since it discerned that here, as everywhere else (but here especially), the Spirit, though invisible and silent, was invisibly and silently present rather than absent. Quite deliberately in this chapter, other than by way of secondary reference, I have avoided any detailed discussion of the contemporary critics of Augustine: one can only attempt so much in a single chapter, or even a single book, and (with others) I deem readings of Augustine and the Cappadocians more basic to our purposes. I suspect, however, the work of Jürgen Moltmann to be one of the more obvious targets in the sights of Steve Holmes in his recent discussion of the Trinity.[42] Whatever else can be said concerning Moltmann's contribution (and being, like Steve Holmes, a former student of Colin Gunton, I believe much should be), towards the beginning of *The Trinity and the Kingdom of God* Moltmann offers what I take to be a helpful exposition of the mediating role of the Spirit within the gospel story.[43] Albeit usually invisibly and silently, the Spirit is nonetheless explicitly present at Jesus' conception and baptism, as the means of his ministry and the mediation of his sacrifice, as the power of his resurrection and the mediation of his continuing presence and power within and through his disciples.[44] The communion between Father and Son in this high-priestly prayer, in Gethsemane, and even at the cross (according to John's account) is a communion mediated by the Spirit, a mediated intimacy. And if this is the manner of the intimacy of Father and Son here, ought we not to confess this as the manner of their eternal intimacy? A mediator, as distinct from a power or mutual love, is a personal agency, a person, a subsistence. And as I have argued at greater length elsewhere,[45] as the mediator of the intimacy of the Father and the Son, maybe we should think of the Spirit, not just in typically Western terms as the one who holds them together, but as the one who, as the mediator of their mutual love, holds them in their distinctiveness as Father and Son and preserves them from an indistinct oneness. Both Colin Gunton and Wolfhart Pannenberg speak of the Spirit as the one who maintains the particularities of creation; could it not be that this is not just his function but his distinctive person, that this is who he is eternally in relation to the Father and the Son?

The prayer of Jesus, and the gospel story as a whole, speak of a unity in distinction – and this must remain the control for our responsive Trinitarian language. And, criticisms aside, it was the control for Augustine as much as for the Cappadocians. Neither we nor they have the possibility of saying that which is wholly adequate as a response: our reasonable and responsible aim should be to avoid saying that which is plainly inadequate or misleading – it would be better otherwise to come to silence and to allow the story to speak for itself.

Bibliography

Aquinas, Thomas. *Summa Theologica* (trans. Fathers of the English Dominican Province; Westminster, MD: Christian Classics, 1981).

Augustine. *On the Holy Trinity*. Pages 17–228 in *A Select Library of the Nicene and Post-Nicene Fathers of the Christian Church*, series 1, vol. 3 (ed. Philip Schaff; Buffalo, NY: Christian Literature Company, 1887).

Ayres, Lewis. *Augustine and the Trinity* (Cambridge: Cambridge University Press, 2010).

Barth, Karl. *Church Dogmatics*, vol. I, part 1 (ed. G.W. Bromiley and T.F. Torrance; Edinburgh: T&T Clark, 2nd edn, 1975).

Basil of Caesarea. *Letter to Amphilochius* (Letter 236). Pages 276–9 in *A Select Library of the Nicene and Post-Nicene Fathers of the Christian Church*, series 2, vol. 8 (ed. Philip Schaff and Henry Wace; New York: Christian Literature Company, 1895).

Calvin, John. *Institutes of the Christian Religion* (2 vols; ed. J.T. McNeill; trans. F.L. Battles; Philadelphia: Westminster Press, 1960).

Colwell, John E. *Promise and Presence: An Exploration of Sacramental Theology* (Milton Keynes: Paternoster Press, 2005; reprinted Eugene, OR: Wipf & Stock, 2011).

Dempsey, Michael T., ed. *Trinity and Election in Contemporary Theology* (Grand Rapids: Eerdmans, 2011).

Fiddes, Paul S. *Participating in God: A Pastoral Doctrine of the Trinity* (London: Darton, Longman & Todd, 2000).

Gavrilyuk, Paul L. *The Suffering of the Impassible God: The Dialectics of Patristic Thought* (Oxford: Oxford University Press, 2006).

Green, Brad. 'The Protomodern Augustine? Colin Gunton and the Failure of Augustine'. *International Journal of Systematic Theology* 9 (2007): pp. 328–41.

Gregory Nazianzen. *Oration 21: On the Great Athanasius, Bishop of Alexandria* 35. Pages 269–80 in *A Select Library of the Nicene and Post-Nicene Fathers of the Christian Church*, series 2, vol. 7 (ed. Philip Schaff and Henry Wace; New York: Christian Literature Company, 1894).

— *Oration 40: On Holy Baptism* 43. Pages 360–77 in *A Select Library of the Nicene and Post-Nicene Fathers of the Christian Church*, series 2, vol. 7 (ed. Philip Schaff and Henry Wace; New York: Christian Literature Company, 1894).

— *Oration 42: 'The Last Farewell'*. Pages 385–95 in *A Select Library of the Nicene and Post-Nicene Fathers of the Christian Church*, series 2, vol. 7 (ed. Philip Schaff and Henry Wace; New York: Christian Literature Company, 1894).

— *The Fifth Theological Oration: On the Holy Spirit* 32. Pages 318–28 in *A Select Library of the Nicene and Post-Nicene Fathers of the Christian Church*, series 2, vol. 7 (ed. Philip Schaff and Henry Wace; New York: Christian Literature Company, 1894).

— *The Third Theological Oration* 3. Pages 301–9 in *A Select Library of the Nicene and Post-Nicene Fathers of the Christian Church*, series 2, vol. 7 (ed. Philip Schaff and Henry Wace; New York: Christian Literature Company, 1894).

Gregory of Nyssa. *Against Eunomius* 1. Pages 35–100 in *A Select Library of the Nicene and Post-Nicene Fathers of the Christian Church*, series 2, vol. 5 (ed. Philip Schaff and Henry Wace; New York: Christian Literature Company, 1893).

— *Against Eunomius* 2. Pages 101–34 in *A Select Library of the Nicene and Post-Nicene Fathers of the Christian Church*, series 2, vol. 5 (ed. Philip Schaff and Henry Wace; New York: Christian Literature Company, 1893).

— *Against Eunomius* 8. Pages 200–10 in *A Select Library of the Nicene and Post-Nicene Fathers of the Christian Church*, series 2, vol. 5 (ed. Philip Schaff and Henry Wace; New York: Christian Literature Company, 1893).

— *On 'Not Three Gods': To Ablabius*. Pages 331–6 in *A Select Library of the Nicene and Post-Nicene Fathers of the Christian Church*, series 2, vol. 5 (ed. Philip Schaff and Henry Wace; New York: Christian Literature Company, 1893).

— *On the Holy Spirit: Against the Followers of Macedonius*. Pages 315–25 in *A Select Library of the Nicene and Post-Nicene Fathers of the Christian Church*, series 2, vol. 5 (ed. Philip Schaff and Henry Wace; New York: Christian Literature Company, 1893).

Gunton, Colin E. *Act and Being: Towards a Theology of the Divine Attributes* (London: SCM Press, 2002).

— *The One, the Three and the Many: God, Creation and the Culture of Modernity*. The Bampton Lectures 1992 (Cambridge: Cambridge University Press, 1993).

Hemming, Laurence Paul. 'Analogia non Entis sed Entitatis: The Ontological Consequences of the Doctrine of Analogy'. *International Journal of Systematic Theology* 6 (2004): pp. 118–29.

Jenson, Robert W. 'A Decision Tree of Colin Gunton's Thinking.' Pages 8–16 in *The Theology of Colin Gunton* (ed. Lincoln Harvey; London: T&T Clark, 2010).

— *Systematic Theology, vol. 1: The Triune God* (Oxford: Oxford University Press, 1997).

— 'What Is the Point of Trinitarian Theology?' Pages 31–43 in *Trinitarian Theology Today: Essays on Divine Being and Act* (ed. Christoph Schwöbel; Edinburgh: T&T Clark, 1995).

Moltmann, Jürgen. *The Trinity and the Kingdom of God: the Doctrine of God* (trans. M. Kohl; London: SCM Press, 1981).

Schwöbel, Christoph and Colin Gunton, eds. *Persons, Divine and Human: King's College Essays in Theological Anthropology* (Edinburgh: T&T Clark, 1991).

Weinandy, Thomas. G. *Does God Suffer?* (Edinburgh: T&T Clark, 2000).

8.

The Biblical Foundations of the Trinity: Evaluating the Trinitarian Exegesis of Stephen R. Holmes

Michael F. Bird

Introduction

I consider it an immense privilege to be able to engage Stephen Holmes on the subject of the biblical foundations of Trinitarian doctrine. Holmes is a leading British theologian in the Baptist tradition and his chapter '"In Your Light, We See Light": the Trinity in the Bible' raises a host of good questions about exactly how biblical the doctrine of the Trinity is. In the end, Holmes effectively shows that the doctrine of the Trinity emerges from 'exegetical pressures' pregnant within the biblical materials themselves.

Holmes correctly notes that while the doctrine of the Trinity was largely derived from biblical exegesis the precise method of exegesis undertaken by the church fathers would strike modern readers as 'unconvincing, obscure, or seemingly arbitrary'.[1] That is because patristic authors employed hermeneutical methods that are different from contemporary ones and they had a tendency to major on details that strike us as relatively minor points of note. That said, Holmes is open to the prospect that there might be more convincing exegetical arguments for the doctrine of the Trinity 'even if they were unknown to the fathers'.[2] Indeed, Holmes takes up this challenge to provide a kind of exegetical précis which demonstrates that the doctrine of the Trinity is sufficiently rooted in the Old and New Testaments.

What I intend to do in this short chapter is evaluate Holmes's suggestion for a biblical basis for the doctrine of the Trinity and prosecute my own proposal for mapping Trinitarian faith in relation to the biblical witness. This will hopefully lead to a wholesome and 'Holmesome' way of understanding how the doctrine of the Trinity emerges from a deep and deliberate reading of Holy Scripture.

Biblical Exegesis and Trinitarian Doctrine

The Trinity and the Old Testament

The central issue is whether the doctrine of the Trinity is derived from biblical exegesis or arrives from esoteric philosophizing. Orthodox theology has always maintained the former, while rationalist critics have dismissed the Trinity as the philosophically incoherent ramblings of the church fathers. In the minds of critics, the church fathers were trying to force biblical materials to say what could never be said about them – i.e. they affirm God's three-and-oneness – by way of importing some highly fanciful philosophical categories and terms like *homoousios* and *hypostasis*. Rationalistic critics have the most bite when it comes to tracing the relationship of Trinitarian doctrine to the Old Testament. If we can hardly have expected the first Christians to arrive at the conclusion that in the 'Godhead there be three Persons, of one substance, power, and eternity; the Father, the Son, and the Holy Ghost'[3] from a cursory reading of the New Testament, it would be hideously rude to expect anything better from the most learned of Jewish scribes or even from the most knowledgeable of rabbis from reading the Old Testament. In which case, moving from the Torah to Tertullian to the Trinity is never going to be a simple ride as there are tectonic interpretive plates that must shift for such theological claims to have any textual legitimacy and internal coherence. But there are plausible reasons for suggesting that textual legitimacy can be found and intellectual coherence is at hand.

First, revelation is progressive, so that God's most recent revelation of himself always forces the believing community to revise their understanding of what has gone before. Indeed, this is exactly what we find stated in the prologue to the Gospel of John and in the opening proem of the Epistle to the Hebrews (John 1:1–18; Heb. 1:1–4). The old religion must be renegotiated in light of new revelation. According to Gregory Nazianzen:

> The Old Testament proclaimed the Father openly, and the Son more obscurely. The New manifested the Son, and suggested the deity of the Spirit. Now the Spirit himself dwells among us, and supplies us with a clearer demonstration of himself. For it was not safe, when the Godhead of the Father was not yet acknowledged, plainly to proclaim the Son; nor when that of the Son was yet

received to burden us further . . . with the Holy Spirit . . . [I]t was necessary that, increasing little by little, and, as David says, by ascensions from glory to glory, the full splendor of the Trinity should gradually shine forth.[4]

Second, doctrine is always deductive. Doctrine emerges from reflection on the mode and message of divine revelation. Moreover, the early church's effort in reasoning from Scripture about the nature and being of God was never going to be a simple exercise. Such a process of deduction was always going to have a complex road towards consensus. That is because the church had to wrestle not only with open texts, but with various debates about God's immanent being in relationship to his economic action, grope after the best terminology they could find to meaningfully explain the biblical phenomenon, and employ the philosophical categories available to them to best make their conclusions coherent within their own resident context.

The real issue is what provided the catalyst for members of a Jewish sect to revise extant assumptions about revelation and to begin a deductive train of thought that would eventually crystallize into Nicene-Chalcedonian clarifications about God's divine nature subsisting in three distinct but equal persons. Holmes touches briefly upon it when he says that Christian readings of the Old Testament were decisively christological because 'the person, and story, of Jesus Christ was seen as the key to understanding the various scriptures. Scripture was seen primarily as God's revelation, and what God had revealed was the gospel of Jesus Christ.'[5] I concur and we need to remember that the event and experience of the gospel of Jesus Christ led to a radical reconfiguration of how God's nature was understood and described. According to Kevin Vanhoozer: 'The very logic of the gospel – the declaration that God enables believers to relate to God the Father in Jesus Christ through the Spirit – implies the divinity of the Son and Spirit as well.'[6] Vanhoozer elsewhere claims that the 'integrity of the gospel is fatally compromised if either the Son or the Spirit is not fully God. If the Son were not God, he could neither reveal the Father nor atone for our sin. If the Spirit were not God, he could unite us neither to the Father and Son nor one another. The gospel, then, requires a triune God.'[7] On this reading, the Trinity emerged as a way of articulating the internal coherence of the gospel. The effective history of Jesus' life, death, and resurrection led to the formation of a community that believed that Jesus was sent by the Father, he was the Father's agent of redemption, he was exalted beside the Father, and he was the dispenser of the Holy Spirit. The gospel conceived the church's theocentric worldview, its christocentric faith, and pneumatic experience and yet it was only internally consistent if the Father's divinity was somehow shared with the Son and the Spirit. While the ordering of relationships within the Godhead was to be long disputed and the configuration of the Son's human and divine natures likewise was not immediately resolved, even so, the basic genetic components for the doctrine of the Trinity are well and truly encoded in the event and experience of the gospel. This gospel-faith thus created a hermeneutical framework for a reading of the Old Testament that was both affirming and yet revisionary, so the Old Testament could be seen to support in manifold ways a belief in a triune God.

I believe this observation, that the gospel announces a new revelation leading to a revised view of the old religion, supports Holmes's thesis that what makes Christian exegesis of the Old Testament plausible is that it was working with a 'different hermeneutic.'[8] The genesis of Trinitarian doctrine derives from no mere hearing of texts, but gains traction from the hermeneutical horizon in which the texts are heard. Holmes rightfully acknowledges that one of the benefits of the postmodern turn has been a sober recognition of the contingency and situatedness of all literary appropriations of texts. What texts 'mean' is very much a matter of context. Interpretation is created by the fusion of authorial intention which generates a text, the manifold cognitive connections that lie dormant within a text, and the experience of the readers around the text. If that is the case, then the patristic exegesis leading to the development of Trinitarian doctrine might not be quite so specious or vacuous as often thought. Patristic exegesis becomes plausible when the biblical texts are read in light of certain religious experiences, in view of a received hermeneutical tradition where the Messiah is the key and climax to Israel's sacred literature, and when an individual text is placed within a wider literary corpus so that the co-location of texts will inevitably foster a mutually interpretive spiral of intertextual illumination and theological illocution. In other words, given the right hermeneutical context, Scripture will drive some readers to believe in a triune God and to live out a Trinitarian faith.

Holmes refers to Psalm 2, one of the most frequently cited psalms in early Christian literature, as an example of how an Old Testament text can become conducive to a Christian interpretation. If a 'text has a certain fluidity, and . . . its meaning can be determined by its later reception' then a text such as Psalm 2 can 'properly be interpreted as a part of the Christian canon, and the echoes of Christology that Christian readers hear in it are – in this reception – not improper.'[9] I think this accounts for the clear phenomenon which we find in the New Testament and in later Christian literature where Psalm 2 is employed principally for the purpose of gospel proclamation and in christological exploration.[10] The scriptural exposition is neither wooden nor convoluted when understood within the mosaic of wider Christian beliefs about God the Father, Jesus the Son of God, and the Holy Spirit as the Spirit of Christ.

Unlike Holmes, however, I am less enthusiastic about the early church's use of Proverbs 8 and Wisdom 7 in their christological exegesis.[11] Such texts have long been read as accounts of the divine generation of the Son, affirmations of the Son's pre-existence, and the descent–ascent journey of wisdom into the world and back has been compared to the incarnation and ascension of Christ. Indeed, such wisdom motifs have been readily used as a backdrop to explain much of the christological claims of the New Testament authors.[12] Though I do not deny the relevance of wisdom motifs for New Testament Christology (see e.g. Col. 1:15–20),[13] I nonetheless have reservations. For, as Simon Gathercole points out, the identification of Jesus as wisdom would at best mean that he is in some sense an embodiment of God's creative activity rather than an incarnation of a divine person. What is more, the personification of a divine attribute is not the same as the incarnation of a divine person.[14] Wisdom traditions are at best narrative analogues to the story of Jesus rather than complete descriptions of a christological ontology.

Regarding the Old Testament as a whole in relation to the Trinity, Holmes is spot-on that a metaphysical monotheism is a modern and malleable construct and cannot be read back into ancient Israelite religion without anachronism. The theism of the Old Testament is shaped principally by God's supremacy and sole authorship of creation and by God's unique relationship to Israel through his covenanting activity. Such theism is expressed chiefly in monolatry with the exclusive worship of God and is sustainable irrespective of whether the ancient Israelites were genuine monotheists or de facto henotheists. That said, I'm not convinced that Old Testament theism is purely doxological rather than metaphysical as Holmes alleges.[15] The claim that God exists is after all a metaphysical claim! There seems to be also a strong emphasis on God's oneness, unity, and even simplicity, which are metaphysical claims about the divine nature.[16] In addition, the common refrain 'there is no other' (Deut. 4:35, 39; Isa. 44:8; 45:5–6, 14, 18, 22; Joel 2:27) certainly edges towards a strict and exclusive form of theism (i.e. monotheism) and this strictness was varyingly negotiated in second temple Jewish literature.

Therefore, I disagree with Holmes that the nature of Old Testament theism means that 'Trinitarian devotion could develop so rapidly after the ascension [because] there was no need to overcome a developed and defended metaphysical conception of deity.'[17] I think the early church's Trinitarian devotion, was metaphysically messy as it made a radical claim about God. It was radical because it staked a metaphysical claim about God's identity in relation to the story of Jesus of Nazareth. That claim was said to be consistent with the Old Testament and could be uncovered by way of a christolic exegesis of the Old Testament. However, such exegesis could only be undertaken under the auspices of a new revelation that fostered a hermeneutical rupture in the minds of Old Testament readers, who would be driven towards new, fresh, and even surprising ways of interpreting Scripture by a particular revelatory experience.

I hasten to add that the Trinitarian hermeneutical framework of the ealy church was erected and energized by a reading of the Old Testament. While their interpretive conclusions were in some sense radical, they were nonetheless regarded as existing in deliberate continuity with the divine voice speaking in the Old Testament. How so? First, the Old Testament fosters a tension between God's transcendence and immanence, or balancing his otherness from creation with his continual action within it. The primary way that the God of heaven is active upon the earth is not direct, but indirect, taking place through various agents like angels, word and wisdom, glory and temple, or *memra* and Messiah. Such agents, like 'the angel of the Lord', always stood in ambiguous relation to the divine identity and existed on a plane somewhere between representation, personification, and presence. This ambiguity, in some sense, paves the way for a theology of incarnation. Second, and with Holmes, several passages like Genesis 1:24–26 are suggestive of a potential plurality within God's being. As Holmes says, such readings are not 'demanded by the text' but are 'at least faithful to the text'.[18] However, the decision to adopt readings that are possible as preferable will depend upon one's hermeneutical disposition and ideational orientation. So while I think the metaphysical problem remains – just ask a rabbi or imam about Trinitarian monotheism – there exists within the Old Testament particular modes of divine presence and divine action that do provide the grounds for a *praeparatio ad incarnationem*. As such, I prefer to think of the Old Testament as providing analogies and intimations of God's tri-personal nature, and such claims become fully coherent in light of the event of the gospel and the worship experience of the early church.

The Trinity and the New Testament

Holmes is aware that the New Testament is a much more fertile soil to cultivate Trinitarian doctrine. Developers and defenders of God's triunity have found the New Testament far more conducive to staking such a theological claim. Unlike the Old Testament, one is not reliant upon creative or canonical readings in order to give textual currency to the doctrine since, as Holmes points out, the New Testament authors themselves exhibit 'exegetical pressure' to formulate a theology God's triunity.[19]

A fourfold taxonomy of arguments supporting a Trinitarian understanding of God is then given by Holmes. First, the gospels present the relationship between Jesus and the Father as unique and central. In this relationship is a complex mix of 'intimacy, union, shared knowledge and action, and subordination.'[20] Moreover, there is a reference to a change of state from one of pre-existence to one of an earthly appearance (e.g. John 1:14, 'The Word became flesh'. Phil. 2:6–8, 'Though he was in the form of God . . . beng made in human likesess and found in appearance as a human being'). Second, a further strand of the argument is that Jesus is said to perform divine works normally thought to be the sole prerogative of the Father. These works include revelation, redemption, providential ordering, judgement, and eschatological fulfilment. Taken together, these works imply that Jesus undertakes functions normally thought to be the exclusive actions of God. Third, Holmes highlights the divine titles given to Jesus and the Spirit, titles which indicate that Son and Spirit share divine honours and therefore share in the divine identity. Fourth, and finally, there are a series of proto-creedal formulations in the New Testament that hint towards Jesus' participating in the divinity identity like 1 Corinthians 8:6 and Matthew 28:19.

Generally speaking, I think Holmes is right in his conclusion. A close reading of these texts does not yield an account of the Trinity as laid out in fourth- and fifth-century formulations. What does emerge, however, is 'exegetical pressure' to find ways of speaking about the Father, Son, and Spirit that preserves divine monotheism and the divinity of the three persons. Thus, the New Testament clearly puts us on a trajectory towards the Trinity, a trajectory that at its logical end point will inevitably lead one to affirm the shared divinity of Father, Son, and Spirit in tandem with their separate personalities. In other words, the New Testament gives us the ingredients for a Trinitarian theology even if it is left to others to subsequently bake the cake so to speak. The subsequent christological and Trinitarian formulations of the early church were not sandcastles in the sky. The patristic church simply employed the language and frameworks available to them to summarize what they understood Scripture to be saying. Thus a term like *homoousios* for 'same substance' is not foreign philosophical impositions read into the text, but is a valid attempt to express in ontological language what Scripture says, that Jesus was 'equal' with God (John 5:18; Phil. 2:6).

That said, I would probably want to construct a taxonomy of New Testament arguments for the Trinity with a little more rigor and depth than Holmes does in his all too brief treatment. Others have done that work elsewhere and I have developed my own taxonomy in a previous work where I drew attention to a different way of organizing the biblical materials.[21] In my approach, one could start off with Old Testament affirmations of God's oneness and unity, then examine intimations of the Trinity in the Old Testament, address the binitarian and pneumatic nature of early Christian worship, analyse and unpack New Testament statements about the divinity and personhood of the Father, Son, and Spirit, then examine an incipient Trinitarianism pregnant within many traditional pieces of material, and finally find a climax in the Gospel of John where the evangelist is, I would argue, a proto-Trinitarian theologian.[22] In the end, the biblical materials, both the Old and New Testament, proffer a view whereby there is one God, the Holy One of Israel, who is also the God of Jesus, and in the experience of the church and in the event of the gospel, this God is known as Father, Son, and the Holy Spirit.

Still, we have to acknowledge the problem with moving from the New Testament directly to the Trinity is that there are some minor embankments along the way that require negotiation. Such obstacles do not receive much attention from Holmes even though it is clear that he is aware of their existence. For a start, there are some texts that seem to have a subordinationist orientation in their Christology, like 'The Father is greater than I' (John 14:28) and 'Then the end will come, when he hands over the kingdom to . . . the Father' (1 Cor. 15:24). These were the texts that Arians clung to and often quoted in their theological disputations. Also, whether the Son is in some sense just an apparition of the Father could be inferred from Jesus' words to Philip: 'Anyone who has seen me has seen the Father' (John 14:9). In addition, the fact that imagery like 'wind' and 'power' is used for the Holy Spirit leaves grounds for the prospect of his impersonal nature (Luke 24:49; John 3:8; Acts 2:2). Some have also asked whether the reference to 'gods' in the plural by Jesus (John 10:34) and by Paul to a separate 'Lord' and 'God' (1 Cor. 8:6) opens the door to ditheism or tritheism.

The early church recognized that, even with these textual tensions, modalism, tritheism, and subordinationism were weak and lazy answers to hard exegetical questions. A coherent doctrine of God required some sophisticated reasoning *with* Scripture (i.e. exegesis) and reasoning *from* Scripture (i.e. theological formulation) in order to affirm what Scripture affirms, namely, God's one-in-threeness. In other words, while the New Testament does not spell out a precise doctrine of the Trinity, we are forced by biblical pressures to develop such a doctrine in order to make sense of the New Testament. In this case, Donald Bloesch was entirely correct that 'the doctrine of the Trinity is both an analytical development of the central facts of divine revelation (as Barth maintained) and a synthetic construction drawn from the church's reflection upon this revelation.'[23]

Conclusion

In sum, Holmes gives a good appraisal of the biblical roots of the doctrine of the Trinity. He is sufficiently aware of the relevant scholarly discussions about monotheism and intermediary figures, he provides a reasoned defence of the appropriateness of patristic exegesis, and affords a way of showing how Trinitarian theology can be mapped in relation to the New Testament witnesses. My own criticisms are admittedly only minor points of disagreement or else suggestions for variations upon a similar theme. In any case, Holmes provides a thoughtful engagement with the biblical materials on his way to providing a critical assessment of contemporary trends in Trinitarian theology; trends that should be constantly measured against the teaching of Scripture and the testimony of tradition.

Bibliography

Bird, Michael F. *Colossians and Philemon*. New Covenant Commentary Series (Eugene, OR: Cascade, 2009).

— *Evangelical Theology: A Biblical and Systematic Introduction* (Grand Rapids: Zondervan, 2013).

Bloesch, Donald G. *God the Almighty: Power, Wisdom, Holiness, Love* (Downers Grove, IL: InterVarsity Press, 1995).

Dunn, James D. G. *Christology in the Making: A New Testament Inquiry into the Origins of the Doctrine of the Incarnation* (Grand Rapids: Eerdmans, 2nd edn, 1989).

Dunne, John Anthony. 'The Regal Status of Christ in the Colossian Hymn "Christ Hymn": A Re-evaluation of the Influence of Wisdom Traditions'. *Trinity Journal* 32 (2011): pp. 3–18.

Emery, Gilles, and Matthew Levering, eds. *The Oxford Handbook of the Trinity* (Oxford: Oxford University Press, 2011).

Gathercole, Simon J. *The Pre-Existent Son: Recovering the Christologies of Matthew, Mark, and Luke* (Grand Rapids: Eerdmans, 2006).

Janse, Sam. *'You Are My Son': The Reception of Psalm 2 in Early Judaism and the Early Church*, BET 51 (Leuven: Peeters, 2009).

Letham, Robert. *The Holy Trinity: In Scripture, History, Theology, and Worship* (Phillipsburg, NJ: Presbyterian & Reformed, 2004).

Levering, Matthew. *Scripture and Metaphysics: Aquinas and the Renewal of Trinitarian Theology* (Malden: Blackwell, 2004).

Rowe, C. Kavin. 'Biblical Pressure and Trinitarian Hermeneutics'. *Pro Ecclesia* 11 (2002): pp. 295–312.

Thiselton, Anthony C. *The Hermeneutics of Doctrine* (Grand Rapids: Eerdmans, 2007).

Vanhoozer, Kevin J. *Drama of Doctrine: A Canonical-Linguistic Approach to Christian Theology* (Louisville, KY: Westminster John Knox Press, 2005).

— 'The Triune God of the Gospel.' Pages 17–34 in *The Cambridge Companion to Evangelical Theology* (ed. Timothy Larsen and Daniel J. Treier; Cambridge: Cambridge University Press, 2007).

Walton, John H. *Ancient Near Eastern Thought and the Old Testament: Introducing the Conceptual World of the Hebrew Bible* (Grand Rapids: Baker, 2006).

Witherington, Ben. *Jesus the Sage: The Pilgrimage of Wisdom* (Minneapolis: Fortress Press, 2000).

9.

Does the Emperor Have New Clothes? Is Modern Trinitarian Theology a Revival or a Repudiation of Fourth-Century Settlements?

Graham J. Watts

Stephen Holmes's recent book *The Holy Trinity* has caused something of a stir. In essence the book attempts to argue three theses.[1]

First, the most commonly held view of the historical distinctions between Eastern and Western views of the Trinity is flawed and largely the result of the way in which the work of a nineteenth-century Jesuit theologian, Theodore de Régnon, has been interpreted. The so-called 'de Régnon hypothesis' argues that the Western approach, articulated most authoritatively by Augustine, starts with the unity of God and asks how one God can be three. The Eastern approach, typified by the Cappadocian fathers, begins with the threeness of God as revealed and asks how three can be one. This has become the received paradigm for most theological education during what became known as the 'Trinitarian revival' of the mid-late twentieth century. This hypothesis has been seriously challenged in recent literature, notably by Lewis Ayres and Michel Barnes, and Holmes follows this revisionist reading of the history of the doctrine of the Trinity.[2] Partly this involves a rehabilitation of Augustine. For much of the later twentieth century, Augustine was often held to be the father of all that is wrong in Western theology. Colin Gunton is renowned for his scathing critique of Augustine's views on the Trinity.[3] Bearing in mind that Gunton was Holmes's doctoral supervisor and theological mentor, to read that Holmes now regards Augustine as the 'greatest interpreter of Cappadocian theology' highlights the extent to which Holmes has moved in his own theology.[4]

Second, the so-called Trinitarian revival of the twentieth century not only assumed without question this East–West split, but developed an understanding of the relationship between God and creation which, Holmes argues, is very different from that of Nicene theology. Whereas patristic writers sought to retain a clear distinction between God and creation, maintaining a sense of God's mystery and otherness, twentieth-century theologians have, in the main, sought to explore a much closer link, notably by bringing God and history much closer together.

Third, the overall thrust of the book argues that with these two major departures from patristic theology, the modern 'Trinitarian revival' is not a revival at all, but a renegotiation, even a repudiation of the early-church doctrine of the Trinity. This begs the question whether modern Trinitarian doctrine is a legitimate recasting of Nicene thought, or a fateful move away from a theology which took the early church several centuries to conceive as consistent with biblical witness.

For the purposes of this chapter I will focus on the second hypothesis: the relationship between God, creation and history. Of all the themes identified by Holmes this seems to me to lie at the heart of the matter. I begin by exploring Holmes's thesis in relation to our understanding of being – ontology. In particular I will address the key question of the interpretation of the incarnation and the ways in which this has been expounded in ancient and modern theology. I will follow this with a briefer excursion into Reformation Christology, as a way of highlighting the process of doctrinal development. I will argue that greater attention is required here than is often identified. The final section will look at issues relating to eternity, space, and time. This is ambitious in a short chapter, but necessary if we are to examine the changing ways in which the relationship between God and history has been expounded. My primary conversation partners from the modern era will be T.F. Torrance and Wolfhart Pannenberg. I choose Torrance partly because his own theology is thoroughly steeped in patristic theology as well as Barth's *Church Dogmatics*. He seems to me to offer a counterpoint to Holmes's thesis. By contrast, Pannenberg represents one significant attempt to renegotiate the relationship between God and history on the basis of a revised ontology. Both are theologians of the Trinity; their approaches are very different.[5] When referring to fourth-century Nicene thought, my sources will vary, but I will pay particular attention to Athanasius. The point is not simply to offer commentary, but to elucidate and suggest ways of expanding the debate. In particular I will argue that Torrance remains an underutilized resource for contemporary theology.

The Thesis Explored: A Question of Being

As Holmes argues, it has become accepted dogma in much modern Trinitarianism to regard the fourth-century language of being as a problem rather than a resource. The primary reason for this is the widespread acceptance of another nineteenth-century narrative, most often ascribed to Harnack, of the infiltration of Greek static concepts of being into the doctrine of God. Examples of the way in which this has won wide acceptance in modern theology are too numerous to quote, but Moltmann would be a classic case.[6] Holmes questions this reading of fourth-century theology. In this Holmes is clearly influenced by the historical reconstruction offered by Lewis Ayres.[7]

Ayres offers a compelling argument to show that the most theologically significant linguistic development in the Nicene Creed is the appearance of the terms *ousia* and *hypostasis*.[8] The historical origin of these terms is debated, but it is instructive to examine the way in which these terms are used in the Creed. Ayres argues, cogently in my view, that the term *ousia* was not primarily regarded as a philosophical stand-alone concept, but rather as a particular way of describing the eternal generation of the Son. Primarily it clarifies the meaning of 'only-begotten' – affirming that the Son is of the same essence of the Father; Father and Son are thus described as *homoousios*. It is only later, sometime in the mid-350s, that Athanasius clarifies his understanding of this Nicene terminology.[9] His main argument rests on an exegesis of Scripture. If we are to ascribe biblical terms such as Power, Wisdom and Word to the Son it is necessary that the Son is understood to be 'from the Father' and thus 'of the essence of the Father'. This is seen as justifying the term *homoousios*, which thereby excludes any possibility of regarding the Son as a created being, against Arius; *homoousios* is thus a necessary supplement to the phrase 'from the *ousia* of the Father'. A second way in which Athanasius deploys the term is to defend divine simplicity. To speak of the essence of God is to speak simply of uncompounded eternal existence. To then describe the Word as 'of the essence of God' is to speak of the eternal generation of the Son without making the Son a created being. In the background is an assumption of a clear break between God and creation; the placing of the Word on the uncreated side of the divide precludes any blurring of that God–creation distinction, such as was found in Arius.[10]

From the perspective of the fourth century it is clear that the language of *homoousios* can be used to secure the nature of the Father–Son relationship by expressing both divine simplicity and the biblical truth that the Word has taken human flesh while not ceasing to be fully divine. This significance is not lost on T.F. Torrance. The incarnation means that God is not closed to us, but has drawn near in the Word become flesh. Yet, as Torrance takes from the Nicene understanding, to know God in Christ does not mean we can fully know what the being of God is. Our knowledge of God is grounded in his eternal being; we have access to some grasp of the eternal being of God, but not in any way which exhausts the being of God.[11] Torrance goes on to argue that, far from representing a Hellenization of Christian theology, the fathers took over certain Greek terms and renegotiated their meaning to facilitate language about God as Creator and Redeemer, eternally triune yet incarnate, thus making possible concepts such as divine providence while retaining divine simplicity and immutability. Torrance asserts in the strongest terms that this was 'not the Hellenising of Christianity, but the Christianising of Hellenism', an achievement which he attributes primarily to Athanasius.[12]

In the twentieth century it was T.F. Torrance who consistently employed the same terminology. For him 'the *homoousion* is the ontological and epistemological linchpin of Christian theology.'[13] It is vital since it conveys the scriptural concept that what God is towards us in Christ, he really is in his transcendent being, without denying divine aseity. Torrance maintains that the term *ousia* has an inward reference, whereas *hypostasis* refers to being in otherness – the outward reference.[14] So, the Father is God *in se*, but also Father for others as *hypostasis*. This enables Torrance to express the Nicene intention, that God is one *ousia*, three *hypostases*. The importance of the *homoousion* is impossible to over-estimate here. It ensures that in the incarnation we really do meet with God; God is the content of his own revelation, thus preserving us from mythological speculation. Because the Son is *homoousios* with the Father, our salvation is secured by God, something that no creature could ever secure. Yet, because the Son is *homoousios* with us in his humanity, he can stand in our place to secure our salvation. This is the evangelical import of *homoousion* theology.

By contrast, Pannenberg offers a far more radical reworking of the doctrine of God. As a student of Barth he learned the centrality of revelation, yet here the similarities end. From the outset Pannenberg was concerned that Barth's emphasis on the otherness of God left theology cut adrift from other forms of intellectual discourse. For Pannenberg, theology has to find a *via media* between faith and reason and thus find ways of interacting with philosophy and science.

Pannenberg's Trinitarian theology finds fullest expression in his *Systematic Theology*, but some of the conceptual groundwork is laid in his earlier collection of essays, *Metaphysics and the Idea of God*.[15] Here he laments the tendency among theologians to abandon metaphysics, arguing that any theology which lacks such a foundation inevitably lapses into subjectivism or demythologization. Yet he is clear that a new form of metaphysics is required. He cites a number of reasons for this, but his primary critique tends to follow the narrative of the Hellenistic infestation of early theology. His criticism here is nuanced, and he is prepared to question whether Harnack's account is accurate, yet he still finds fault with Nicene theology for the way the language of *ousia* is used. First, the importing of such an alien philosophical concept led to unhelpful discussions about the derivation of the persons of the Trinity. 'Any derivation of the Trinitarian persons from the essence of the one God leads either to modalism or subordinationism.'[16] This is a very different reading from that of Torrance. Whereas Torrance sees Nicene theology as reinterpreting the language of *ousia* and *hypostasis* in the light of biblical revelation, Pannenberg sees it as an alien import. In fact, Pannenberg goes so far as to criticize Nicaea for failing to take seriously the significance of the incarnation for the being of God. He thus accuses pro-Nicene theology of breaking the link between the immanent Trinity and history.

History has always been central in Pannenberg's theology. This reflects his commitment to understanding the being of God in relation to the totality of God's acts in history. Perhaps the most important reason for this is his attempt to construct a metaphysic built upon the concept of the infinite. He traces this back to Gregory of Nyssa and suggests that this concept can be used to secure the idea of the unity of God. The infinite has nothing beyond it, nothing to circumscribe it; it is the ultimate One. Hegel is credited with adopting the idea in relation to his dialectical method. The true Infinite is that which finds expression in that which is other – the finite.

The later *Systematic Theology* explores these themes with a more specifically Trinitarian focus.[17] Since Pannenberg rejects the traditional understanding of personal distinctions in terms of relations of origin, he argues that the Father–Son distinction has to be grounded in the historical message of Jesus and the coming of the kingdom of God. This facilitates a construction of the doctrine of the Trinity which is grounded in the historical revelation of Christ, emphasizing personal distinction, while employing the eschatological dimension of the coming of the kingdom of God. With regard to personal distinctiveness, Pannenberg uses the concept of mutual self-distinction. The historical Jesus witnesses to the Lordship of the Father and thus distinguishes himself from the Father. Similarly, the Father, in sending the Son distinguishes himself from the Son, and again, the Spirit distinguishes himself from Father and Son in the unique role of uniting them in the power of love. With regard to eschatology, Pannenberg does not abandon the idea of the monarchy of the Father but reinterprets this as the outworking of the agency of the Son and the Spirit in creation. He is quite clear that this is not simply a description of the economy of salvation; it is true of the immanent being of God. The monarchy of the Father is true 'not merely in the event of revelation. On the basis of the historical relation of Jesus to the Father we may say this of the inner life of the triune God.'[18] Again we should be clear that Pannenberg nuances his comments with great care. While it seems that the monarchy of the Father, and in some sense the unity of God, is posited as an outcome of the historical process, he seeks to avoid the pitfalls of process theology by affirming the overall sovereignty of God within the process. God cannot be reduced simply to an outcome of the historical process. In order to secure this, Pannenberg utilizes one of his most difficult concepts – the ontological priority of the future. If God is in some way dependent on the outcome of the process of history, yet sovereign over the process, then securing the ontological primacy of the future is a way of securing the transcendent otherness of God. Whether this actually makes sense seems to me at least debatable. At the very least we have here an indication of how far we have come from the classical doctrine of God.

Two points are worth noting in the context of this chapter. First, if we are to accuse fourth-century theologians of imbibing alien philosophical forms of thought, we ought to ask a similar question of Pannenberg. The influence of Hegel is clear in his deployment of the idea of God as the true Infinite. To paraphrase a recent critique, is the being of God essentially self-sufficient and immutable, as in classical doctrine, or is the being of God essentially self-unfolding and self-manifestation, as in Pannenberg? In classical formulations, the identity of the divine essence as three persons is understood as a relation of origins. In Pannenberg it is dialectical and eschatological.[19] Barth's critique of Hegel is apposite: 'the divine act of self-differentiation, of positing an Other over against himself and then reconciling that Other to himself, is a necessary rather than a free act. This means that creation and reconciliation are both necessary for God, which completely undermines the graciousness of those activities.'[20]

Second, by utilizing the concepts of self-manifestation and mutual self-distinction, Pannenberg seems to be guilty of projecting a very human, finite idea into the eternal being of God. It is one thing to take the history of Jesus seriously as a revelation of God, but quite another to reduce the immanent being of God to the sum total of God's self-revelation. For all Pannenberg's protestations that Nicene theology severs the immanent Trinity from history – and I do not believe it does – it is quite another thing to reduce the immanent Trinity to the economic Trinity. Pannenberg argues that he does not do that, maintaining the transcendence of God, but in order to secure this he resorts to the difficult futurity principle.

To return to my purpose, it seems that Holmes is correct in his critique of modern theology with regards to Pannenberg. Torrance is a different matter; on the question of ontology, it seems he is not susceptible to the critique of Holmes.

A Question of History: What of the Reformation?

According to Holmes, there are two important contributions within twentieth-century theology which lay the ground for this closer relating of history to the being of God: Barth's denial of the *logos asarkos* and Rahner's equating of the economic and immanent Trinities. The concept of the *logos asarkos* came to prominence during the Reformation debates over the incarnation. Calvin asserted that in taking human flesh the eternal Word of God was not fully contained spatially within the human body of Jesus. In this he was following Athanasius; the body of Jesus does not fully circumscribe the eternal being of the Word of God. The incarnation does not involve the Son of God relinquishing his governing of the universe. Luther did not agree, believing that this entailed some lack in the fullness of deity in the incarnate *Logos*. What was it that could be left behind? The so-called remainder – the *Logos* without flesh – was dubbed the 'Calvinist extra'. The main focus of debate was on the presence of Christ in the Eucharist, but the distinctions within Christology were sharp. Luther's Christology employed the idea of the communication of attributes, the intermingling of divinity and humanity in the person of Jesus. Luther's concern was perhaps understandable in seeking to avoid a lapse into a Nestorian Christology; yet, as Torrance argues, Luther's approach tended towards a divinization of the humanity of Christ. In effect he imported the Trinitarian language of *perichoresis* into the person of Christ.

Rahner's axiom regarding the identity of the economic and immanent Trinity has also seemingly become *de rigueur* in contemporary writing. I will return to this later. It is sufficient to note at this stage that this has had a profound influence on the understanding of the relationship between God and creation.

Barth and Rahner cannot be taken in isolation from other developments; Holmes is also clear that it is to Hegel that we must look for a key influence in modern Trinitarian theology. We have already noted this in Pannenberg. Hegel's dialectical method, expressed within a Trinitarian framework, inevitably ties the being of God to the world. The Father creates a world that is not God; the Son becomes that which is not God and embraces otherness from God; the Spirit brings everything to final consummation so that God is all in all. I take it that most modern theologians are not unaware of their philosophical influences and thus consider that there is a mesh somewhere here with the theological tradition. That link comes from the Lutheran tradition, something which I am certain Holmes recognizes, but which may be more significant than is often acknowledged.

My point is a relatively straightforward one. If we look at many of the main theologians of the twentieth century, especially those who most clearly tie the being of God to the process of world history, they are all avowedly Lutheran – the exception of course being the far more Reformed Barth and Torrance. That they are also heavily indebted to a form of Hegelian dialectic should not be surprising. Hegel is regularly cited as being proud of his Lutheran heritage. One recent article expressed it thus: 'The . . . Christological doctrine of the "communication of attributes" (*communicatio idiomatum*) between the divine and the human in Jesus Christ, along with the implications of this doctrine for sacramental theology, were important theological resources that Hegel saw as paralleling his philosophical project.'[21]

One of the oft-noted consequences of Luther's emphasis on the communication of attributes is the ubiquity of Christ's body. Luther's well-known axiom, 'Where you can say: Here is God, there you must say: Christ the man is here also', inevitably implies that the body of Christ participates in divine omnipresence. Now it should be noted that Luther related this primarily to eucharistic theology, but later Lutheran theology developed this in other ways. I am indebted to Holmes for his constructive comments at this point. The key question is: at what point in the history of the man Jesus is this communication of attributes understood to apply? At the incarnation? Clearly that presents difficulties. After the resurrection? At the ascension? These are important questions, but I would maintain that, for many modern Lutherans, these distinctions have become rather blurred. The consequence seems to be that Lutheran doctrines of incarnation, adopted within a Hegelian context, frequently lead to a much closer relationship being drawn between God and creation.

I would argue that the strength of the Lutheran influence is often underplayed in mapping the history of twentieth-century Trinitarian theology. It is no surprise that it is modern Lutheran theologians who are engaged in a radical reworking of a divine ontology – Pannenberg, Moltmann, and Jenson, to name three. I would tentatively suggest that more attention to the significant differences in Christology at the Reformation would add something to the understanding of the directions of contemporary theology and add weight to Holmes's argument.

A Question of Space and Time

Clearly, any discussion of the nature of God's relationship to history must engage with some understanding of space and time. Here our two modern theologians offer similar analyses of Nicene theology, but articulate significantly different solutions.

The diagnosis common to both is that Nicene theology decisively rejected what is often referred to as the container model of space. This can be traced as far back as Aristotle and in many ways is the most common-sense understanding from everyday experience. We pour water into a glass and it is contained by the shape of the glass – its space is determined by the shape of the container. As I recall from my days as a physics teacher, one definition of a liquid is that it takes the shape of the container which holds it. Both Torrance and Pannenberg argue that this is problematic for an understanding of God's relationship to the world.

Pannenberg rejects this concept of space, preferring to explore the nature of God's transcendence and immanence, once again, via the concept of the infinite. This is understood to be an expression of the Whole which, it is argued, gives the essential precondition for our perception of any particular event in space and time. Understanding particular events is only possible because these are part of the infinite whole. Pannenberg sees this as closely paralleled by a Plotinian view of eternity. He rejects the idea that eternity is timelessness; rather, eternity is seen as the simultaneous possession of all things. In God's eternity space and time are simultaneous, while for creatures they must remain distinct since they are a condition of their finite existence. The relationship between them is best expressed through the idea of the true Infinite. Creation takes place within the more comprehensive totality of God's eternity; the totality of the process is expressed through the concept of the infinite, which Pannenberg sees as expressing God's omnipresence. The presence of the infinite, eternal God, is expressed in terms of the Spirit as a field of force within creation, mediating the presence of God but also moving all things to the final consummation.

There are problems here. First, expressing an understanding of eternity as simultaneity is fashionable but difficult. It should at least be acknowledged that such a view runs counter to the Christian tradition as represented by Augustine, Aquinas, and Calvin. Second, by resorting to the idea of God as the true Infinite, and then by tying the being of God to the eschatological consummation, Pannenberg resorts to his problematic ontological priority of the future. The contrast here with Nicene theology and also with Torrance is stark. Whereas Pannenberg uses the concept of the infinite, Torrance follows fourth-century thought by developing an understanding of space and time based on the incarnation.

Torrance's view is most comprehensively worked out in his slim volume *Space, Time and Incarnation*.[22] In a densely argued construction he suggests that the Nicene view of the incarnation broke away from the inherited model of space as a container, replacing it with what he refers to as a relational model.

So how does the incarnation enable us to conceive of a relational view of space and time? And what does this mean for the relationship between God, creation and history? Fundamentally, it requires us to think of the incarnation as the place of meeting between God and humanity. In Jesus Christ the reality of God enters this world; the God who cannot be understood or observed becomes observable and enters into created space and time. 'The interaction of God with us in the space and time of this world sets up, as it were, a coordinate system between . . . the space and time of this world and . . . the vertical dimension, relation to God through His Spirit.'[23] In Jesus Christ we have to do with both divine and human centres of reference, yet in one person. He is the 'place of contact and communication between God and man in a real movement within physical existence, involving interaction between God and nature, divine and human agency.'[24]

In an extremely important passage, Torrance explains that, since the incarnation is the place of intersection between divine and human, eternal and temporal, invisible and visible, it is tempting for theology to use the same language to describe both types of reality. To quote Torrance, 'this is exactly what we cannot do . . . to do so is to introduce confusion into theology.'[25] Interestingly, Torrance draws a parallel here with one of the key problems of modern science – to find common ground between language referring to quantum mechanics and relativity theory – a quest still ongoing today. So how do we express an understanding of the incarnation which does justice to both divine and human co-ordinates? Torrance proposes the use of topological language, used in science and mathematics, as a way of bringing into relation two quite different kinds of activity in space. Torrance argues that this was the implication of the teaching of the Greek fathers. In Jesus Christ human *topos* and divine *topos* are found together. The Son of God has assumed flesh without being confined or circumscribed by it. In other words, in Christ, we meet the observable and unobservable, the temporal and the eternal, in a way that affirms their co-ordination without reducing them to a form of logical rationality determined by other means. The incarnation is something entirely new; it marks the intersection of divine and human fields of energy in a new relation, without conflating or confusing them.

The import of this way of thinking can be seen in Torrance's understanding of the relationship between the immanent and economic Trinity.

It is fundamental to Torrance that what God is towards us in the economy is what he is in his eternal being. Yet he also insists that we cannot read back from our own experience of God into the immanent Trinity. Although his early response to Rahner was positive, he later criticized Rahner's axiom, since he found him guilty of reading back human self-transcendence into the being of God. Consequently, although through the incarnation God has identified himself fully with the finitude and space-time limitation of creation, this cannot be read as a limitation of the very being of God. There remains inscrutability and unknowability. Thus, for Torrance, to read the history of creation back into the being of God in such a way as to diminish the gulf between God and creation is simply untenable. It is an attempt to think of God in ways that are not grounded in God.

The contrast with Pannenberg is clear. Both understand the significance of the Nicene understanding of space revealed through the incarnation. Pannenberg, committed to a reformulating of metaphysics, chooses to ground his understanding of the relationship between God and creation through the concept of the infinite. Torrance reaffirms the language of the fourth century, seeing that the full ramifications of the relational understanding of space and time have not been fully appreciated.

Implications

If the concern of the early church was proper worship, biblical exegesis, and the life of piety, so we should not waver in that intent. Holmes I know shares that view. It does seem to me that these debates are far from arcane; they impact the real world of Christian life and witness. Here I mention three areas of concern.

1. Monarchy, subordination, and ecclesiology

The question of subordination of the Son to the Father remains a contentious matter of debate, not least among those seeking to use this as a basis for Trinitarian ecclesiology. Some form of economic subordination is clearly biblically rooted (e.g. Phil. 2); to read this back into the inner life of God has been a constant temptation, arguably made possible by the language of *begotten* and *arche*. This clearly has a bearing on the question at hand.

Torrance's view follows that of Gregory Nazianzen, whom he sees as countering an element of Origenist subordination which was creeping into the Cappadocian doctrine of the Trinity. The problem he identified was the application of the term *arche* in a way that distinguished the

Father from the Son, leading to some form of unequal Deity within the Trinity. Torrance follows Gregory by insisting that Father, Son, and Spirit are relations eternally subsisting in God beyond all origin. Torrance takes this as a 'far more satisfactory view of the Triunity of God.'[26] On the basis of the *homoousios*, the monarchy is 'not limited to one Person: it is a unity constituted in and by the Trinity.'[27] In a footnote Torrance make his position clear: 'This means that the Trinity as a whole must be thought of as the one divine Principle or *arche*.'[28] This is not to deny that there is a proper order between the persons of the Trinity, as disclosed in revelation. Father, Son, and Spirit are distinguished 'by position and not status, by form and not being'; the Father is not the cause of the divine being.[29]

By contrast, those modern theologians who tie the being of God more closely to the historical process tend to reinterpret the monarchy of the Father. For Pannenberg, the monarchy of the Father is the eschatological outcome – the goal of the Trinitarian relationships. Yet he still seems to secure the final unity of God via the concept of monarchy. He states categorically that it is 'in his monarchy that the Father is one God.'[30] This has led some to conclude that, although Pannenberg does seek to steer around the problem by identifying the Spirit and the Son as mediators of the Father's monarchy, he is at least open to the charge of an implicit subordinationism.[31] More generally, to tie God and creation too closely together inevitably runs the risk of importing the economic condescension into the immanent Trinity.

2. The truth of the gospel and Christian mission

There can be no doubt that the challenge of world faiths and the diminishing of religious claims to truth to the realm of matters of personal, private opinion present the church with huge challenges in the presentation of the gospel. It is therefore understandable and perhaps laudable that Pannenberg has taken the debatability of truth-claims as the starting point for his theology. Yet his methodology is seriously open to question. Because he is committed to tying the revelation of God to the totality of world history, he employs the concept of a universal religious awareness as a foundation for expounding the distinctive truth-claims of the Christian faith. There is clearly the risk that theological foundations are being built on non-theological concepts.[38]

From Torrance I believe we can learn at least three lessons. First, the church stands and falls on the confession of Christ in his unique identity with God. As soon as we lose the centrality of Christ we lapse into various forms of psychology, sociology, or therapeutic community activity. This is not to diminish the importance of these fields of study, simply to resist defining the gospel in terms other than the self-revelation of God. We also risk compromising the unique claims of the gospel by entering into inter-religious dialogue from a position of weakness rather than conviction. It is far more productive to debate with a Muslim or indeed an atheist from a position of firm belief than some desire for common ground located in human rationality. Second, a proper understanding of Nicene theology will enable us to avoid any form of dualism between God and Christ, between God and creation, and between theology and science. Since Einstein, modern science has blown apart the false Kantian dualism between subject and object. Sadly, this has not always been the case in theology and biblical studies. Third, by holding to the Nicene theology of hypostatic union and reserving the use of *perichoresis* to intra-Trinitarian relations, we preserve the true humanity of Christ and pave the way for a distinctive understanding of the meaning of person which is grounded in the being of God rather than a projection of human individualism. Trinitarian theology of this sort is the ground of true humanism.[33]

3. Rewriting the narrative

A brief comment will suffice with regard to the received narrative of the infestation of early theology by Greek philosophy. There are growing numbers of voices who simply do not believe the story any more. Sadly it remains a dominant paradigm, not least among some evangelical theologians in a mistaken desire to be 'simply biblical'. As Hans Boersma states, 'this says a great deal more about contemporary evangelicalism than it does about the history of Christian thought.'[34] In rejecting the language of the tradition many are simply embracing a metaphysical framework which assumes that a theology of persons in relation exhausts all there is to say about God. As Boersma states, 'the result is a radical historicising of our understanding of God and thus a loss of transcendence.'[35]

So what is the way forward? If Holmes and others are correct, perhaps one important step will be to mirror the approach of the early fathers by paying greater attention to the biblical witness. The historic divide between biblical studies and systematic theology needs to be bridged in an attempt to read the biblical narrative theologically. This is an urgent task for theology if the language of Trinitarian theology is to be reframed for the contemporary church.

Conclusion

I stated at the outset that I believe that the general tenor of Holmes's argument is correct. This comparison of Torrance with Pannenberg not only highlights the problem identified in the book, but also shows that not all twentieth-century theologians are susceptible to Holmes's critique. Torrance articulates a strong Nicene theology and sees the importance of retaining many of the key concepts within the modern context. Greater attention to his work would prove fruitful for future work on the Trinity.

The significance of the Reformation debates over the incarnation would repay closer attention. These distinctives are lightly covered in books on the Trinity, but the decisions made with regard to the doctrine of Christ, for reasons not initially to do with the doctrine of God, have had far greater influence than is often recognized.

Finally, the complex debate about space, time, and eternity remains a field that offers opportunity for fruitful dialogue with modern science. It is certainly true that the so-called Trinitarian revival has seen this, but too often has preferred to explore this on grounds other than those so clearly identified by pro-Nicene theology. Again Torrance points the way.

I close with a word of thanks to Stephen Holmes for provoking and challenging received wisdom. My main worry is that now, I fear, I will have to revise some of my lecture material.

Bibliography

Ayres, Lewis. *Nicaea and Its Legacy* (Oxford: Oxford University Press, 2004).

Barnes, Michel. 'De Régnon Reconsidered'. *Augustinian Studies* 26 (1995): pp. 51–79.

Boersma, Hans, *Heavenly Participation: The Weaving of a Sacramental Tapestry* (Grand Rapids: Eerdmans, 2011).

Gunton, Colin E. *The Promise of Trinitarian Theology* (London: T&T Clark, 2nd edn, 1997).

Mattes, M. 'Hegel's Lutheran Claim'. *Lutheran Quarterly* 14 (2000): pp. 249–79.

McCormack, Bruce. 'Grace and Being.' Pages 92–110 in *The Cambridge Companion to Karl Barth* (ed. John Webster. Cambridge: Cambridge University Press, 2000).

Min, Anselm K. 'The Dialectic of Divine Love: Pannenberg's Hegelian Trinitarianism'. *International Journal of Systematic Theology* 6 (2004): pp. 252–69.

Molnar, Paul D. *Thomas F. Torrance: Theologian of the Trinity* (Farnham: Ashgate, 2009).

Moltmann, Jürgen. *The Trinity and the Kingdom of God* (trans. M. Kohl. London: SCM Press, 1981).

Olson, Roger, 'Wolfhart Pannenberg's Doctrine of the Trinity'. *Scottish Journal of Theology* 43 (1990): pp. 175–206.

Pannenberg, Wolfhart. *Metaphysics and the Idea of God* (trans. Philip Clayton; Edinburgh: T&T Clark, 1990).

— *Systematic Theology* (3 vols; trans. G.W. Bromiley; Edinburgh: T&T Clark, 1991–8).

Schwöbel, Christoph. 'Wolfhart Pannenberg.' Pages 257–92 in *The Modern Theologians* (ed. David F. Ford; Oxford: Blackwell, 1989).

Torrance, T.F. *The Christian Doctrine of God* (Edinburgh: T&T Clark, 1996).

— *The Ground and Grammar of Theology* (Edinburgh: T&T Clark, 2001).

— *Space, Time and Incarnation* (Oxford: Oxford University Press, 1978).

— *The Trinitarian Faith* (Edinburgh: T&T Clark, 1988).

— *Trinitarian Perspectives: Toward Doctrinal Agreement* (Edinburgh: T&T Clark, 1994).

Part II

Stephen R. Holmes's Rejoinder

10.

Reponse: In Praise of Being Criticized

Stephen R. Holmes

I recall, as a young scholar, being involved in organizing a day conference in the Research Institute for Systematic Theology at King's College, London; this day was to celebrate the sixtieth birthday of my *Doktorvater*, Colin Gunton. Among others, Christoph Schwöbel, then of Heidelberg, and Robert Jenson, then of Princeton, gave papers discussing aspects of Colin's work; it was a good day, and ended (as those RIST conferences generally did) in a meal at Colin's favourite Italian restaurant, on the Strand. I commented to Colin as we walked to the meal that it was a strange profession in which we worked, where the way we honoured and celebrated someone was to gather their friends from across the world to explain in detail and in public why they were wrong.

I was beginning to know then, of course, and know far better now, that serious, critical, interaction with our work is the greatest gift anyone can give to those of us who work as scholars. It is not just that we can ask for nothing more than to be read and discussed by our peers; it is that the readings and reflections – and criticisms, however sharp – of others help us to know our own thoughts – always better; sometimes for the first time.

So it is both a duty and a pleasure to begin this response with gratitude; I am deeply grateful, first, to Jason Sexton and Tom Noble, who organized a Tyndale Fellowship study group in 2013 in response to my book on the Trinity, and who have collected most of those papers, and several others, in this publication. I am grateful to all those who presented and joined in the discussion at that meeting, and to those others who have since written reflections for this book; I am particularly grateful to Graham Watts, who graciously agreed to devote his 2013 Tyndale Lecture to the theme, particularly as the first serious airing of some of the ideas in my *The Holy Trinity* was in my own Tyndale Lecture in 2009. To be taken so seriously by friends, and by people I have never met, by former teachers

(John Colwell), and by former students (Jon Mackenzie), is a great gift, and I am thankful.

It would be tedious, repetitive and prolix to work through each essay in turn in response, so I will here draw out several themes which arise in one or more of the essays in this book, and seek to respond to them. I should first say that the thesis of my book is deliberately, and limitedly, historical;[1] I argue that the doctrine of the Trinity presented and promoted by a number of writers in the second half of the twentieth century was a radical departure from an earlier, and remarkably stable, classical doctrine. Clearly this historical thesis suggests a systematic thesis, that the twentieth-century doctrine was a mistake, but this claim is not entailed, only suggested, by the historical claim I make, and I do not attempt to argue it in the book.[2] One could accept everything I have to say in the book and nonetheless assert that the revision of the doctrine that occurred in the twentieth century was correct and required; Schleiermacher would approve of such a claim. If several of the essays in this volume, and some of my comments in response, move beyond a merely historical thesis to such constructive work, I see no problem; I neither object to others so moving nor apologize for so doing myself; but that discussion, useful and fruitful though I hope it will be, will then have moved beyond the claims of *The Holy Trinity* itself.

The Bible and the Doctrine of the Trinity

Appropriately, the question of biblical revelation recurs in these pages. Fred Sanders is deeply concerned to 'render the doctrine of the Trinity . . . as a biblical doctrine, or to speak more precisely, as a doctrine that is in the Bible.'[3] He offers hermeneutical proposals, visibly based in the recent tradition of theological exegesis, to suggest ways forward for this work. Mike Bird raises the same question, 'whether the doctrine of the Trinity is derived from biblical exegesis or arrives from esoteric philosophizing.'[4] John Colwell takes us to a specific text, the prayers of the incarnate Son recorded in the fourth gospel, and asks what Trinitarian proposal makes most sense in their light; Kevin Giles suggests that my book was less generous than it might have been to patristic exegesis. We all share a commitment to the authority of Scripture; in different ways, all four are asking how that commitment relates to our understanding of the doctrine of the Trinity.

I return first to my comment above: my purposes in the book were simply historical. As a result, I recorded a concern, which seemed (and still seems) to me to be legitimate, that the history of the doctrine of the

Trinity displays a certain exegetical deficit: broadly, the doctrine was exhaustively defended in the fourth century, on the basis, however, of hermeneutical assumptions that we would find rather implausible now; it then became accepted as orthodoxy, but the necessary re-narration in the light of differing hermeneutics has only intermittently and patchily been done. This is not, of course, to say that the work cannot be done, or that the efforts of the fourth-century fathers are irrelevant or unhelpful to it; but we cannot simply rest on the assumption that their arguments were wholly right, and will be found wholly convincing to readers from different ages.

In this, certain hermeneutical questions are raised acutely: it seems to me that history strongly suggests that any attempt to derive a doctrine of the Trinity on the basis of the New Testament alone is unlikely to be helpful: tritheism and subordinationism seem inevitably to result. Until rather recently, however, a particular hermeneutic mode that assumed *a priori* that the Old Testament/Hebrew Bible texts could not be referring to the Trinity reigned unquestioned in the academy (its hegemony was rather less evident in devotional and homiletic practices of Bible reading); if my historical suggestion is right, this made it almost impossible to offer an academically acceptable exegetical defence of the doctrine of the Trinity.

The breaking of this hermeneutic hegemony has opened many different possibilities, and Fred Sanders's essay pushes at some of them in ways I find to be helpful and suggestive; constructively, however, the full working out of an exegetical defence of the doctrine in our day remains an incomplete task; this is unquestionably a matter of serious concern. That said, I do wonder how much would be proved by such exegesis: one might list a series of careful doctrinal statements that span the doctrine and could each be defended exegetically ('Father, Son, and Holy Spirit are each truly God;' 'The divine essence is simple, unrepeatable, and so in some crude sense one'; . . .); I very much doubt whether the underlying logic of the doctrine – the relationship of *ousia* to *hypostasis*; the particular account of divine simplicity at play; . . . – could be derived exegetically.

In the historical narrative I offered in *The Holy Trinity*, I proposed that this distinction, between Trinitarian claims and Trinitarian logic or grammar, was of some interest, in that there is evidence that from its earliest apostolic foundations the church knew tacitly or instinctively the claims that should be made, but struggled until the Cappadocian settlement with the problem of how to speak about God in a way that was responsible to these various claims. If that – admittedly here vastly over-simplified – narrative is even broadly correct, and my claims above about what can and cannot be established exegetically are also right, then a striking conclusion follows: *what we call 'the doctrine of the Trinity' is not a biblical idea, and is not defensible exegetically.*

Let me be clear precisely what I am asserting and denying here: there are a set of propositions concerning the relationship of Father, Son, and Spirit in the eternal life of God, and the true revelation of God's eternal life given in the gospel narratives, that I believe are clearly derivable exegetically; what we tend to call 'the doctrine of the Trinity', however, is not these first-order propositions, but the claims we make about God's life which give us the logic/grammar which allows us to understand how all these various claims can be made without our lapsing into simple incoherence. So what we call 'the doctrine of the Trinity' consists of claims like 'a spiritual substance may have a subsistent relation to itself which does not compromise its simplicity' or 'in the single divine ousia there are three hypostases, distinguished by relations of origin and not otherwise'; there is, I strongly suspect, no way of demonstrating such claims exegetically.

This result is not trivial, although nor is it devastating. It is a commonplace that the developed fourth-century doctrine relies on borrowing and adapting the vocabulary, and some of the arguments, of middle Platonic philosophy. It is not unreasonable for us to ask, as a thought-experiment, would another borrowed philosophical system have served as well? (Or even, perhaps, better?) Were we to attempt to make sense of the various exegetically derived claims about God's life using the categories of Vedic philosophy, or Xhosan philosophy, would we inevitably fail, or would there be the possibility, after much deep thought, careful redefinition and hard argument, that we might succeed?[5] If we claim that the doctrine of the Trinity is necessarily biblical (or if we accept a certain, broadly Catholic, account of dogmatic development), then we must answer that such a quest would fail: the language and arguments we have are simply right, and so irreplaceable. I think, however, that the alternative view has something to commend it, and that we might imagine that our Trinitarian formulations are in some measure, under God, historically contingent.

To refine this further, let me propose one more distinction, a common one, between those things which may be proved exegetically and those things which are necessary consequences of what may be proved exegetically. The unity of the Father and the Son in the Godhead is straightforwardly demonstrated exegetically; the unity of Father, Son, and Spirit in the Godhead is a deduction from several exegetical propositions; no single text teaches this unambiguously. We thus have three sorts of theological claim: direct results of exegesis; derived results of exegesis; and that class of propositions of which I have been writing, which are neither direct results of exegesis nor derivable from such results, but which are creative proposals – *epinoiae*, in Basil's language – designed to offer plausible accounts of the underlying logic of exegetical results.

It may not be straightforward to decide which of these categories a concept fits into. Take, for example, the doctrine of eternal generation. There is certainly a patristic tradition of finding it to be a direct result of exegesis: the psalmist's prophecy 'You are my son, today I have begotten you' might be read this way, for example (reading, as the fathers often did, with some justification, 'today' as a continuous present, and so a reference to divine eternity). As I read Origen, his primary defence was in the second category: the doctrine of the generation of the Son is exegetically demonstrable, as is the claim that the divine life is eternal; eternal generation is the necessary logical result of considering these two claims. It might be argued, however, that eternal generation is a possible and plausible, but not a necessary, way of making simultaneous sense of those two exegetical claims, which would place it in my third category – along with, I submit, much traditional Trinitarian doctrine. The location of particular examples is less important than the schema which I am proposing.

If we do understand the relation of doctrine and exegesis like this, it relieves at least some, but not all, of the exegetical pressure I described above. Historically, it seems to me that in the early church the specifically exegetical task concerning the Trinity was found to be fairly simple; the complexity came in the 'epinoic' task of imagining how to speak of God in such a way that the various exegetical claims could all be true. It was, that is, apparently just obvious to most readers (of whom we have any record) that the Bible affirmed the singularity of the divine life, and also the inclusion of Jesus of Nazareth in that life; the problem was how to speak of that singularity in a way that did not make the deity of Christ impossible to conceive.

Even the 'difficult' exegetical texts fit in this narrative: it was apparently equally obvious to most readers that the incarnate Son deferred to the Father, and so is subordinate to the Father; the Arian problem was not whether this was a biblical truth, but whether the best way to speak about the divine life was to prioritize this exegetical discovery and seek to make other texts conform to it, or to relativize this point by making it conform to other texts; Hilary's 'form of God / form of a servant' distinction did the latter, claiming that the fact of incarnation offered a good reason to understand that this subordination, although true and biblical, was not in fact an insight into the divine life.

All that said, it is very noticeable that at other points in history – early modern Europe might be a good example – those who have sought most assiduously to read the biblical texts without allowing inherited categories to be their guide have not discovered the exegesis to be quite so straightforward; the claim, then, that the single divine life must include Jesus of Nazareth seems to have been less obvious than in the first centuries of the church's history. Of course, the completeness of the historical record is very different in the two cases, and I would certainly be open to a claim that I am privileging eccentric voices in focusing on anti-Trinitarians in the early modern period; I suspect, however, there is a difference. This difference may have to do with ontological assumptions; it may be (as I suggested in *The Holy Trinity*) that it has more to do with a certain, and I would argue improper, privileging of the New Testament over the Old; it may, as Fred Sanders argues in this book, have to do with a failure to adopt an explicitly soteriological hermeneutic.

What, then, would a contemporary biblical/exegetical defence of the doctrine of the Trinity look like? We would first want to do the basic exegetical work: what propositions about the divine life, the relationship of the Son to the Father, and the relationship of both to the Holy Spirit, are required by the text? The results will be inevitably somewhat messy, and would possibly appear to be incoherent; we would then need to set about the theological work of imagining what sort of things might be true of God's life in order to allow all these exegetically derived propositions to be true. We could pretend to start from scratch in doing this, paying no heed to the tradition but claiming to listen only to the biblical text. Such pretence would inevitably be mendacious; we cannot escape the historical fact of our immersion in the tradition – it is a part of what it is to be a creature. Instead, then, we would be better to take the historically proposed doctrines and see whether, in fact, they serve to make good sense of our jumble of results of exegesis. I cannot claim to have done this work exhaustively, or to have the philological skills required for it; what work I have done in this direction leads me to hope that the classical doctrine will in fact be found adequate, however.

It is at this level that I would want to engage with John Colwell's reflections on the prayers of Jesus in the fourth gospel. Robert Jenson points to these texts and claims that here we overhear an inner-triune conversation, and so that what we derive exegetically about the Father–Son relation here deserves to be privileged; I am not convinced that this is the best way of reading the texts. We overhear the incarnate Son praying to the Father; I take it (I know Jenson would disagree) that prayer is an intrinsically human, or at least creaturely, act, and so that we do better to read these texts through the lens of Christology, not Trinity. The rightness or wrongness of either view can only be established by doing the reading, and aligning the results with other readings in a wider and wider circle, exploring the coherence and explanatory power of either position; historically, it seems to me, such a task is adequately accomplished over decades or centuries by communities, not over hours or even years by individual scholars. Reading the Bible well is extraordinarily hard work!

Philosophy, Language, and the Doctrine of the Trinity

I have already reflected above that the history of the doctrine of the Trinity that I find is deeply philosophically implicated. Classical Trinitarianism borrows technical philosophical language and puts it to new use; at the heart of the debate between Eunomius and the Cappadocians was a theory of language and reference; my reconstruction of the classical doctrine foregrounds categories, notably that of divine simplicity, which these days seem to belong to the philosophy faculty far more than to theologians. To talk well about the Trinity we are going to need to know how to talk well about philosophy. These themes come up in several of the essays in this book, with Ryan Mullins giving the most sustained discussion.

My book, as noted above, was historical in form, not philosophical. The relation of history to philosophy is an interesting one; Ryan Mullins assumes in his chapter the philosopher's prerogative to judge the adequacy, or coherence, of historical claims: Augustine (or whoever) argued like this and stated that; was this argument logical, or that statement coherent? Clearly this is a valid thing to do, and Ryan, displaying the careful and clear thought that is characteristic of the developing school of analytic theology, does it very well. There is, however, also a way in which the historian can judge the adequacy – and indeed coherence – of philosophical claims; to take an example that is germane to Ryan's chapter, if not directly drawn from it, it is not uncommon to hear a certain sort of philosopher of religion conclude that the doctrine of the Trinity is incompatible with divine simplicity.

This conclusion, I suggest, can be shown historically to be necessarily false, and indeed actually meaningless. This is a bold claim, I accept, but an important one. My argument for it would go something like this: 'the doctrine of the Trinity' is only meaningfully definable historically; it is historically demonstrable that divine simplicity is an integral part of the doctrine of the Trinity; therefore, to claim that the doctrine of the Trinity necessarily denies divine simplicity is effectively to claim that both p and not-p are simultaneously true.

Now, I know my more philosophically minded friends will be impatient with this; if my historical claim is accepted, all that is necessary is a careful definition of what is meant by 'the doctrine of the Trinity' at the beginning of the argument, which was almost certainly there anyway. Well, yes – but words are not, or should not be, so susceptible to redefinition. With the right piece of definition at the beginning of the argument it would no doubt be possible to demonstrate that 'racism' is always virtuous, or that 'democracy' is necessarily evil; the one offering these definitions and arguments would – rightly – be accused of doing something seriously improper, though. As a historian, I want to claim that 'the doctrine of the Trinity' means something fairly concrete and describable, and so I want to insist that philosophers should be historically responsible in their use of the term, and indeed of other terms which have significant historical meaning.[6]

As I tried to show in *The Holy Trinity*, problems like these became very important at certain times in history. The assumption that words like 'substance' or 'essence' carried contemporary meaning in the ancient formulas led at various points, particularly in the early modern period, to serious misunderstanding. Of particular interest, perhaps, is the word 'person'; in Greek Trinitarianism, it is a fairly minor concept; the standard technical term is *hypostasis* ('subsistence'); *prosopon* ('person') is used, but infrequently; my sense is that other terms, such as *tropos hyparxeos* ('mode of being'), are used more frequently. The same is true, I think, of scholastic Latin Trinitarianism; *subsistentia* became the most common term; it was not, however, available in the patristic period, being a later coinage, and so from Tertullian down *persona* became the standard term, then imported into vernacular languages – 'person' in English; 'Person' in German, etc.

This history should alert us to the fact that investing heavily in the particular meaning of 'person' in our doctrine of God is probably going to lead us away from, not towards, the patristic and scholastic traditions of thought. This problem became acute with the rise of the Romantic movement, because being personal was then invested with a particular existential value: it was a great good, that is, to be a person rather than not. There was inevitable pressure to apply something like perfect being theology, and so to find in God, particularly in the three divine hypostases, the perfection of Romantic personhood. In this narrative, I think, lie the roots of social Trinitarianism . . .

Now, I suppose that Ryan would not disagree with any of this, at least at the level of methodological claim; he works on divine simplicity and ineffability in his chapter, and in each case quickly reaches for historical examples of use to give meaning to the terms. As a historian, however, I would want to make a further claim, that meaning is not always easy to grasp. Ryan quotes Augustine from *De doctrina* in what readers of Augustine will recognize is a characteristic mode, reflecting that what he has just said has led him into a logical morass, and despairing before God of his ability to speak. Ryan reads this straightforwardly, and expresses impatience with it ('This makes no sense'); I would suggest rather that we should see here a relatively common Augustinian rhetorical move, in which he deliberately lapses into incoherence to alert his reader to the fact that he has begun to speak of things which are at the edge of that to which human language can meaningfully refer, and so his statements should be taken as much more partial and allusive and hesitant than they might seem, or than his normal mode of argument might imply.

Now, I am no specialist in Augustine, and this might be completely wrong; but my point is general, not specific. To extract meaning from an ancient writer requires extensive knowledge of context, rhetorical style, and use of terms; it is certainly a non-trivial task. Further, I would want to insist on a proper respect for historical figures: to be blunt, to have been guilty of meaning what Ryan claimed he meant, Augustine would have had to be quite extraordinarily stupid – and he wasn't.

Of course, there are things we know now that were not known in earlier ages. In some cases these are facts (scientific knowledge, or in theology text-critical or philological discoveries); in others they may be (things we regard as) methodological advances (the notation of formal logic, which makes exploring the structure of syllogisms much easier; hermeneutical moves that give us a different view of the right way to read texts; increased consciousness of the reality of historical change; . . .). In such cases we properly privilege our thoughts over theirs; but on a subject such as divine ineffability, I do not see that we have any advantage over Augustine, other perhaps than a longer tradition of reflection on the subject to explore. Given that, and given the undoubted quality of his mind, I think we must accord him a certain respect: he may well have been wrong, but if he was, it would not have been in a trivial or obvious manner and, I suggest, if we think we have spotted a trivial or obvious problem in Augustine, we should more readily assume that we have misunderstood him, and read further, than assume that that problem is in fact real.

Writing in historical mode, I can sit relatively lightly to Ryan's criticisms: maybe ineffability is self-referentially incoherent; that does not change the fact that it was very regularly appealed to in substantive ways in the tradition, which is all that I claim in the book. As a theologian, committed to working in recognizable continuity with the historical tradition that I explore, I want to push back rather harder, and reclaim terms like simplicity and ineffability, on the basis that their historical usages are not as obviously incoherent as Ryan would have us believe; there is not space to enter fully into this argument here, but let me sketch some directions in which I think the discussion might develop.

I start with ineffability because it illustrates a point that will help us to think about simplicity, which is this: as lexicographers now universally insist, meaning is determined by use, not by etymology. Ryan's argument about ineffability, or its synonym unknowability, repeatedly turns on the point that, etymologically, these claims must be absolute; his fundamental argument is that if I say God is 'unknowable', I am claiming to know something about God, and so my claim is necessarily incoherent. He contrasts this absolute claim with what he calls a 'doctrine of partial comprehension'.

Now, it should be clear even from the examples Ryan cites that this was not how a doctrine of ineffability functioned in the writers he cites, or those I cite;[7] all of them, albeit in different ways, use the doctrine to caution presumption about our – adequate but imperfect – capacity to speak about the divine. Now, Ryan might protest that this is partial comprehension, not ineffability, but it is what everyone meant when they said 'ineffability', so it is ineffability for any responsible reader.

Ryan offers two cautions against the use of ineffability: one that it is a 'cheap card to play' because it leaves objections unanswered, and the other that there is a danger of elision between a full doctrine of ineffability (in his sense) and a doctrine of partial comprehension. On the former, the use of ineffability to avoid having to respond to an objection could well be an abdication of intellectual responsibility; but there is also a proper modesty about what we do, or can, know. The classic deployment of ineffability in Trinitarian history comes when Gregory of Nazianzus refuses to speculate on the difference between generation and procession, save only to insist that they are different, in his Fifth Theological Oration; this does not look to me like an improper evasion; Gregory knows he is at the limit of what human language can say about the life of God, and refuses to be drawn into speculation beyond that. (The precise delineations of apophaticism in Thomas Aquinas's treatise on the Trinity work in a very similar way.)

Ryan offers no examples of his latter criticism; I suspect some, at least, of those he had in mind will be answered by my point of definition above. That said, we might recast the criticism slightly and acknowledge and address it: appeals to ineffability become inappropriate when they are inconsistent. Suppose in his next sermon Gregory had refuted an opponent by tracing the detail of how generation and procession differ; we would rightly accuse him of inconsistency. There are, unquestionably it seems to me, occasions where this sort of double standard does appear to be in play in theological history (the examples that spring to mind are mostly from Calvinist theologians discussing the justice or otherwise of the divine decrees), and they are deserving of criticism. On the doctrine of the Trinity (and on the divine perfections), however, it seems to me that generally the great theologians have been careful to specify what they believe can be known, and have worked consistently within their self-defined limits.

Now, I suspect that there is more to be said here; I suspect that at root the difference Ryan and I have is more about a philosophy of language than any of these doctrines; I suppose, however, that our operative philosophies of language will owe something to our accounts of the knowability, and 'speakability', of God. (I completely accept, incidentally, Ryan's criticism that I oversimplified my account of recent analytic theology in this area; I plead only that in a book covering two thousand years of intellectual history, a certain degree of oversimplification is inevitable.)

On simplicity it seems to me that there is a significant work of historical retrieval to be done; there are visibly different doctrines of divine simplicity at work across the tradition.[8] (Ryan or another analytic theologian might protest that the word obviously means the exclusion of all metaphysical complexity, but I would again respond that use trumps etymology in the determination of meaning.) With some sense of the different doctrines that have been used, the question of the coherence of the doctrine can be properly addressed; I note and completely agree with Fred Sanders's comment in his chapter that this work will be done best by analytic theologians like Ryan; I hope, however, that historians of doctrine will be allowed, will perhaps even be invited, to test the concepts being analysed against the historical record to make sure that what is being judged coherent or incoherent is a concept that is actually in play in theological reasoning.

Some historical questions: Augustine, Luther, and Torrance

John Colwell challenged me on reading Augustine, citing a well-known passage from Robert Jenson; I confess that I struggle to know the right way to deal with this passage, although I have had it quoted against me in other places also.[9] It throws down a series of charges, some of which I simply do not recognize as being Augustinian, while the rest are certainly Augustinian but are things Augustine held in common with the Cappadocians. Let me again separate the historical and the dogmatic tasks: writers within the Trinitarian revival often made a series of historical claims: the Cappadocians thought in personal and relational terms; this was radically different from Augustine's doctrine of the Trinity, which was basically an exercise in metaphysics. There is then a dogmatic claim, that focusing on personal and relational categories is the right way to construct a doctrine of the Trinity. This dogmatic claim draws support from the historical claims, but is not entailed by them (and in turn does not entail them); it is not inappropriate, therefore, to consider the claims separately.

As I have said, in *The Holy Trinity* I considered only the historical claims; in describing Augustine (deliberately provocatively, of course) as 'the greatest interpreter of Cappadocian Trinitarianism' I did not intend to suggest that the 'personalist' reading of the Cappadocians had been right, and that we should read Augustine as a 'personalist' also; I think, in fact, that in the recently common caricatures of Latin versus Cappadocian Trinitarianisms, Augustine has been read reasonably well, but the Cappadocian doctrine has been distorted almost beyond recognition; in the recent shorthand, my claim for a close similarity of doctrine does not rely on a proposition that Augustine should be read as a 'social Trinitarian' but a proposition that the Cappadocians are best read as 'Latin Trinitarians'.

How, then, have they been so badly misread? Zizioulas's interpretation, which it seems to me is basically misguided, has been deeply influential; the old de Régnon thesis was still widely assumed; the cultural pressure for a personalist doctrine was very strong (see comments above on Romanticism); the Cappadocian texts were difficult to access[10] – all these were, no doubt, contributory factors. At the same time, a generation of patristics scholars largely lost interest in doctrinal claims and so genuinely specialist help was in short supply. My work builds obviously and gratefully on the return to doctrinal history in the work of a number of brilliant patristics specialists of recent years, Lewis Ayres being pre-eminent among them.

So perhaps my basic response to Jenson's criticisms of 'those who bash us Augustine-bashers' is to say that it is not his (and others') interpretation of Augustine that I want to 'bash', but their interpretation of the Cappadocians and their consequent claim that Augustine's theology was a falling away from a prior high-point. To borrow Jenson's colloquialism, I come to bash Basil-praisers far more than Augustine-bashers.

I should say, however, that on one point I accept John Colwell's criticisms without demur, and that is the suggestion that I so emphasized unity of divine action that I did not adequately represent the specifically triune character of that action, and the proper ordering of it: in each single divine act, the Father initiates, the Son executes, the Spirit perfects. In an admittedly controversial work I overstated my case badly on this issue, and I am grateful for John's corrective (and for the same point made by Robert Letham in his chapter).[11]

This takes us to the dogmatic point: suppose I am right, that (to put it anachronistically, to make the point clear) the Cappadocians look very like Augustine on Trinitarian theology; this still does not make social Trinitarianism wrong – it merely makes it innovative. The degree to which this conclusion is found to be worrying will vary according to the ecclesiology of the writer; for John Zizioulas, an Orthodox bishop, a claim that his theology is an innovation unknown to, or even opposed to, the tradition would be unacceptable; as I noted above, for a Schleiermachian (or, perhaps, a certain sort of contemporary feminist theologian) the same claim might well be worn as a badge of honour.

For most of us who self-identify as evangelical, I suppose the reality would be somewhere between these two; we would rather, all else being equal, be able to stand in comfortable continuity with the tradition, or at least with significant portions of it; but fidelity to Scripture trumps this desire, and we would generally be prepared, at least in principle, to stand for the need for the tradition to be reformed on this or that point. John Colwell and I are both Baptist ministers; on questions of congregational government, religious liberty, church–state relations and (to a lesser extent for us both, I think) the proper mode and subjects of baptism, we are (more or less) comfortable in belonging to a community that takes a principled and prophetic stand against the majority witness of the tradition. The basic claim of my book is not 'you cannot be a social Trinitarian' but 'if you are a social Trinitarian, you are separating yourself decisively from a remarkably united traditional witness'. If I thought the Bible clearly taught social Trinitarianism, I would stand by everything I said in the book, and then embrace that position; it happens that I do not presently think this, however.

A quote from Robert Jenson occasioned these reflections; Jenson is a Lutheran theologian, whose work I read as being profoundly Lutheran in tradition, in the sense that he presses the Lutheran christological inno-vations to a logical conclusion, and reconstructs the whole of Christian doctrine in the light of that. For Jenson, the fact of incarnation entails a complete and mutual real communication of attributes; Jesus, the true Israelite, is the divine Son, and that statement does not admit any quali-fication or reserve. On this basis, every other doctrine in theology looks radically different.

I do not say this by way of objection, but by way of critical analysis. I regard Jenson's project as one of the two most interesting and intellec-tually powerful in contemporary Anglophone theology (alongside Bruce McCormack's confessionally Reformed but otherwise interestingly similar developing system). I happen to disagree with it, not least because on the christological questions my dogmatic convictions are essentially Reformed, not Lutheran, but such disagreement hardly lessens my appreciation. I mention these confessional divides because it is a useful link into the next issue to which I want to respond, Jon Mackenzie's suggestion that Luther is the presiding genius of the sort of Trinitarianism that I want to reject.

Jon's starting point is to notice the preponderance of Lutheran (whether confessional or merely familial) theologians in the Trinitarian revival that I criticize; specifically, the path of identifying the triune life with the events of the gospel history is, on Jon's reading, populated almost entirely by Lutherans. He identifies Hegel as the crucial mediator, and locates Hegel as the one who – long before Jenson – actually understood the ways in which Luther's christological innovations necessarily transformed our understanding of theology proper.

As will have been clear from my comments on Jenson above, I have a certain amount of sympathy for this account, although I suspect it can be overplayed. It is always tempting, in exploring the history of ideas, to surrender to a sort of 'idealist fallacy', whereby we assert or assume that a single powerful idea exhaustively explains great social movements. I accept completely that Hegel's account of divine self-realization in history would not have been what it was without the influence of Luther, but that is not to say that Luther's Christology is adequate explanation, on its own, for Hegel's ideas – otherwise Hegel would have been pre-empted by some sixteenth-century Swabian; I am sure that the later twentieth-century theology I explore is deeply influenced in complex ways by Hegel's philosophy, but the existence of Hegel's thought is not adequate explanation for Jenson or Moltmann; otherwise they would have been pre-empted by some precocious student in Berlin who was pushed into the orbit of Hegel by an intense dislike for Schleiermacher's piety.

Of course Jon is not suggesting such a simplistic account of intellectual causation, but nor does he explore the other streams that lead into Hegel's philosophy, or the turn to history in Pannenberg and others, and so his narrative could be read as asserting that Luther via Hegel was the crucial influence, which, it would seem to me, would be a significant overstatement. Further, I wonder whether Jon is not missing a significant development of Lutheran theology which Luther himself resisted, but which began to become popular in the nineteenth century, and became almost endemic in the twentieth. In describing Luther's 'innovative Christology', Jon rightly points towards the doctrine of the *communicatio idiomatum* as the decisive move (Graham Watts makes the same move) – but of course that needs further specification. The Reformed and the Lutherans distinguished three forms of the *communicatio*, and were agreed on two of them: the *genus idiomatum* and the *genus apotelesmaticum*; the Lutherans further affirmed the *genus maiesticum*, the Lutheran claim that the human nature shares in the properties of the divine nature (and so, to get to the original point, transcends locality and is able to be physically present on many altars at the same time).

Jon's linkage of Lutheran Christology with the *theologia crucis* and the involvement of God in history, however, depends on a fourth form of the *communicatio*, the *genus tapeinoticum*, the doctrine that the divine nature shares in the properties of the human nature, and so, paradigmatically, can suffer. I believe that this was first affirmed by Gess in the nineteenth century, although cannot claim to have investigated the history at all thoroughly; Jon's and Graham's argument turns on an assumption that the affirmation of the *genus maiesticum* requires, or at least strongly encourages, the affirmation of the *genus tapeinoticum*; I am, simply, not sure that this is true (although Jenson, for one, seems to claim as much); certainly the carefully logical Lutheran scholastic theologians of the seventeenth century denied the point. (That said, there is more work to be done here on Lutheran orthodoxy; if precursors of this move are to be found, I suspect it will be among the Swabian Lutherans, and some serious research in that direction would be valuable.)

What, finally, of my omission of T.F. Torrance? Kevin Giles, Robert Letham, and Jason Radcliff all express surprise at this, as did a number of others in conversation elsewhere.[12] Torrance does not, as Radcliff traces clearly, fit the story I tell concerning the twentieth-century Trinitarian revival; at various points in the book I note that I am tracing broad currents, and that there are many outliers, often brilliant; should I just locate Torrance there? In my first responses to questions about this omission, that was my broad reply; as I have read the criticisms in this book and talked to others, however, I have come to the conclusion that this response is inadequate; the story I tell is broadly one of a misappropriation of fourth-century Trinitarianism in the twentieth century, and Torrance's work is too close to that story to make his omission excusable.

I reflect that I learned my Trinitarianism almost exclusively from the school that gathered around King's College, London. My two early doctrine tutors, Nigel Wright and John Colwell, both took their doctorates from KCL. I went there for my own doctoral work, under Colin Gunton, and stayed on to teach there for something over six years. During this time, John Zizioulas was regularly present (there was an arrangement which brought him to KCL for six weeks each year, as I recall); Robert Jenson and Christoph Schwöbel would come for every conference; and so on. Reflecting on those days, it strikes me that the story of Trinitarian renewal that I imbibed did not give a starring, or even a significant, role to T.F. Torrance (something visible in the various publications to come out of that school). I fear that in rejecting the correctness of the story I learned then, I did not spend enough time questioning the contours of it. Torrance should have been more prominent in my mind and in my narrative (as, rather differently, should Catherine Mowry LaCugna).

First, as Jason Radcliff demonstrates well, Torrance offers a doctrine of the Trinity that is in visible continuity with the classical doctrine; he does not fall under the strictures I heap on others of his period (and nor do those who have been particularly influenced by him, such as Paul Molnar). Second, however, I fear that his construction of the doctrine does not offer adequate resources to guard against the developments I have criticized. Systematically – and here I am conscious of painting in very broad brushstrokes – Torrance makes the *homoousion to Patri* do the work that divine simplicity did for the Cappadocians.[13] This is interesting and in some ways attractive; Ryan Mullins's critique of the coherence of divine simplicity is hardly unusual in recent philosophy of religion, and to sidestep all those debates with a move like this would be an excellent option if it works; but does it?

Let me make, once again, a distinction between historical and dogmatic reasoning; historically, it seems clear that the *homoousion* never had the significance which Torrance attaches to it; Athanasius's thought was fully formed, and his opposition to Arianism clearly articulated, well before he hit upon the strategy of appealing to the Council of Nicaea, and so to the *homoousion*;[14] the term played little formal part in the construction and articulation of Cappadocian doctrine. Further, the immediate aftermath of the Council of Nicaea demonstrated that the word was not carefully defined and rather capacious; several opinions which would later be regarded as unacceptable could shelter under the term. Its historical usefulness at Nicaea was essentially to be a word that Arius would not say, and so that allowed him to be distinguished from the varied and not always well-formed Trinitarian theories of the collected bishops.[15] For some, *homoousion* implied strict metaphysical identity, certainly; for others it was much looser, implying little more than shared membership of a class.[16]

Of course, this strictly historical reflection does not prevent Torrance's dogmatic claims; as Radcliff points out, Torrance redefines the *homoousion* in essentially Barthian terms, and it may well be that this redefinition allows the term to do the work it needs to. I have two concerns, however. The first is, once again, that I find the redefinition of significant historical terms unhelpful. Athanasius was largely successful in his campaign to make *homoousion* a necessary badge of orthodoxy, and its inclusion in the Creed has continued this; as with 'the doctrine of the Trinity', I think we need to be rather hesitant in redefining words which carry such ecclesial weight.

Second, however, and more theologically, I question (and this is a genuine question; I am presently unsure of the answer) whether Torrance's *homoousion* is precise enough to do the work he needs it to do; it seems to me to be a fundamentally revelatory term for Torrance, stressing that because Jesus is one with God, we can know and be sure that God is actually like Jesus. (Put like this, we might think of it as a better way of stating 'Rahner's rule'.) This is absolutely right, of course, but I wonder whether it is a strong enough affirmation of the utter unity of Father and Son – of the simplicity of the Godhead? Torrance obviously was not a social Trinitarian, but I wonder whether his theology provides the resources to criticize adequately those who are. Paul Molnar has in several publications tried to show that it does, certainly, and he knows Torrance's work better than I do; but I remain more comfortable confessing simplicity, as the Fathers and Reformers did.

On the *filioque* and the Great Schism

Robert Letham queries whether I reflect adequately the depth of the division over the *filioque*; his points are well made, but largely refer to the contemporary context. Any of us who have been involved in formal ecumenical work know the phenomenon of the growing apart of separated traditions; even when it is possible to resolve completely the original points of division (as, differently, the international Roman Catholic–Lutheran *Joint Declaration on Justification* or the British *Anglican–Methodist Covenant* might each be held to have done), there are generations of separate development that need to be reconciled, and this is extraordinarily difficult and messy. I see the present situation concerning the *filioque* in these terms to some extent: I stand by my claims that it was not a major point of difference originally, but a millennium of separate development has made it an extraordinarily difficult problem to unravel now.

Historically, it seems clear that the inclusion of the *filioque* in the Creed was normal in the West from Charlemagne's reign; the evidence of Photius confirms that this was known in the East from about the middle of the ninth century, or two centuries before the formal schism; other than Photius's *Mystagogy*, which comes from a very particular political context, the only criticisms of the position of which we know before the Schism are from two late tenth-century patriarchs, Sisinnius and Sergius. The evidence seems to suggest that for two centuries or more there was broad acceptance that the *filioque* was a matter of dogmatic indifference. As I argue in *The Holy Trinity*, this makes sense: developed patristic Trinitarianism in fact left the question unanswered, and so both sole procession and double procession are compatible with it. Now, once an answer to this open question was given, and was given the status of dogma, that indifference was no longer possible, and schism was inevitable; following the Great Schism, there have been centuries of development, in which the divergent positions have on both sides been assumed, repeated, and so have become involved in many other doctrinal definitions. Unravelling all this will be a Herculean task (or perhaps better a Zerubbabelian one, since if it is to be achieved it will only be through the extraordinary help of God); but we should not project all these centuries of development back on to the original difference which, I continue to believe, was rather minor.

Worship, gender, and practical theology

I turn finally to two more practically orientated topics. Robert Letham suggests that we stand in need of a Trinitarian revival in our practices of worship and extempore prayer. I am less sure, I confess; in small prayer-groups I sometimes hear infelicitous expressions, but I genuinely cannot recall the last time I heard something said or sung in public worship that seemed to me to be unorthodox in Trinitarian terms. This, of course, is anecdotal and impressionistic, but so is the original complaint; we do not have hard data in this area, and it would not be easy to gather. We could trade words of songs, of course, but (as I have argued elsewhere) songs function as a part of a wider construction of liturgy, and so can only be criticized in the context of their use. My general impression is that hymnody ancient and modern, and the public prayers and preaching that I encounter, confess the triune economy in fairly rich ways, but are rather reticent about the eternal life of God; Gregory of Nazianzus would have approved. I accept of course that my experience may be much better than the average on this, and that there may be regional, national or denom-inational differences; but in the absence of hard evidence I can only cite my own experience.[17]

Kevin Giles raises the issue of the popularity of 'eternal functional subordination' in certain evangelical circles today, and asks why I did not address it. He is right that it is impossible to square this idea with classical Trinitarian orthodoxy; this seems to me to be merely obvious. The fact is that the concept only makes any sense with an excessively 'social' doctrine of the Trinity; considered against the classical doctrine, it falls into that celebrated class of ideas that are 'not even wrong' but just utterly incoherent.[18] This has been demonstrated carefully and charitably by Millard Erickson.[19] Should I have considered this in the book? As with Robert Letham's comments on worship, I can only respond that the issue does not loom as large in my eyes as it clearly does in Kevin's. Here, though, I am very conscious that he has done the careful work of documenting the prevalence of such views, and so has good evidence to back up his estimate of how significant an issue this is. I am happy, anyway, to record my complete agreement with his view that both eternal functional subordination and a denial of eternal generation are significant departures from classical Trinitarian orthodoxy.

I end as I began, by recording my genuine and heartfelt gratitude to all the contributors to this book. Even where I still presently disagree with one or another, I have benefited greatly from considering the interaction; my thinking has been sharpened, and my knowledge deepened; these are the greatest gifts a would-be scholar can receive, and I am thankful. I look forward to continuing many of these conversations in other places.

Conclusion

Jason S. Sexton and T.A. Noble

The slow, careful work of reflection on the doctrine of the Trinity continues. In this volume, evangelical theologians work through a number of critical issues raised by Stephen Holmes in his important book. As Fred Sanders suggests in his opening chapter, this may very well end up being a pivotal point in the wider conversation in the West. The work of this volume takes place, if Holmes's argument from *The Holy Trinity* is convincing, after a period of hasty generalizations about the history of the doctrine. And perhaps both poor readings and superfluous associations and assertions have been made far too frequently in recent history.

But the writers in this volume, along with other scholars writing in the aftermath of Holmes's book, have significant questions to raise. This leaves us wondering precisely which reader (in this volume) is correct about Holmes's contribution. And which writer has a better grasp on where things have come from, where they stand, and where they may be heading. These are significant questions about no small doctrinal matter of the Christian faith. The doctrine of the Trinity is not a marginal element of Christian belief, nor is it a mere peccadillo to ill-treat the doctrine in any form, whether past or present.

It seems best for this brief conclusion to offer a few remarks about where this leaves us. How shall we best bring the present conversation into a proper perspective that may help us continue to situate Trinitarian theology in the best light in order that it may flourish for the good of the church? What are the critical issues and the points of tension in the debate? These will probably continue to revolve around the questions of how the doctrine is to be understood in relation to its historical expressions, its shape given by divine revelation in Holy Scripture, and how the doctrine should be given contemporary confession in both ecclesial and missionary perspectives.

An Historical Matter

At the end of *The Holy Trinity*, Holmes is right to take note that the historians of doctrine will need to give account of the present moment of Trinitarian theology. Holmes noted repeatedly that his own argument in the book is 'deliberately, and limitedly, historical', showing that there has been a very significant departure from a largely consistent tradition.[1] But, the question may yet be raised, why does history (i.e. historical investigation and reconstruction) receive a special place for this sort of critical doctrinal scrutiny, as a critical approach wielding a kind of authority spanning the traditions? Historical investigation itself is a relative newcomer in academic discourse (although not as green as, say, sociology or the performing arts). To be sure, we have extant texts, and can constructively imagine the situations that gave birth to them. But we do not have everything from the tradition; we do not see all the conversations in their entirety, nor all points of earlier critical scrutiny; nor do we see other wider cultural and ecclesial factors giving birth to the earliest patristic doctrine. And the moments of the past are not exactly our moments; nor were their concerns entirely the ones of pressing importance in our contemporary era. Perhaps they should be; but that is another matter.

So while historians will account for the current conversation in Trinitarian theology, and its relationship to the tradition (and to Scripture and culture), so will theologians. And so, as those entrusted with the primary task of serving the church for the sake of its confession, this may be the more significant matter. Trinitarian theology is, of course, not the mere restatement of historical claims or commitments: it is about truth-claims for today. Holmes does not think the recent innovations are necessarily right or helpful, a point he makes repeatedly. But it is worth repeating yet again. And what of developmental latitude in Trinitarian discourse? This raises the question whether repeating the same words and concepts in a different (e.g. present) context really allows one to continue saying the same thing in any meaningful sense. Do the concepts have the same kind of pressure or wider cultural purchase?[2] On the other hand, if the same thing is being translated into the present (whether it is the approach of Eunomius or any another) and aims to repeat the same exact thing, then precisely what should be said, for example, in places in the Global South, or in Boston, Los Angeles or greater Manchester, or using the thought-categories (again Holmes's examples) of Vedic or Xhosan philosophy? And can we appropriate the designation of heresy in such a way that allows for the avoidance of the charge of anachronism which often snares the novice historian? While the conversation in this book is set out around Holmes's particular claims, and while it seems that new insight generated from observing various texts and trends is being yielded, the question remains precisely how much of the present state of conversation about Trinitarian theology should be loaded and located with historical description and various expressions of the doctrine in the past.

As all theology does, Holmes's work seems to have had a few weaknesses that some essays in this volume have highlighted, some of which Holmes concedes. By his own admission, he also left a few things out, perhaps even leaving a few gaps in the research. He therefore did not capture the entirety of doctrinal history in his book. This is a fair point. He missed some of Luther and the Lutherans; he missed the major contribution of Thomas Torrance; and he could perhaps have investigated other voices with greater nuance. But of course Holmes is tracing a general mood, and is not alone, since other patristic scholars make similar points. Assuming he is right in his reading and relating of the ancient heresies to recent developments, one still wonders whether saying the same thing today is actually saying the same thing if it is stated with different rationale and in the light of different reasons and in different thought-categories. It seems that whatever our own particular social histories might say of the present moment and its relationship to the past, there will be quite a lot of issues to consider about how our present moment of theological reflection relates to the earlier traditional statements and arguments. So, there is more work to be done.

A Biblical Doctrine

Perhaps most intriguing is the engagement Holmes is receiving from the biblical scholars, some of whom we later learned would have loved to have been part of the current project. There appears to be a point of tension between his argument and what many (perhaps most) of the confessional scholars are seeking to find, namely, whether the doctrine of the Trinity is itself a *biblical* idea. In the strict sense Holmes denies this. This is not to say that what we later have as a codified doctrine of the Trinity is not derived, even primarily, from the biblical witness. What Holmes sees, however, is that 'what we tend to call "the doctrine of the Trinity" . . . is . . . the claims we make about God's life which give us the logic/grammar which allows us to understand how all these various claims can be made without our lapsing into simple incoherence.'[3]

While some evangelical biblical scholars may find Holmes's proposal uncomfortable, there seems to be support for it in recent arguments made for a kind of implicit Trinitarianism found in the sophisticated forms of Trinitarian descriptions that were used early on.[4] And as biblical scholarship continues its work into the second century of Christian theology, in conjunction with patristic scholarship, this may also find that Holmes's proposal sufficiently accounts for what happened there.

A lingering question is whether the grammar and logic of Trinitarian descriptions can change. Holmes thinks they do, in theory, noting that just as early Trinitarian doctrine borrowed from the middle Platonic philosophical system of the day, so also current symbols and thought-systems may also give sound, plausible, and good accounts of the triune life. But in different worlds, borrowing from Wittgenstein's notion of language games, precisely *how does* and *when can* this Trinitarian description change? For understanding how this may occur, the reality of the scriptural witness gives substance to the shape of the tradition. Most of the earliest forms of Trinitarian reflection came about as expositions of the biblical texts. And so good historical work needs to be done to see how this has happened, and this may indeed affirm Holmes's argument that 'such a task is adequately accomplished over decades or centuries by communities, not over hours or even years by individual scholars. Reading the Bible well is extraordinarily hard work!'[5] Again, with this more slow, hard work is needed.

A Constructive Dogma

Is Trinitarian doctrine always hard work? It depends what, of course, we understand by 'doctrine', and whether it is primarily passed down and carried on (preserved) or constructed. A question that remains in the light of Holmes's critique concerns precisely *how* we will in the contemporary world continue to construct the doctrine further, and whether it may be driven largely by the tools of the academic exercise and discourse, or by something else. Some may fear that forms of the new school of analytic philosophy may end up pulling us towards various forms of tritheism. Perhaps there are other forms of both classical and relational doctrines of the Trinity which may yield more modalistic models or may perhaps compromise a personal God altogether. Trinitarian construction does not take shape merely by the tools of academic discourse, but with the priority of Scripture governing the enterprise, as noted above. The core truths of Trinitarian theology are irreducibly *biblical* insofar as they are revealed truths about divine economic action of the God who is the Father, the Son, and the Holy Spirit. God cannot be anything less than this. As such, the divine being in economic action is first and foremost a *revealed* reality.

In these ways, Trinitarian reflection finds its proper expression, as James Torrance and Lesslie Newbigin insisted, in the dynamic life of the church – in the personal and communal lives of those who commune with this God in worship and who speak of this God in evangelism. The doctrine of the Trinity, then, is an *exposition* or *explication* of the God revealed in Scripture.[6] Accordingly, Holmes's work turned on its head becomes a clarion call for the missionary task in our day. We are not merely to work out the Trinitarian confession in our own context, nor merely to get the historical details right. For if indeed our confession of the Trinitarian shape of faith takes place in the public place, it yields a public faith for anyone wishing to peer into it for whatever expositional and gospel-oriented explanatory value it may have. Holmes gifts us then with a call to better confession of the God revealed in the gospel and in the entirety of Scripture, as well as to being responsible heirs of our own traditions. In this way, contemporary readers may very well think hard about their particular traditions, incorporating and perhaps replacing them with an earlier and more substantial one that may have carried out this missionary task more faithfully.

In whatever era, if it is really 'God' we speak of in the Trinitarian confession, then the power in our confession of the Trinity is the power of the gospel, the power and presence of God. In this way a developing doctrine of the Trinity may itself be able to speak into a range of traditions, from the analytic to the continental, to the evangelical and the Catholic, and everything in between. But coming to this conviction must proceed by way of a recapitulation that this is the way it happened in the tradition, indicating a deeper consideration of the shape the earlier Trinitarian description took and how this shape occurred and, more generally, develops. This may be the profound significance of the work Steve Holmes has prodded us with. Holmes invokes us: 'Imagine, however, a situation analogous to the patristic history, a slow communal argument and development, testing and refining every particular proposal over decades, until after some centuries a broad consensus emerged that the categories thus understood could be deployed usefully to speak of God's life.'[7] In this way, we may indeed find ways of speaking of the historical phenomena as ways of better waging the debate over Trinitarian descriptions, and for the shaping of our confession today.[8]

This work is not slow of necessity, and sometimes will invoke sharp responses, whether pastoral, apologetic, or otherwise. Sometimes it must indeed be quite urgent as in the forms of migrant communities making sense of displacement, or where God might be in events such as the Holocaust, or persecution under the governance of the radical Islamic state, or for some other reasons. In this way, however, the ontological reality of the triune God's real presence is acknowledged to be available both in love and action.

Considering where to go from here, both constructively and methodo-logically, one wonders whether Holmes is after something similar to what is after all displayed in the work of the late Wolfhart Pannenberg, with its reciprocally top-down/bottom-up dialogical approach exhibiting the relationship between revelation and other thought-forms and developing conceptual categories. This indeed seems like something that Torrance succeeded at admirably in his work with theology and science. It also seems as if Colin Gunton and those from the earlier tradition (including the Cappadocians and Augustine) were committed to something like this: specifically, that theology works through the various thought-forms of the day, with the pertinently expressed challenges and opportunities these bring to Christian theology, and especially to a Christian doctrine of God. In turn this development might indeed yield a better understanding of the doctrine, and perhaps assist in cultivating a better communion with this triune God of the gospel. The contributors in this volume are indeed open to such a possibility, believing that Scripture can point us there. Perhaps the slow, communal argument which we have been privileged to enjoy in the pages of this volume, then, flowing from the earlier conversation in Cambridge and provoked by Stephen Holmes's book, may itself contribute in a small way to being part of exploring better ways to speak of God's life in Trinity.

Jason S. Sexton
T.A. Noble

Endnotes

Introduction

1. Stephen R. Holmes, *The Holy Trinity: Understanding God's Life* (Milton Keynes: Paternoster, 2012), p. 2.
2. See a more structured debate between what are deemed 'classical' and 'relational' views of the Trinity – the classical represented by Stephen R. Holmes and Paul D. Molnar and the relational represented by Thomas H. McCall and Paul S. Fiddes in *Two Views on the Doctrine of the Trinity* (ed. Jason S. Sexton; Grand Rapids: Zondervan, 2014).

1. Redefining Progress in Trinitarian Theology: Stephen R. Holmes on the Trinity

1. Jürgen Moltmann, *The Trinity and the Kingdom of God* (trans. M. Kohl; London: SCM, 1981).
2. Catherine LaCugna, *God For Us: The Trinity and Christian Life* (London: HarperOne, 1993).
3. Robert W. Jenson, *Systematic Theology* (2 vols; New York: OUP, 1997–9).
4. Stephen R. Holmes, *The Holy Trinity: Understanding God's Life* (Milton Keynes: Paternoster, 2012), p. xv.
5. Holmes, *Holy Trinity*, p. xviii.
6. Holmes, *Holy Trinity*, p. 2.
7. Holmes, *Holy Trinity*, p. 2.
8. Holmes, *Holy Trinity*, p. 2.
9. Matthew Levering and Gilles Emery, eds, *The Oxford Handbook on the Trinity* (Oxford: OUP, 2012).

10 Holmes, *Holy Trinity*, p. 200.

11 1 John 5:7 AV.

12 Benjamin B. Warfield, 'Trinity', in *The International Standard Bible Cyclopedia* (ed. James Orr; Chicago: Howard-Severance Co., 1915), 5:3012–22.

13 Irenaeus, *On the Apostolic Preaching* (New York: St Vladimir's Seminary Press, 1997).

14 C. Kavin Rowe, 'Biblical Pressure and Trinitarian Hermeneutics', *ProEccl* 11 (2002): pp. 295–312, esp. p. 308.

15 T.F. Torrance, *The Christian Doctrine of God: One Being Three Persons* (Edinburgh: T&T Clark, 1996).

16 Bernard Lonergan, *The Triune God: Systematics* (trans. Michael G. Shields; ed. Robert M. Doran and H. Daniel Monsour; Toronto: University of Toronto Press, 2007).

17 Lewis Ayres, *Nicaea and Its Legacy: An Approach to Fourth-Century Trinitarian Theology* (Oxford: OUP, 2006).

18 R.W. Dale, *Christian Doctrine: A Series of Discourses* (London: Hodder & Stoughton, 1894), p. 151.

19 Bruce D. Marshall, 'The Unity of the Triune God: Reviving an Ancient Question', *Thomist* 74 (2010): pp. 1–32, citing p. 7.

20 Marshall, 'The Unity of the Triune God', p. 7.

21 Marshall, 'The Unity of the Triune God', pp. 7–8.

22 Marshall, 'The Unity of the Triune God', p. 8.

23 E.g. Gilles Emery op, *The Trinity: An Introduction to Catholic Doctrine on the Triune God* (Washington, DC: Catholic University of America Press, 2011).

24 Holmes, *Holy Trinity*, p. 200.

25 Holmes, *Holy Trinity*, p. 146.

26 Holmes, *Holy Trinity*, p. 120.

27 C.S. Lewis, 'De Descriptione Temporum', in *Selected Literary Essays* (Cambridge: CUP, 1969), p. 2.

28 Lewis, 'De Descriptione Temporum', pp. 7–10.

29 Holmes, *Holy Trinity*, p. 146.

30 Scott R. Swain, http://thegospelcoalition.org/book-reviews/review/the_quest_for_the_trinity (accessed 21 April 2014).

31 Wolfhart Pannenberg, *Systematic Theology*, vol. 1 (trans. G.W. Bromiley; Grand Rapids: Eerdmans, 1991), p. 320.

32 Thomas Aquinas, *Summa Theologiae* I.Q43.2 http://www.newadvent.org/summa/1043.htm#article2.

2. Old and New, East and West, and a Missing Horse

[1] Stephen R. Holmes, *The Holy Trinity: Understanding God's Life* (Milton Keynes: Paternoster, 2012), pp. 9ff.

[2] Paul D. Molnar, *Divine Freedom and the Doctrine of the Immanent Trinity: In Dialogue with Karl Barth and Contemporary Theology* (London: T&T Clark, 2002).

[3] Holmes, *Holy Trinity*, pp. 199–200.

[4] Robert Letham, *The Holy Trinity: In Scripture, History, Theology, and Worship* (Phillipsburg, NJ: Presbyterian & Reformed, 2004), pp. 291–321.

[5] Letham, *Holy Trinity*, pp. 298–312.

[6] Kevin J. Bidwell, *The Church as the Image of the Trinity: A Critical Evaluation of Miroslav Volf's Ecclesial Model* (Eugene, OR: Wipf & Stock, 2011).

[7] Letham, *The Holy Trinity*, p. 6.

[8] Keith and Melody Green, 'There Is a Redeemer', from *Songs for the Shepherd* (© 1990 Sparrow Records); emphasis mine.

[9] Letham, *The Holy Trinity*, pp. 59–60.

[10] Geerhardus Vos, *The Pauline Eschatology* (Grand Rapids: Eerdmans, 1972), p. 163.

[11] Holmes, *Holy Trinity*, pp. 129–39; Lewis Ayres, *Augustine and the Trinity* (Cambridge: CUP, 2010).

[12] Basil Studer, *The Grace of Christ and the Grace of God in Augustine of Hippo: Christocentrism or Theocentrism?* (Collegeville, MN: Liturgical Press, 1997), p. 106.

[13] Augustine, *Letter* 169 (PL 33:740–41).

[14] Gregory Nazianzen, *Oration* 31, pp. 8, 31–3 (PG 36:141, 169–72).

[15] Holmes, *Holy Trinity*, p. 164.

[16] Theodore de Régnon, *Études de théologie positive sur la Sainte Trinité* (3 vols; Paris: Retaux, 1892–8).

[17] Michel René Barnes, 'De Régnon Reconsidered', *AugStud* 26 (1995): pp. 51–79; Michel René Barnes, 'Rereading Augustine on the Trinity', in *The Trinity: An Interdisciplinary Symposium on the Trinity* (ed. Stephen T. Davis; Oxford: OUP, 1999), pp. 145–76.

[18] See Kristin Hennessy, 'An Answer to De Régnon's Accusers: Why We Should Not Speak of "His" Paradigm', *HTR* 100 (April 2007): pp. 179–97.

[19] Lewis Ayres, *Nicaea and Its Legacy: An Approach to Fourth-Century Trinitarian Theology* (Oxford: OUP, 2004).

20 Robert Letham, *Through Western Eyes: Eastern Orthodoxy; A Reformed Perspective* (Fearn: Mentor, 2007); Andrew Louth, *John Damascene: Tradition and Originality in Byzantine Theology* (Oxford: OUP, 2002); Robert Letham, 'The Trinity between East and West', *JRT* 3 (2009): pp. 42–56.

21 Letham, *Through Western Eyes*, pp. 143–71.

22 Dumitru Staniloae, *The Experience of God: Orthodox Dogmatic Theology, vol. 1: Revelation and Knowledge of the Triune God* (Iona Ionita; Brookline, MA: Holy Cross Orthodox Press, 1994), pp. 95–7.

23 Photios, *On the Mystagogy of the Holy Spirit* (PG 102:280–391); Saint Photios, *On the Mystagogy of the Holy Spirit* (n.p.: Studion, 1983), pp. 73–6.

24 Gregory Palamas, *The Triads* 3.2.5 – 3.3.6.

25 Deno John Geanakoplos, *Byzantium: Church, Society, and Civilization Seen through Contemporary Eyes* (Chicago: University of Chicago Press, 1984), p. 219.

26 Holmes, *Holy Trinity*, p. 159.

27 Timothy Ware, *The Orthodox Church* (London: Penguin, 1969), p. 63.

28 Saint Photios, *Mystagogy*, pp. 73–6, 84–6.

29 Ware, *Orthodox Church*, pp. 218–19.

30 *The Festal Menaion* (trans. Mother Mary and Archimandrite Kallistos Ware; South Canaan, PA: St Tikhon's Seminary Press, 1998); *Service Book of the Holy Orthodox-Catholic Apostolic Church* (ed. Isabel Florence Hapgood; Brooklyn, NY: Syrian Antiochene Orthodox Archdiocese of New York and All North America, 3rd edn, 1956), pp. 456–7; *The Lenten Triadion* (trans. Mother Mary and Archimandrite Kallistos Ware; South Canaan, PA: St Tikhon's Seminary Press, 2002).

31 Gerald Bray, 'The Filioque Clause in History and Theology', *TynBul* 34 (1983): pp. 142–3.

32 Ware, *Orthodox Church*, pp. 59–60, 222–3.

33 Holmes, *Holy Trinity*, p. 145.

34 Holmes, *Holy Trinity*, p. 147.

35 Holmes, *Holy Trinity*, pp. 162–3.

36 M. Edmund Hussey, 'The Palamite Trinitarian Models', *SVTQ* 16 (1972): pp. 83–9.

37 Jeremy D. Wilkins, '"The Image of His Highest Love": The Trinitarian Analogy in Gregory Palamas's Capita 150', *SVTQ* 47 (2003): pp. 383–412.

38 Wilkins, 'Trinitarian Analogy', p. 410.

39 Wilkins, 'Trinitarian Analogy', p. 411.
40 Wilkins, 'Trinitarian Analogy', p. 411.
41 Wilkins, 'Trinitarian Analogy', p. 412.
42 Kallistos Ware, 'Foreword', in Staniloae, *Experience of God*, p. xxiv.
43 Holmes, *Holy Trinity*, p. 163.
44 Holmes, *Holy Trinity*, p. 155.
45 Holmes, *Holy Trinity*, p. 161.
46 Holmes, *Holy Trinity*, p. 162.
47 Ware, *Orthodox Church*, p. 9.
48 T.A. Noble, 'Paradox in Gregory Nazianzen's Doctrine of the Trinity', *StPatr* 27 (1993): pp. 94–9.
49 *Service Book*, pp. 456–7.
50 Sir Arthur Conan Doyle, *The Complete Sherlock Holmes* (Garden City, NY: Doubleday, 1927), p. 347.
51 Aristotle Papanikolaou, 'Is John Zizioulas an Existentialist in Disguise? Response to Lucian Turcescu', *Mod Theol* 20 (October 2004): p. 605.
52 Staniloae, *Experience of God*, p. 246.
53 Staniloae, *Experience of God*, p. 247.
54 Holmes, *Holy Trinity*, pp. 199–200.
55 John of Damascus, *On the Orthodox Faith* 1.8 (PG 194:808–33).
56 Gilles Emery, *The Trinity: An Introduction to Catholic Doctrine of the Triune God* (trans. Matthew Levering; Washington, DC: Catholic University of America Press, 2011), p. 27.
57 Emery, *The Trinity*, pp. 183–4.
58 Staniloae, *Experience of God*, p. 249.
59 Staniloae, *Experience of God*, p. 258.
60 Holmes, *Holy Trinity*, p. 200.

3. A Personal Response to Stephen R. Holmes's *The Holy Trinity*

1 I take the liberty in this chapter of addressing Dr Holmes as 'Stephen'. I am an Australian; this is my excuse! To speak of 'Holmes's' seems to me to be a very impersonal way to address a brother Christian. When I sent him this essay in draft before publication for him to read, I asked for permission to use his Christian name.
2 *The Nicene and Post-Nicene Fathers*, series 2 (ed. Philip Schaff and Henry Wace; New York: Christian Literature Co., 1892), *Four Discourses*

against the Arians 4.24 (p. 443); cf. 1.5.14 (p. 314), 1.5.16 (p. 316), and 1.9.31 (p. 325). (Henceforth in this chapter abbreviated as *NPNF*[2] with the volume number and then the page number.)

3 Holmes, *Holy Trinity*, p. 146.

4 Athanasius, *Four Discourses against the Arians* 3.26.29 (*NPNF*[2] 4:409).

5 Holmes, *Holy Trinity*, pp. 87–92.

6 Holmes, *Holy Trinity*, pp. 113.

7 Holmes, *Holy Trinity*, pp. 144–64.

8 See T.F. Torrance, *Trinitarian Perspectives: Toward Doctrinal Agreement* (Edinburgh: T&T Clark, 1994), pp. 115–22.

9 Charles Hodge, *Systematic Theology* (3 vols; Grand Rapids: Eerdmans, 1960), 1:467.

10 Hodge, *Systematic Theology* 1:460. See also pp. 445, 460, 461, 462, 464, 465, 467, 468, 474.

11 Hodge, *Systematic Theology* 1:445, 461.

12 Hodge, *Systematic Theology* 1:469.

13 Holmes, *Holy Trinity*, p. 33.

14 Holmes, *Holy Trinity*, p. 47.

15 Holmes, *Holy Trinity*, p. 51.

16 Athanasius, *Council of Nicaea* 1.2 and n. 3 (*NPNF*[2] 4:75). See also *Discourses against the Arians* 1.3.8 (*NPNF*[2] 4:310).

17 Thomas G. Weinandy, *Athanasius: A Theological Introduction* (Aldershot: Ashgate, 2007), p. 135.

18 Athanasius, *Letter 2, Easter* 330 5 (*NPNF*[2] 4:511ff.).

19 Athanasius, *Discourses* 3.26.26–9 (*NPNF*[2] 4:409).

20 Athanasius, *Discourses* 3.26.26–9 (*NPNF*[2] 4:409).

21 Holmes, *Holy Trinity*, p. 3.

22 Wayne A. Grudem, *Systematic Theology: An Introduction to Biblical Doctrine* (Grand Rapids: Zondervan, rev. edn, 2000). In my *Jesus and the Father: Modern Evangelicals Reinvent the Doctrine of the Trinity* (Grand Rapids: Zondervan, 2006) I give a full bibliography of the many evangelical theologians promulgating this doctrine. For recent particularly egregious examples of this teaching and replies to it, see Dennis W. Jowers and H. Wayne House, eds, *The New Evangelical Subordinationism?* (Eugene, OR: Pickwick, 2012).

23 George W. Knight III, *New Testament Teaching on the Role Relationship of Men and Women* (Grand Rapids: Baker, 1977).

4. A Double-Headed Luther? A Lutheran Response to *The Holy Trinity* by Stephen R. Holmes

¹ Stephen R. Holmes, *The Holy Trinity: Understanding God's Life* (Milton Keynes: Paternoster, 2012).

² Holmes, *Holy Trinity*, p. xv.

³ Holmes, *Holy Trinity*, p. xv.

⁴ Holmes, *Holy Trinity*, p. 2.

⁵ Holmes, *Holy Trinity*, p. 2.

⁶ Holmes, *Holy Trinity*, p. 166.

⁷ Holmes's reading is clearly motivated by Christine Helmer's recent study on Luther's doctrine of the Trinity to which we shall return in due course. See Christine Helmer, *The Trinity and Martin Luther: A Study on the Relationship between Genre, Language, and the Trinity in Luther's Works (1523—1546)*, Veröffenlichungen des Institutes für europäische Geschichte/Abteilung abendländische Religionsgeschichte 174 (Mainz: Verlag Philipp von Zabern, 1999).

⁸ Helmer, *Trinity and Martin Luther*, p. 168.

⁹ Paul Althaus, *The Theology of Martin Luther* (trans. R.C. Schultz; Philadelphia: Fortress, 1966), pp. 199–200.

¹⁰ See Dennis Ngien, *The Suffering of God According to Martin Luther's 'Theologia Crucis'* (New York: Peter Lang, 1995), pp. 135–74; Bernhard Lohse, *Martin Luther's Theology: Its Historical and Systematic Development* (trans. Roy A. Harrisville; Edinburgh: T&T Clark, 1999), pp. 207–15; Oswald Bayer, *Martin Luther's Theology: A Contemporary Interpretation* (trans. Thomas H. Trapp; Grand Rapids: Eerdmans, 2008), pp. 334–42.

¹¹ Holmes, *Holy Trinity*, p. 166.

¹² Karl Rahner, *The Trinity* (trans. Joseph Donceel; Tunbridge Wells: Burns & Oates, 1970), p. 22.

¹³ George Hunsinger has remarked upon the confluence between Barth's thinking and the theology of Martin Luther in his essay 'What Karl Barth Learned from Martin Luther'. See George Hunsinger, 'What Karl Barth Learned from Martin Luther', *LQ* 13 (1999): pp. 125–55.

¹⁴ Karl Barth, *Church Dogmatics* I/1 (Edinburgh: T&T Clark, 1936), p. 315.

¹⁵ Robert W. Jenson, *The Triune Identity: God According to the Gospel* (Philadelphia: Fortress, 1982), p. 138.

¹⁶ Holmes, *Holy Trinity*, p. 16.

[17] See e.g. his essay 'Luther's Contribution to Christian Spirituality', *Dialog* 40/4 (2001): pp. 284–9. See further Anselm K. Min, 'The Dialectic of Divine Love: Pannenberg's Hegelian Trinitarianism', *IJST* 6 (2004): pp. 252–69.

[18] Moltmann consciously adopts a Lutheran register in implementing the theological tropes of a 'theology of the cross' and 'God crucified'. Nevertheless, as Burnell F. Eckardt Jr has argued, Moltmann has a tendency to depart from a stringent reading of Luther's own understanding of these theological ideas. See Burnell F. Eckardt Jr, 'Luther and Moltmann: The Theology of the Cross', *CTQ* 49 (1985): pp. 19–28.

[19] Robert W. Jenson, *Systematic Theology* (2 vols; Oxford: OUP, 1997, 1999).

[20] Isaak Dorner, who has been relatively overlooked in the scholarship, is enjoying something of a renaissance with a number of works being dedicated to his thinking. Principally, Jonathan Norgate's book, *Isaak A. Dorner: The Triune God and the Gospel of Salvation* (Edinburgh: T&T Clark, 2009) is a great gain to the world of theological scholarship. Beyond this, Piotr Małysz's article 'Hegel's Conception of God, and Its Application by Isaak Dorner to the Problem of Divine Immutability', *ProEccl* 15 (2006): pp. 448–71, gives a good introduction to the sort of issues concerning divine triunity that we have been discussing.

[21] Relatively little research has been devoted to assessing the place of Schleiermacher within the Protestant heritage within which he developed. No doubt this says more about the reception of Schleiermacher in the context of a post-Barthian theological milieu, but there are some points of progress which should encourage an optimism with respect to future research particularly in terms of the Lutheran element within Schleiermacher's thinking. The best extant illustration of this kind of scholarship is Brian Gerrish's study on Schleiermacher and the naissance of modern theology. See Brian A. Gerrish, *A Prince of the Church: Schleiermacher and the Beginnings of Modern Theology* (Eugene, OR: Wipf & Stock, 1988).

[22] Holmes, *Holy Trinity*, p. 16, n. 52.

[23] Holmes, *Holy Trinity*, p. 16, n. 52.

[24] See Frederic Jameson, 'The Vanishing Mediator: Narrative Structure in Max Weber', *NGC* 1 (1973): pp. 52–89.

[25] Holmes himself is careful to include a discussion of Hegel in the final chapter of the book. See *Holy Trinity*, pp. 184-6.

[26] There can be little doubt that Cyril O'Regan's book *The Heterodox Hegel* (New York: State University of New York, 1994) has the most to offer in exploring the theological underpinnings of Hegel's wider project. Beyond this, Ulrich Asendorf's *Luther und Hegel: Untersuchung zur Grundlegung einer neuen systematischen Theologie* (Wiesbaden: Franz Steiner Verlag, 1982) approaches the topic from a theological angle, Asendorf being a noted scholar of Luther, and offers important insights into the relationship between the two giants of German intellectualism.

[27] *Dr Martin Luthers Werke* [WA] (Weimar: Böhlau, 1883–1993), 6, 305, 24–6.

[28] Holmes references Helmer's book in his brief treatment of Luther: *Holy Trinity*, p. 167, n. 6.

[29] See Helmer, *Trinity and Martin Luther*, pp. 8–25.

[30] Helmer, *Trinity and Martin Luther*, pp. 8–9.

[31] Helmer, *Trinity and Martin Luther*, p. 15.

[32] Helmer, *Trinity and Martin Luther*, pp. 15–17.

[33] Holmes, *Holy Trinity*, p. 16, n. 52.

[34] *Luther's Works* [LW] (ed. Jaroslav Pelikan and Helmut T. Lehmann; St Louis: Concordia and Philadelphia: Fortress, 1955–86), 26:29; WA 40^1, 77, 28 – 78, 1.

[35] In this sense, both Helmer and the Finnish School are correct – contemporary readings of Luther have a tendency to conflate post-Kantian epistemology with Luther's methodological approach in the *theologia crucis*.

[36] Holmes discusses this facet of Robert Jenson's work in Holmes, *Holy Trinity*, pp. 23–4.

[37] The most helpful contemporary treatments of the Lutheran doctrine of *communicatio idiomatum* are Robert W. Jenson, 'Luther's Contemporary Theological Significance', in *The Cambridge Companion to Martin Luther* (ed. Donald K. McKim; Cambridge: CUP, 2003), pp. 272–88 and Piotr J. Małysz, 'Storming Heaven with Karl Barth? Barth's Unwitting Appropriation of the Genus Maiestaticum and what Lutherans Can Learn from It', *Mod Theol* 9 (2007): pp. 73–92.

[38] Ingolf Dalferth has argued against Luther's mode of argument here, suggesting that he conflates a concept of real presence with a concept of bodily presence, missing the force of the theological rule of faith that Chalcedon implemented. See Ingolf U. Dalferth, *Becoming Present: An Inquiry into the Christian Sense of the Presence of God* (Leuven: Peeters, 2006), p. 92.

[39] It is arguable that Luther himself allows this to happen in his frequent references to the 'hidden God' which arise across his theological writings and draw him away from the focal point of Christ Crucified as the moment at which God is seen as he is. Alister McGrath writes of this tendency in *de servo arbitrio*, '[Luther's] dilemma is his own creation, and his failure to resolve it in *de servo arbitrio* an indictment of his abandonment of his own principle: *Crux sola est nostra theologia!*' Alister E. McGrath, *Luther's Theology of the Cross* (Oxford: Blackwell, 1985), p. 167.

[40] Eberhard Jüngel, *God as the Mystery of the World* (Edinburgh: T&T Clark, 1983), p. 100.

5. T.F. Torrance and the Patristic Consensus on the Doctrine of the Trinity

[1] Colin E. Gunton, *Father, Son, and Holy Spirit: Essays toward a Fully Trinitarian Theology* (London: T&T Clark, 2003), p. 51.

[2] George Dragas, 'The Significance for the Church of Professor Torrance's Election as Moderator of the General Assembly of the Church of Scotland', *EP* 58 (1976): p. 216.

[3] See T.F. Torrance, *The Trinitarian Faith: The Evangelical Theology of the Ancient Catholic Church* (Edinburgh: T&T Clark, 1988); T.F. Torrance, *The Christian Doctrine of God: One Being Three Persons* (Edinburgh: T&T Clark, 1996).

[4] See Stephen R. Holmes, *The Holy Trinity: Understanding God's Life* (Milton Keynes: Paternoster, 2012), pp. 2, 200.

[5] Holmes, *Holy Trinity*, pp. 144–6.

[6] Torrance, *Trinitarian Faith*, p. 2.

[7] Torrance, *Christian Doctrine of God*, p. ix.

[8] See *Itinerarium Mentis in Deum: T.F. Torrance – My Theological Development*, The Thomas F. Torrance Manuscript Collection, Princeton Theological Seminary, box 10.

[9] Holmes, *Holy Trinity*, p. 199.

[10] See e.g. T.F. Torrance, *Theology in Reconciliation: Essays towards Evangelical and Catholic Unity in East and West* (Eugene, OR: Wipf & Stock, 1996), p. 9.

[11] Torrance, *Theology in Reconciliation*, pp. 7–14.

[12] See Torrance, *Theology in Reconciliation*, p. 14.

[13] *Torrance Manuscript Collection*, box 172.

[14] T.F. Torrance, *Theology in Reconstruction* (Eugene, OR: Wipf & Stock, 1996).

[15] See Torrance, *Trinitarian Faith* for the flowering of Torrance's reconstruction. See further Jason Radcliff, *Thomas F. Torrance and the Church Fathers* (Eugene, OR: Pickwick, 2014) for a more extensive exploration of Torrance's use of the fathers.

[16] Dragas, 'The Significance for the Church of Professor Torrance's Election', p. 226.

[17] Torrance, *Christian Doctrine of God*, p. 7.

[18] See Torrance, *Theology in Reconciliation*, p. 264.

[19] A reading of any chapter in *Trinitarian Faith* portrays this; the entire book is organized around this patristic concept. However, see particularly the chapter on this, pp. 110–90.

[20] T.F. Torrance, *Preaching Christ Today: The Gospel and Scientific Thinking* (Grand Rapids: Eerdmans, 1994), pp. 55–6; *Trinitarian Perspectives: Toward Doctrinal Agreement* (Edinburgh: T&T Clark, 1994), p. 86.

[21] Torrance, *Theology in Reconciliation*, p. 241; *Trinitarian Faith*, pp. 66–8, 72.

[22] See e.g. Torrance, *Trinitarian Faith*, pp. 149–59 and *The Mediation of Christ* (Colorado Springs: Helmers & Howard, 1992).

[23] Torrance, *Christian Doctrine of God*, p. 7.

[24] See further Elmer Colyer, *How to Read T.F. Torrance: Understanding His Trinitarian and Scientific Theology* (Downers Grove, IL: IVP, 2001), p. 360.

[25] Torrance, *Reality and Evangelical Theology* (Eugene, OR: Wipf & Stock, 1999), pp. 14–15; *Preaching Christ Today*, p. 20; *Theology in Reconciliation*, pp. 235–7; 285; *Theology in Reconstruction*, p. 267.

[26] Torrance, *Theology in Reconstruction*, p. 225. Torrance considers grace to be intrinsically personal as it was connected to the person of Christ. See Torrance, *Preaching Christ Today*, pp. 20–21.

[27] Torrance, *Trinitarian Perspectives*, pp. 21–2.

[28] Torrance, *Theology in Reconstruction*, p. 265. See also Torrance, 'Karl Barth and the Latin Heresy', *SJT* 39 (1986): pp. 462–3.

[29] T.F. Torrance, *Karl Barth: An Introduction to His Early Theology* (London: SCM, 1962), p. 146.

[30] See Torrance, *Trinitarian Faith*, p. 72.

[31] Torrance, *Christian Doctrine of God*, p. 149. See also *Mediation of Christ*, p. 40.

32 See Torrance, *Christian Doctrine of God*, p. 28.

33 See *God and Rationality*, pp. 100–01.

34 See *Reality and Scientific Theology*, pp. 86–93.

35 Torrance, 'Athanasius: A Study in the Foundations of Classical Theology', in *Theology in Reconciliation*, pp. 215–66.

36 T.F. Torrance, *Theological Dialogue between Orthodox and Reformed Churches*, vol. 1 (Edinburgh: Scottish Academic Press, 1985), p. 13.

37 Torrance's attack is typically more on Augustinian thought than Augustine himself. See e.g. T.F. Torrance, *Gospel, Church, and Ministry* (ed. Jock Stein; Eugene, OR: Wipf & Stock, 2012), p. 209 and *Theological Dialogue* 1:12.

38 T.F. Torrance, *Theological Dialogue between Orthodox and Reformed Churches*, vol. 2 (Edinburgh: Scottish Academic Press, 1993), pp. 32, 119; *Trinitarian Faith*, pp. 316–17.

39 See Torrance, *Trinitarian Faith*, pp. 38–9, esp. n. 69 on p. 38. Torrance is critical of the way in which Maximus the Confessor, John of Damascus, and Gregory Palamas used the distinction between essence and energies introduced by Basil.

40 Holmes, *Holy Trinity*, p. 199.

41 Holmes, *Holy Trinity*, pp. 5–9.

42 Holmes, *Holy Trinity*, pp. 9–12.

43 Torrance, 'Karl Barth and the Latin Heresy', p. 464.

44 Torrance, 'Karl Barth and the Latin Heresy', p. 476.

45 Torrance, *Reality and Evangelical Theology*, pp. 14–15; *Preaching Christ Today*, p. 20; *Theology in Reconciliation*, pp. 235–37, 285; *Theology in Reconstruction*, p. 230.

46 Torrance, *Trinitarian Perspectives*, pp. 77–102.

47 Torrance, *Trinitarian Perspectives*, p. 81. High praise indeed from Torrance.

48 Torrance, *Trinitarian Perspectives*, p. 81.

49 Torrance, *Trinitarian Perspectives*, pp. 79–80.

50 Torrance, *Trinitarian Perspectives*, p. 79.

51 See throughout his book, but he states this view explicitly on p. 144.

52 Holmes, *Holy Trinity*, pp. 147–64.

53 Holmes, *Holy Trinity*, p. 164.

54 See further Jason Radcliff, 'Thomas F. Torrance's Conception of the Consensus Patrum on the Doctrine of Pneumatology', *StPatr* 69 (2013): pp. 417–34.

55 Torrance, *Christian Doctrine of God*, p. 129. See also Torrance, *Trinitarian Perspectives*, pp. 9, 218–19.

56 Torrance, *Christian Doctrine of God*, p. 104; Torrance, *Trinitarian Perspectives*, p. 15.

57 See Torrance, *Theology in Reconciliation*, pp. 243–44.

58 Torrance, *Trinitarian Faith*, p. 238.

59 Torrance, *Trinitarian Faith*, pp. 304–5.

60 Torrance, *Trinitarian Faith*, p. 313.

61 Torrance, *Trinitarian Faith*, p. 236.

62 Torrance, *Trinitarian Faith*, pp. 338–9.

63 Torrance, *Christian Doctrine of God*, pp. 112–13, 182.

64 Torrance, *Trinitarian Faith*, pp. 221, 210; *Christian Doctrine of God*, p. 189.

65 Torrance, *Trinitarian Perspectives*, p. 22.

66 Torrance, *Theological Dialogue* 2:32, 119.

67 Torrance, *Theology in Reconstruction*, pp. 219, 224.

68 Torrance, *Theology in Reconstruction*, p. 252.

69 Holmes, *Holy Trinity*, pp. 12–16.

70 Holmes, *Holy Trinity*, pp. 145–6.

71 'Harnack read through Hanson' according to Wilken. See Robert L. Wilken, 'Review of Divine Meaning: Studies in Patristic Hermeneutics by T.F. Torrance', *TS* 57 (1996): p. 744. See also Matthew Baker, 'The Place of St. Irenaeus of Lyons in Historical and Dogmatic Theology According to Thomas F. Torrance', *Participatio: The Journal of the Thomas F. Torrance Theological Fellowship* 2 (2010): p. 43.

72 Adolf von Harnack, *History of Dogma*, vol. 4 (London: Williams & Norgate, 1894), pp. 80–107.

73 For example, J.N.D. Kelly, *Early Christian Doctrines* (London: A&C Black, 1958), pp. 263–5. However, there are patristics scholars today who are similar to Torrance, even Orthodox. See John Behr, *The Nicene Faith: Part I* (Crestwood, NY: St Vladimir's Seminary, 2004), pp. 27–8.

74 See e.g. Lewis Ayres, *Nicaea and Its Legacy* (Oxford: OUP, 2004); Khaled Anatolios, *Retrieving Nicaea: The Development and Meaning of Trinitarian Doctrine* (Grand Rapids: Baker, 2011).

75 Torrance, *Theological Dialogue* 1:x.

76 Torrance, *Theological Dialogue* 1:10.

77 According to the Minutes, in the discussion, Emialonos from the Orthodox side states: 'Is not Torrance in danger of over-absolutizing

Athanasius in relation to the Cappadocians?' See Torrance Manuscript Collection, box 170.

[78] Torrance, *Theological Dialogue* 1:xxiii.

[79] Torrance, *Theological Dialogue* 1:11.

[80] Torrance, *Theological Dialogue* 1:10–11.

[81] Torrance, *Theological Dialogue* 1:219–26; *Trinitarian Perspectives*, pp. 115–22.

[82] Torrance, *Theological Dialogue* 2:xxi.

[83] See John Meyendorff, *Byzantine Theology: Historical Trends and Doctrinal Themes* (London: Mowbrays, 1974), p. 128.

[84] James Ernest, *The Bible in Athanasius of Alexandria* (Boston: Brill, 2004), p. 17. See also Paul D. Molnar, *Thomas F. Torrance: Theologian of the Trinity* (Farnham: Ashgate, 2009), p. 325 for an account of this critique put forward by Muller.

[85] Gunton, *Father, Son, and Holy Spirit*, pp. 44–52.

[86] Torrance applies the ὁμοούσιον and other patristic terms much more broadly than the fathers did themselves by combining it with his own Reformed commitments.

[87] See T.A. Noble, *Holy Trinity: Holy People: The Theology of Christian Perfecting* (Eugene, OR: Wipf & Stock, 2013), pp. 201–3 for an excellent summary of the debate.

[88] See e.g. Edward Siecienski, *The Filioque: History of a Doctrinal Controversy* (Oxford: OUP, 2010).

[89] Or, at least not necessarily contradictory to one another. See Ayres, *Nicaea and Its Legacy*; Lewis Ayres, *Augustine and the Trinity* (Cambridge: CUP, 2010); Anatolios, *Retrieving Nicaea*; Michel René Barnes, 'Rereading Augustine's Theology of the Trinity', in *The Trinity: An Interdisciplinary Symposium on the Trinity* (ed. Stephen T. Davis, Daniel Kendall, and Gerald O'Collins; Oxford: OUP, 1999), pp. 146–76.

[90] Cf. Noble, *Holy Trinity: Holy People*, pp. 215–17.

[91] Noble, *Holy Trinity: Holy People*, p. 215, n. 41.

[92] However, perhaps Torrance also shows that patrology today is not theologically constructive enough (or, put negatively, too historically static). John Behr's statement that patristic scholarship has become more a study of late antiquity than theology highlights this point precisely. See John Behr, *The Mystery of Christ* (Crestwood, NY: St Vladimir's Seminary, 2006), p. 18. Torrance's approach shows how patrology can (and, indeed, should) be much different from classics; one could suggest that

the current trajectory of patrology is not substantially different than classics.

6. An Analytical Response to Stephen R. Holmes, with a Special Treatment of his Doctrine of Divine Simplicity

1 Stephen R. Holmes, *The Holy Trinity: Understanding God's Life* (Milton Keynes: Paternoster, 2012), pp. 30–32.

2 Holmes, *Holy Trinity*, p. 32.

3 William Alston, 'Religious Language', in *The Oxford Handbook of Philosophy of Religion* (ed. William J. Wainwright; Oxford: OUP, 2005). Janet Soskice, 'Religious Language', in *A Companion to Philosophy of Religion* (ed. Philip L. Quinn and Charles Taliaferro; Malden: Blackwell, 1997).

4 William P. Alston, *Divine Nature and Human Language: Essays in Philosophical Theology* (Ithaca, NY: Cornell University Press, 1989). Richard Swinburne, *Revelation: From Metaphor to Analogy* (New York: 2nd edn, OUP, 2007).

5 A sampling is as follows: Nicholas Wolterstorff, *Inquiring about God: Selected Essays*, vol. 1 (New York: CUP, 2009); Richard Cross, 'Idolatry and Religious Language', *Faith and Philosophy* 25 (2008); Thomas Williams, 'The Doctrine of Univocity Is True and Salutary', *Mod Theol* 21 (2005); David K. Clark, *To Know and Love God: Method for Theology* (Wheaton, IL: Crossway, 2003), ch. 12.

6 Nick Trakakis, 'Does Univocity Entail Idolatry?' *Sophia* 49 (2010); Daniel Bonevac, 'Two Theories of Analogical Predication', in *Oxford Studies in Philosophy of Religion*, vol. 4 (ed. Jonathan Kvanvig; Oxford: OUP, 2012).

7 John Hick, 'Ineffability', *RelS* 36 (2000); William J. Wainwright, 'Theology and Mystery', in *The Oxford Handbook of Philosophical Theology* (ed. Thomas P. Flint and Michael C. Rea; Oxford: OUP, 2009); William J. Wainwright, 'Theistic Mystical Experiences, Enlightenment Experiences, and Ineffability', in *Philosophy and the Christian Worldview: Analysis, Assessment, and Development* (ed. David Werther and Mark D. Linville; New York: Continuum, 2012).

8 For a thorough critique of ineffability see Keith Yandell, 'The Ineffability Theme', *IJPR* 4 (1975). Also Yandell, *The Epistemology of Religious Experience* (New York: CUP, 1993), ch. 3.

⁹ R.T. Mullins, 'Simply Impossible: A Case against Divine Simplicity', *JRT* 13 (2013).

¹⁰ *Sentences*, bk 1, dist. 8.3. Lombard is explicitly following several Christian theologians: Augustine, Hilary of Pointers, Boethius, and Jerome.

¹¹ Augustine, *The Trinity* 6.8.

¹² Augustine, *The Trinity* 5.5.

¹³ Augustine, *The Trinity* 6.6.

¹⁴ Augustine, *The Trinity* 6.8.

¹⁵ Boethius follows Augustine on the doctrine of divine simplicity. See *The Trinity Is One God Not Three Gods* 4. See also Anselm, *Monologion* 16–17. Aquinas does the same throughout *Summa Contra Gentiles*, bk 1. John Duns Scotus seems to be one of the few Christians to dissent from this in the Middle Ages by employing his formal distinction, but this dissent is minimal. He still claims that all of the attributes are identical and that there is no composition in God. He also continues to hold that God is pure act. See his *De Primo Principio* 143–5.

¹⁶ Maximus, *Knowledge of God* 1.83.

¹⁷ Scotus, *God and Creatures* Q5.34. Note that Scotus is innovative in that he allows for the divine attributes to be formally distinct; Richard Cross, *Duns Scotus on God* (Aldershot: Ashgate, 2005), pp. 108–9. James Arminius follows Augustine, but suggests that it might be possible to allow the formal distinction. See his *Disputation* 4.11.

¹⁸ Stock, *A Stock of Divine Knowledge*, being a lively description of the divine nature (London: T.H. for Philip Nevil, 1641), p. 88.

¹⁹ Augustine, *The Trinity* 15.8.

²⁰ Augustine, *The Trinity* 5.11.

²¹ Augustine, *The Trinity* 7.10.

²² Katherin Rogers, 'The Traditional Doctrine of Divine Simplicity', *RelS* 32 (1996): p. 166, see also p. 173. Also Henry Church, *Miscellanea Philo-Theologica* (London: I.N. for John Rothwell, 1638), p. 23.

²³ Augustine, *The Trinity* 5.17. Boethius, *The Trinity Is One God Not Three Gods* 4. Peter Lombard, *Sentences*, bk 1, dist. 30.1; Aquinas, *Summa Contra Gentiles* 2.12; Arminius, *Disputation* 4.14.

²⁴ Aquinas, *Summa Contra Gentiles* 2.12–14.

²⁵ See Rogers, 'The Traditional Doctrine of Divine Simplicity' for more on this. Also, *John of Scythopolis and the Dionysian Corpus: Annotating the Areopagite* (trans. Paul Rorem and John C. Lamoreaux; Oxford: OUP, 1998), p. 220.

²⁶ Aquinas, *Summa Contra Gentiles* 1.16–18.

27 Aquinas, *Summa Contra Gentiles* 1.22.

28 Aquinas, *Summa Contra Gentiles* 2.9.

29 Aquinas, *Summa Contra Gentiles* 2.10.

30 Anselm, *Incarnation of the Word* 7; cf. 4. Avicenna concurs that even conceptual distinctions are foreign to the simple God; Jon McGinnis, 'Avicenna (Ibn Sina)', in *The History of Western Philosophy of Religion, vol. 2: Medieval Philosophy of Religion* (ed. Graham Oppy and Nick Trakakis; Durham: Acumen, 2009), p. 64.

31 *The Works of James Arminius: The London Edition*, vol. 2 (trans. James Nichols; Grand Rapids: Baker, 1986), p. 115.

32 Holmes, *Holy Trinity*, p. 97.

33 Holmes, *Holy Trinity*, p. 104–5.

34 Holmes, *Holy Trinity*, p. 117.

35 Holmes, *Holy Trinity*, p. 108.

36 Keith E. Yandell, 'Universal Religion and Comparative Philosophy', in *Philosophy of Religion for a New Century* (ed. Jeremiah Hackett and Jerald Wallulis; Dordrecht: Kluwer Academic, 2004), p. 289.

37 Augustine, *On Christian Doctrine* 1.6.

38 Holmes, *Holy Trinity*, pp. 117–18.

39 Holmes, *Holy Trinity*, pp. 105–7.

40 This understanding of nature is common to the patristics as well as to some contemporary metaphysicians; John Anthony McGuckin, *The Westminster Handbook to Patristic Theology* (Louisville, KY: Westminster John Knox, 2004), pp. 234–5; Jay Wesley Richards, *The Untamed God: A Philosophical Exploration of Divine Perfection, Simplicity and Immutability* (Downers Grove, IL: IVP, 2003), chs 2, 3.

41 Holmes, *Holy Trinity*, p. 111.

42 Holmes, *Holy Trinity*, p. 200.

43 R.T. Mullins, 'Divine Temporality and the Charge of Arianism' (forthcoming).

44 Holmes, *Holy Trinity*, p. 103.

45 Holmes, *Holy Trinity*, pp. 145–6.

46 Holmes, *Holy Trinity*, p. 112.

47 Holmes, *Holy Trinity*, p. 99.

48 Alasdair I.C. Heron, 'Homoousios with the Father', in *The Incarnation: Ecumenical Studies in the Nicene-Constantinopolitan Creed A.D. 381* (ed. Thomas F. Torrance; Edinburgh: Handsel, 1981), pp. 60–61. See also Michel R. Barnes, 'The Background and Use of Eunomius' Causal Language', in *Arianism after Arius: Essays on the Development of the*

Fourth Century Trinitarian Conflicts (ed. Michel R. Barnes and Daniel H. Williams; Edinburgh: T&T Clark, 1993).

[49] 'Could the Father have not willed the Son?' was a worry that became standard theological prolegomena during the Middle Ages and scholastic era.

[50] Holmes, *Holy Trinity*, pp. 151–2.

[51] For more, see R.T. Mullins, 'Hasker on Divine Procession' (forthcoming).

[52] R.T. Mullins, 'Divine Temporality and the Charge of Arianism'.

[53] Aquinas, *Summa Theologiae* I.Q33.1.

[54] Special thanks to Kate Finely, J.T. Turner, and the editors for feedback on earlier versions of this chapter.

7. A Conversation Overheard: Reflecting on the Trinitarian Grammar of Intimacy and Substance

[1] Robert W. Jenson, 'What Is the Point of Trinitarian Theology?', in *Trinitarian Theology Today: Essays on Divine Being and Act* (ed. Christoph Schwöbel; Edinburgh: T&T Clark, 1995), pp. 31–43, esp. p. 36.

[2] I'm alluding to one of many private conversations with the late Tom Smail.

[3] Laurence Paul Hemming, '*Analogia non Entis sed Entitatis*: The Ontological Consequences of the Doctrine of Analogy', *IJST* 6 (2004): pp. 118–29, esp. p. 119.

[4] Thomas Aquinas, *Summa Theologica* (trans. Fathers of the English Dominican Province; Westminster, MD: Christian Classics, 1981), I.Q13 – hereafter referred to as ST.

[5] ST I.Q29.3.

[6] In this respect I was troubled by Lewis Ayres's not infrequent appeal to what Augustine might have intended. I'm left wondering whether the hermeneutical revolution in biblical studies has eluded historical research and historical theology. Lewis Ayres, *Augustine and the Trinity* (Cambridge: CUP, 2010).

[7] 'I see the twentieth-century renewal of Trinitarian theology as depending in large part on concepts and ideas that cannot be found in patristic, medieval, or Reformation accounts of the doctrine of the Trinity. In some cases, indeed, they are points explicitly and energetically repudiated as erroneous – even occasionally as formally

heretical – by the earlier tradition.' Stephen R. Holmes, *The Holy Trinity: Understanding God's Life* (Milton Keynes: Paternoster, 2012), p. 2.

8 See esp. Paul L. Gavrilyuk, *The Suffering of the Impassible God: The Dialectics of Patristic Thought* (Oxford: OUP, 2006) and T.G. Weinandy, *Does God Suffer?* (Edinburgh: T&T Clark, 2000).

9 '[W]hatever else the tradition is, it is not naive, and that is why the fashionable assumption that we may simply reject certain of the ancient attributes – for example impassibility – is at best patronizing to a tradition that had good reason to say the things that it did about God.' Colin E. Gunton, *Act and Being: Towards a Theology of the Divine Attributes* (London: SCM, 2002), p. 22, cf. pp. 125ff.

10 See e.g. Colin E. Gunton, *The One, the Three and the Many: God, Creation and the Culture of Modernity*, the Bampton Lectures 1992 (Cambridge: CUP, 1993), and various essays in *Persons, Divine and Human: King's College Essays in Theological Anthropology* (ed. Christoph Schwöbel and Colin Gunton; Edinburgh: T&T Clark, 1991).

11 Gregory Nazianzen, *Oration 21: On the Great Athanasius, Bishop of Alexandria* 35 (*NPNF*² 7:269–80, 279).

12 Gregory Nazianzen, *Oration 42: 'The Last Farewell'* 16 (*NPNF*² 7:385–95, 391).

13 Gregory Nazianzen, *The Third Theological Oration* 3 (*NPNF*² 7:301–9, 302).

14 Gregory Nazianzen, *Oration 40: On Holy Baptism* 43 (*NPNF*² 7:360–77, 376): Οὐδὲν γὰρ τῶν ὁμοουσίων τῇ οὐσίᾳ μεῖζον ἢ ἔλαττον.

15 Basil the Great, *Letter to Amphilochius* (Letter 236.6) (*NPNF*² 8:276–9, 278).

16 Augustine, *On the Holy Trinity* 8.4.9 (*NPNF*¹ 3:17–228), hereafter referred to as *De trinitate*.

17 Cf. Ayres, *Augustine and the Trinity*, p. 201.

18 *De trinitate* 7.5.10. Perhaps it should be noted that Thomas Aquinas recognizes the appropriateness of distinguishing between substance and subsistence, the latter being the better rendering of the Greek ὑπόστασις ST I.Q29.2; cf. John Calvin, *Institutes of the Christian Religion* (ed. J.T. McNeill; trans. F.L. Battles; Philadelphia: Westminster, 1960), 1.13.6 (p. 128).

19 *De trinitate* 3.1.1.

20 *De trinitate* 5.9.10.

21 *De trinitate* 5.5.6.

[22] Robert W. Jenson, 'A Decision Tree of Colin Gunton's Thinking', in *The Theology of Colin Gunton* (ed. Lincoln Harvey; London: T&T Clark, 2010), pp. 8–16, esp. p. 12.

[23] Gregory of Nyssa, *On 'Not Three Gods': To Ablabius*, in *Selected Writing and Letters* (NPNF² 5:331–6, 334).

[24] Gregory of Nyssa, *Against Eunomius* 2.2, in *Selected Writing and Letters* (NPNF² 5.101–34, 102).

[25] See e.g. Brad Green, 'The Protomodern Augustine? Colin Gunton and the Failure of Augustine', *IJST* 9 (2007): pp. 328–41.

[26] Augustine anticipates this discussion in his *Confessions* 13.11 (12).

[27] *De trinitate* 12.6.8.

[28] *De trinitate* 15.22.42.

[29] *De trinitate* 14.12.15.

[30] *De trinitate* 15.28.51.

[31] Gregory of Nyssa, *Against Eunomius* 8.1, in *Selected Writing and Letters* (NPNF² 5:200–10, esp. 202).

[32] Gregory Nazianzen, *The Fifth Theological Oration: On the Holy Spirit* 32 (NPNF² 7.318–28).

[33] Gregory Nazianzen, *On the Holy Spirit* 32 (NPNF² 7.318–28).

[34] Karl Barth, *Church Dogmatics* (trans. and ed. G.W. Bromiley and T.F. Torrance; Edinburgh: T&T Clark, 2nd edn, 1975), I/1:333–47.

[35] Karl Barth, *CD* I/1:348–489.

[36] Paul S. Fiddes, *Participating in God: A Pastoral Doctrine of the Trinity* (London: DLT, 2000), p. 34.

[37] Fiddes, *Participating in God*, pp. 41, 72.

[38] Earlier Eastern icons tended to depict Father and Son in equal majesty while, as in Western frescos, depicting the Spirit as a dove.

[39] Robert W. Jenson, *Systematic Theology, vol. 1: The Triune God* (Oxford: OUP, 1997), pp. 152–3.

[40] For a summary of this debate see the collection of essays in *Trinity and Election in Contemporary Theology* (ed. Michael T. Dempsey; Grand Rapids: Eerdmans, 2011).

[41] Gregory of Nyssa, *Against Eunomius* 1.22, in *Selected Writing and Letters* (NPNF² 5:33–100, esp. 61); cf. *On the Holy Spirit: Against the Followers of Macedonius*, in *Selected Writing and Letters* (NPNF² 5:315–25, esp. 315–6).

[42] This is made explicit at the beginning of the book where Pannenberg, Moltmann, and Jenson are (representatively) identified. Holmes, *Holy Trinity*, pp. 19–23.

[43] Jürgen Moltmann, *The Trinity and the Kingdom of God: The Doctrine of God* (trans. M. Kohl; London: SCM, 1981), pp. 64–96.

[44] Thus Lewis Ayres opines that 'Augustine never discusses directly the extent to which we can speak of the Spirit having a role in the Son's generation. But because Augustine envisages the Father eternally constituting the Son through giving him his own personal and active Spirit who is love, we do seem to be able to conclude that the Son is generated in the Spirit. But this supposition remains just that. I suspect Augustine never discusses this question because of the lack of significant scriptural warrant, and because of his commitment to the standard taxis of Father-Son-Spirit.' Ayres, *Augustine and the Trinity*, pp. 265–6.

[45] John E. Colwell, *Promise and Presence: An Exploration of Sacramental Theology* (Milton Keynes: Paternoster, 2005; repr. Eugene, OR: Wipf & Stock, 2011), pp. 35–41.

8. The Biblical Foundations of the Trinity: Evaluating the Trinitarian Exegesis of Stephen R. Holmes

[1] Stephen R. Holmes, *The Holy Trinity: Understanding God's Life* (Milton Keynes: Paternoster, 2012), p. 33.

[2] Holmes, *Holy Trinity*, p. 33.

[3] Thirty-Nine Articles, § 1.

[4] Gregory Nazianzen, *Oration* 31.26 cited from Robert Letham, *The Holy Trinity: In Scripture, History, Theology, and Worship* (Phillipsburg, NJ: Presbyterian & Reformed, 2004), p. 33.

[5] Holmes, *Holy Trinity*, p. 37.

[6] Kevin J. Vanhoozer, 'The Triune God of the Gospel', in *The Cambridge Companion to Evangelical Theology* (ed. Timothy Larsen and Daniel J. Treier; Cambridge: CUP, 2007), p. 17.

[7] Kevin J. Vanhoozer, *Drama of Doctrine: A Canonical-Linguistic Approach to Christian Theology* (Louisville, KY: Westminster John Knox, 2005), p. 43.

[8] Holmes, *Holy Trinity*, p. 34.

[9] Holmes, *Holy Trinity*, p. 34.

[10] Cf. Sam Janse, *'You Are My Son': The Reception of Psalm 2 in Early Judaism and the Early Church*, BET 51 (Leuven: Peeters, 2009).

[11] Holmes, *Holy Trinity*, pp. 39–41.

12 Cf. e.g. James D.G. Dunn, *Christology in the Making: A New Testament Inquiry into the Origins of the Doctrine of the Incarnation* (Grand Rapids: Eerdmans, 2nd edn, 1989), pp. 163–212; Ben Witherington, *Jesus the Sage: The Pilgrimage of Wisdom* (Minneapolis: Fortress, 2000).

13 Cf. Michael F. Bird, *Colossians and Philemon*, NCCS (Eugene, OR: Cascade, 2009), pp. 47–54; though I am recently persuaded by John Anthony Dunne that kingship traditions are very prominent here too. See John Anthony Dunne, 'The Regal Status of Christ in the Colossian Hymn "Christ Hymn"': A Re-evaluation of the Influence of Wisdom Traditions', *TJ* 32 (2011): pp. 3–18.

14 Simon J. Gathercole, *The Pre-Existent Son: Recovering the Christologies of Matthew, Mark, and Luke* (Grand Rapids: Eerdmans, 2006), pp. 193–209, esp. p. 209.

15 Holmes, *Holy Trinity*, p. 46.

16 For case in point, the *shema* includes both God's capacity to relate to the world (*ad extra*) and his inter-Trinitarian relations (*ad intra*). See further Matthew Levering, *Scripture and Metaphysics: Aquinas and the Renewal of Trinitarian Theology* (Malden: Blackwell, 2004), pp. 213–35; C. Kavin Rowe, 'Biblical Pressure and Trinitarian Hermeneutics', *ProEccl* 11 (2002): p. 308; John H. Walton, *Ancient Near Eastern Thought and the Old Testament: Introducing the Conceptual World of the Hebrew Bible* (Grand Rapids: Baker, 2006), p. 91; Anthony C. Thiselton, *The Hermeneutics of Doctrine* (Grand Rapids: Eerdmans, 2007), p. 462. I owe this point to interaction with Mr Paul Maxwell.

17 Holmes, *Holy Trinity*, p. 46.

18 Holmes, *Holy Trinity*, p. 48.

19 Holmes, *Holy Trinity*, p. 53. On the theme of 'exegetical pressures', see also C. Kavin Rowe, 'Biblical Pressure and Trinitarian Hermeneutics', *ProEccl* 11 (2002): pp. 295–312.

20 Holmes, *Holy Trinity*, p. 52.

21 See esp. the early chapters in Gilles Emery and Matthew Levering, eds, *The Oxford Handbook of the Trinity* (Oxford: OUP, 2011).

22 Michael F. Bird, *Evangelical Theology: A Biblical and Systematic Introduction* (Grand Rapids: Zondervan, 2013), pp. 98–113.

23 Donald G. Bloesch, *God the Almighty: Power, Wisdom, Holiness, Love* (Downers Grove, IL: IVP, 1995), p. 167.

9. Does the Emperor Have New Clothes: Is Modern Trinitarian Theology a Revival or a Repudiatin of Fourth-Century Settlements?

1 Stephen R. Holmes, *The Holy Trinity: Understanding God's Life* (Milton Keynes: Paternoster, 2012).
2 See Lewis Ayres, *Nicaea and Its Legacy* (Oxford: OUP, 2004); Michel Barnes, 'De Régnon Reconsidered', *AugStud* 26 (1995): pp. 51–79.
3 E.g. Colin E. Gunton, *The Promise of Trinitarian Theology* (London: T&T Clark, 2nd edn, 1997).
4 Holmes, *Holy Trinity*, pp. 121–2.
5 I borrow the phrase from the title of Molnar's recent monograph on T.F. Torrance: Paul D. Molnar, *Thomas F. Torrance: Theologian of the Trinity* (Farnham: Ashgate, 2009).
6 Jürgen Moltmann, *The Trinity and the Kingdom of God* (trans. M. Kohl; London: SCM, 1981).
7 Ayres, *Nicaea and Its Legacy*.
8 Ayres, *Nicaea and Its Legacy*, pp. 92–8.
9 Ayres, *Nicaea and Its Legacy*, pp. 140ff. for an analysis of Athanasius, *On the Decrees of Nicaea*.
10 Ayres, *Nicaea and Its Legacy*, p. 143.
11 T.F. Torrance, *The Trinitarian Faith* (Edinburgh: T&T Clark, 1988) p. 67.
12 Torrance, *Trinitarian Faith*, p. 68.
13 T.F. Torrance, *The Christian Doctrine of God: One Being Three Persons* (Edinburgh: T&T Clark, 1996) p. 95.
14 Torrance follows Athanasius here. See *Trinitarian Faith*, pp. 130–31.
15 Wolfhart Pannenberg, *Metaphysics and the Idea of God* (trans. Philip Clayton; Edinburgh: T&T Clark, 1990).
16 Wolfhart Pannenberg, *Systematic Theology*, vol. 1 (trans. G.W. Bromiley; Grand Rapids: Eerdmans, 1991), p. 298.
17 Wolfhart Pannenberg, *Systematic Theology* (3 vols; trans. G.W. Bromiley; Grand Rapids: Eerdmans, 1991–8).
18 Pannenberg, *Systematic Theology* 1:324.
19 See A.K. Min, 'The Dialectic of Divine Love: Pannenberg's Hegelian Trinitarianism', *IJST* 6 (2004): pp. 252–69.
20 This summary of Barth's critique is as expressed by Bruce McCormack, 'Grace and Being', in *The Cambridge Companion to Karl Barth* (ed. John Webster; Cambridge: CUP, 2000), p. 99.
21 M. Mattes, 'Hegel's Lutheran Claim', *LQ* 14 (2000): pp. 249–79.

22 T.F. Torrance, *Space, Time and Incarnation* (Oxford: OUP, 1978).

23 Pannenberg, *Systematic Theology* 1:72.

24 Pannenberg, *Systematic Theology* 1:75.

25 Pannenberg, *Systematic Theology* 1:76.

26 Torrance, *Trinitarian Faith*, p. 321.

27 Torrance, *Trinitarian Faith*, p. 321.

28 Torrance, *Trinitarian Faith*, p. 321, n. 94.

29 Torrance, *Trinitarian Perspectives: Toward Doctrinal Agreement* (Edinburgh: T&T Clark, 1994), p. 135.

30 Pannenberg, *Systematic Theology* 1:326.

31 See, for example, Roger Olson, 'Wolfhart Pannenberg's Doctrine of the Trinity', *SJT* 43 (1990): pp. 175–206.

32 See the critique of Christoph Schwöbel, 'Wolfhart Pannenberg', in *The Modern Theologians* (ed. David F. Ford; Oxford: Blackwell, 1989), 1:287.

33 See T.F. Torrance, *The Ground and Grammar of Theology* (Belfast: Christian Journals, 1980).

34 Hans Boersma, *Heavenly Participation: The Weaving of a Sacramental Tapestry* (Grand Rapids: Eerdmans, 2011), p. 35.

35 Boersma, *Heavenly Participation*, p. 35.

10. Response: In Praise of Being Criticized

1 Fred Sanders recognizes this in his essay, and then moves on to consider some of the constructive work that needs to be done.

2 I have argued it in brief elsewhere: Stephen R. Holmes, 'Three versus One? Some Problems of Social Trinitarianism', *JRT* 3 (2009): pp. 77–89; see also the response to my and other criticisms from Gijsbert van den Brink, 'Social Trinitarianism: A Discussion of Some Recent Theological Criticisms', *IJST* 16 (2014): pp. 331–50.

3 p. 13 above.

4 p. 112.

5 I do not have in mind the recent fashion for 'local theologies' in which a single writer attempts a rapid recasting of the whole of Christian doctrine in the thought-forms of his/her culture; these are, in my experience, almost always uninteresting. Imagine, however, a situation analogous to the patristic history, a slow communal argument and development, testing and refining every particular proposal over decades, until after some centuries a broad consensus emerged that

the categories thus understood could be deployed usefully to speak
of God's life . . .

6 This is not merely a point of academic responsibility; when we speak
of 'the doctrine of the Trinity' we speak of something that centrally
defines orthodoxy for many organizations, from the local to the international; redefinition of the term is thus of real ecclesial importance.

7 Or in any theologian I can think of; perhaps the mystical doctrine
of the anonymous medieval *Cloud of Unknowing* comes somewhere
close.

8 Thomas H. McCall has a chapter in the proceedings of the Second Los
Angeles Theology Conference, 'Trinity Doctrine, Plain and Simple', in
Advancing Trinitarian Theology: Explorations in Constructive Dogmatics
(ed. Oliver D. Crisp and Fred Sanders; Grand Rapids: Zondervan,
2014), pp. 42–59, that looks at three different accounts of simplicity,
and the contrasts between them.

9 van den Brink, 'Social Trinitarianism', p. 340.

10 Basil's *Contra Eunomium* did not have an English translation until a
year or so ago, although a good critical edition and a French translation were available; Nyssan's anti-Eunomian writings were trans-
mitted very messily, with chapters being transposed from work to
work in Migne, and so in the standard English translations; Jaeger's
critical edition corrected all this, but again there was genuine difficulty; it was hard for a non-specialist to challenge received interpretations.

11 In my essay in the proceedings of the Los Angeles Theology Conference, 'Trinitarian Action and Inseparable Operations', in *Advancing
Trinitarian Theology* (ed. Crisp and Sanders), pp. 60–74 I explore this
question of the unity, but triune shaping, of divine action at some
length; I hope that this might be an adequate corrective.

12 I am grateful in particular for some conversation on Facebook with
Bobby Grow, which helped me to think through some of the points I
will make here.

13 I should say that I find Jason Radcliff's reading of Torrance's later
criticisms of the Cappadocians as in fact criticisms of Zizioulas to be
convincing.

14 See Lewis Ayres, *Nicaea and Its Legacy: An Approach to Fourth-Century
Trinitarian Theology* (Oxford: OUP, 2004), pp. 105–30.

15 See Ayres, *Nicaea*, pp. 90–98.

16 As, famously, Gregory of Nyssa points out in responding to Ablabius.

17 I have, since my conversion as a student, always worshipped in the geographically closest Baptist church to where I have been living; when away from home, I have tended to worship in the nearest Baptist or other nonconformist church, unless staying with friends who worship elsewhere. I see no reason, then, to assume my experience is not fairly normal. I have heard, and been invited to sing, some quite execrable theology over the years, but my sense is that the failures have mostly been in the areas of soteriology, creation, and pneumatology, not in Trinitarian orthodoxy.

18 The simplest demonstration of this is to consider such central Trinitarian claims as the unity of energy and operation; any sort of functional subordination necessarily requires separate operations, or there are not two things to be in a relationship of subordination.

19 Millard Erickson, *Who's Tampering with the Trinity? An Assessment of the Subordination Debate* (Grand Rapids: Kregel, 2009).

Conclusion

1 p. 140.

2 For Holmes making a similar argument about the (often rapidly) changing meanings of words, see his 'Classical Trinity: Evangelical Perspective', in *Two Views on the Doctrine of the Trinity* (ed. Jason S. Sexton; Grand Rapids: Zondervan, 2014), pp. 26–8.

3 p. 142.

4 For example, see Stuart E. Parsons, 'Very Early Trinitarian Expressions', *TynBul* 65 (2014): pp. 141–52.

5 p. 145.

6 For more on this, see Jason S. Sexton, 'A Confessing Trinitarian Theology for Today's Mission', in *Advancing Trinitarian Theology: Essays in Constructive Dogmatics* (ed. Oliver D. Crisp and Fred Sanders; Grand Rapids: Zondervan, 2014), pp. 171–89.

7 p. 242, n. 5

8 See the point of Torrance's later criticisms of the Cappadocians as really a critique of Zizioulas, a point Jason Radcliff makes with which Holmes concurs (p. 243, n. 13; cf. p. 75).

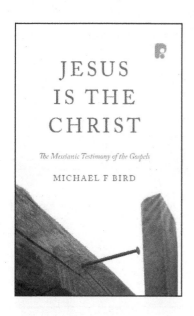

Jesus is the Christ

The Messianic Testimony of the Gospels

Michael F. Bird

In this book Michael Bird engages the subject of the messianism of the four Gospels. While the title and role of 'Messiah' ascribed to Jesus in the Gospels has long been regarded as a late add on, a fabricate claim, or an insignificant feature, Bird argues in contrast that the messianic claims are the most significant for the portrayal of Jesus. Bird proceeds to show how the claim that 'Jesus is the Messiah' drives the purpose and shape of the Gospels. He describes how each Evangelist portrays Jesus as the Messiah of Israel and what they think was at stake in that claim.

> Michael Bird tackles one of the hottest topics currently debated among New Testament scholars – what early believers understood by their confession that Jesus was the Christ, the promised Messiah of Israel. This is a splendid study, written by an expert in the field, in engaging style and displaying clarity of thought. There is much to be learnt on every page – **Paul Foster, lecturer in New Testament, Edinburgh University.**

978-1-84227-446-1

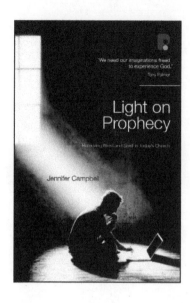

Light on Prophecy

Retrieving Word and Prophecy in Today's Church

Jennifer Campbell

The author correlates the vision and thinking of two powerful prophetic leaders: Hildegard of Bingen, a twelfth-century enclosed nun/mystic, and Dietrich Bonhoeffer, the twentieth-century German pastor/theologian executed by the Nazis. With a view to recovering a balanced and rounded theology of prophecy for the church today, she discusses the closely related workings of both the Word of God (viewed as Christ and the Scriptures) and the Holy Spirit in the works and lives of these famous Christians.

'Rarely do we encounter maturity, depth and wisdom when the subject at hand is the prophetic gift. Jenny Campbell's book is the exception. With rare insight she offers us a workable and thorough theology of Prophecy' – **Mike Breen, 3DM Global Leader.**

Jennifer Campbell is a lecturer in Christian Doctrine at Westminster Theological Centre, Cheltenham, UK. She is also the leader of Eaglesinflight.

978-1-84227-768-3

Multi-Voiced Church

Stuart & Sian Murray Williams

Multi-Voiced Church argues strongly and persuasively for churches in which everyone is important for the well-being and growth of the community. A multi-voiced church is necessary for genuine mission in today's complex world.

'Those who take the book to heart may find they have a share in making a significant contribution to helping local churches enjoy significant and lasting renewal.' – **Stephen Finamore, Principal of Bristol Baptist College.**

'*Multi-Voiced Church* is an important book that addresses the centuries-old abuse that stifles congregations and exhausts clergy – the silencing of the laity. It is bold, original and practical. Together they have written a multi-voiced book on multi-voiced church life. The medium and the message work together. Wonderful.' – **Alan and Eleanor Kreider, Associated Mennonite Biblical Seminary, Elkhart, Indiana (retired); authors** of *Worship and Mission After Christendom* **(2009)**

978-1-84227-766-9

Primitive Piety

A Journey from Suburban Mediocrity to Passionate Christianity

Ian Stackhouse

In *Primitive Piety* Ian Stackhouse takes us on a journey away from the safety and pleasantries of suburban piety and into a faith that is able to embrace the messiness as well as the paradoxes of the Christian faith.

In a culture in which there is every danger that we all look the same and speak the same, Stackhouse argues for a more gritty kind of faith – one that celebrates the oddity of the gospel, the eccentricity of the saints, and the utter uniqueness of each and every church.

Ian Stackhouse is the Pastoral Leader of Millmead, Guildford Baptist Church.

978-1-84227-786-7